ALL TOO SOON…

It's the second week in May and the AP World History Exam looms. Quick, take a look at the **20 Things to Know** section (page 9). Go over how to write the free-response questions then just go through the **practice questions** (page 325), comparing your choices with the correct answers.

Months before the test? Read the **Comprehensive Strategies and Review** (page 63), then get online and review the sites mentioned in the **Strategies for Long-Term Preparation** (page 319) toward the end of this book. Spend some time with the history teachers on your campus or at a local library looking for additional text resources.

Somewhere in between? Take some time to look over your *My Max Score* book and **personalize a plan** for your exam preparation.

My Max Score

AP WORLD HISTORY

Maximize Your Score in Less Time

Kirby Whitehead

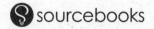 sourcebooks

Published by Sourcebooks, Inc.
P.O. Box 4410, Naperville, Illinois 60567-4410
(630) 961-3900
Fax: (630) 961-2168
www.sourcebooks.com

Library of Congress Cataloging-in-Publication Data

Whitehead, Kirby.
  My max score AP world history : maximize your score in less time / Kirby Whitehead.
     p. cm.
  1. World history—Examinations—Study guides. 2. College entrance achievement tests—United States—Study guides. 3. History—Examinations, questions, etc. 4. Advanced placement programs (Education) I. Title.
  D21.W59 2012
  907.6—dc23

2011041151

Printed and bound in the United States of America.
VP 10 9 8 7 6 5 4 3 2 1

Contents

Introduction

Now that you have made the choice to take the Advanced Placement World History Exam, you need to get ready; or if you have not yet made the choice, say yes now and get registered through your school counselor or contact the College Board, the company that administers the exam, by calling (888) 225-5427 or emailing them at apexams@info.collegeboard.org. You need to ask them how to register to take the exam in your area. Once you are registered you need to prepare. This book should help.

You will find the main content of the book in three sections: the "20 Things to Know," covering key concepts in world history that should be reviewed the week prior to the exam; a comprehensive review of the six periods of world history covered by the exam; and a section suggesting a long-term plan for preparing for the exam. Ultimately, you need to choose how you will use these sections and how much time you will devote to preparing for the exam. To help, here is a little bit about the College Board Advanced Placement World History Exam.

About the Test

The AP World History Exam is divided into two sections: a multiple-choice section with 70 questions and a free-response section with three specific types of essays. The latter includes one document-based question, one change-over-time essay, and one comparative essay. The whole exam lasts three hours and five minutes. Each section of the exam counts for 50 percent of the overall exam grade.

QUESTION TYPE	NUMBER OF QUESTIONS	TIMING
Multiple-Choice Questions	70 questions	55 minutes
Document-Based Question	1 question	50 minutes (including a 10-minute reading period)
Change-over-Time Essay	1 question	40 minutes
Comparative Essay	1 question	40 minutes

The multiple-choice section includes a set number of questions from each of six time periods.

TIME PERIOD	DATE RANGE	APPROX. NUMBER OF MULTIPLE-CHOICE QUESTIONS
Technological and Environmental Transformations	to 600 BCE	3–4
Organization and Reorganization of Human Societies	600 BCE to 600 CE	10–11
Regional and Transregional Interactions	600 CE to 1450	14
Global Interactions	1450 to 1750	14
Industrialization and Global Integration	1750 to c. 1900	14
Accelerating Global Change and Realignments	c. 1900 to Present	14

How the Test Is Graded

AP exams receive a score between 1 and 5, with 5 being the best. Most colleges and universities will give credit for a score of a 5, and many will also award credit for a 4. A 3 on the exam is considered passing, but fewer universities will award credit for a 3. You should contact the universities you are planning to attend and ask them about how they view the AP exams and what credit they offer.

After you complete the exam in May, it goes to be scored by machines for the multiple-choice section (so make your marks clear) and by a team of several hundred readers for the free-response section. Sometime in mid-July, the composite score will be mailed to you. You do not get a report on the individual sections of the exam.

The scores for the 2010 exam broke down as follows.

EXAM COMPOSITE SCORE	% OF TEST TAKERS
5	9.8
4	15.5
3	23.8
2	24.2
1	26.7

Generally, students making a 3 or above get about 50 percent of the multiple-choice questions correct and need to get greater than a 3 on each of the essays (see the Free-Response Questions section on page 79 for an explanation of the essay scoring system). If you are great at memorization, focus on the content but know that many of the questions require you to analyze information and make educated guesses. If you express yourself well in writing, spend more time reviewing the section on writing the free-response questions, because a higher score on the essays can greatly improve your composite grade.

Either way, make a plan, do the work, and go into the test confident that you can make your Max Score.

Visit mymaxscore.com for an additional practice test for the AP World History Exam, as well as practice tests for other AP subjects.

THE ESSENTIALS: A LAST-MINUTE STUDY GUIDE

So the test is this week and you've just picked up this review guide. What next? Don't panic; many AP students find themselves rushing to review just before the exam. While you cannot cram all of history into your head in 24 or even 48 hours, there are some things you can do, and this book will help. Follow this plan and then use the Day before the Exam advice on page 322 as you get ready the night before the test.

First, take some time and go through the **free-response questions** section (page 79). Even an average essay will significantly impact your score. Many years, the average essay score is less than a 3 because numerous students fail to complete some of the basics. For instance, the first paragraph must offer a complete answer to the question, that is, a thesis statement. Take time to review the format of each essay so you will know the basic structure you need for each of the different prompts. Look at the examples for ideas about how to effectively brainstorm an answer and what specific structure to use for each essay.

Second, go through the **20 Things to Know** (page 9), as these make the historical connections between time periods in world history that the change-over-time essay and many of the multiple-choice questions require. These pages cover major themes that occur throughout history and, more important, throughout the course description for the AP World History Exam. Use them as a primer to connect what you already know about history to similar historic circumstances.

Third, go through the **practice exam** (page 325). Pay attention to the types of questions and the answer choices. Review the answer to each question as you go through the exam. You want to take the time to notice what separates a correct and incorrect answer, because many of the AP answer choices may be true statements, just not the best answer for the question presented. This provides the greatest challenge for most students on the exam.

You may finally wish to go through the **content review sections** (starting on page 119), possibly concentrating on periods of time you have not recently reviewed in class. But do not forget to get a good night's sleep before the exam.

The Basics for Maximizing Your Score

What the College Board Says

For each of its tests, the College Board publishes a short booklet (available online at apcentral.collegeboard.com/apc/public/repository/ap-world-history-course-description.pdf) that provides guidelines for what the test may include. This review uses the College Board's guidelines to expand on each of the key areas and to prepare you for getting the highest possible score. Since the booklet is free, you should really look it over. The booklet includes a number of multiple-choice practice questions, free-response questions, and an outline of the content for the test, which you should use to target your content review as you get closer to the test date.

To start, the College Board wants you to view history according to five themes, by asking you to interpret and analyze events based on these overarching historical processes. The first, human and environmental interaction, requires you to evaluate history based on the environment and, more important, how human societies learned to shape or control their environment. Second, you must understand what defines a society's culture and how societies develop over time. The next theme continues to look at societies as they develop into larger political units, nations, and even empires. It also introduces the decline of political states over time through revolutions and invasions. The fourth theme, and one of *maximum* importance, introduces economics to your analysis of continuities and changes in history. More than anything, you will find easy connections between economic factors and political and social change. *Pay attention* to these for both your essays and the multiple-choice answers. Finally, the fifth theme requires you to consider gender and social and family structures when analyzing a society. Gender especially plays an important part in many of the test questions.

The College Board does not suggest you try to study a complete, chronological narrative of history. It suggests that this traditional approach will not equal a good score on the exam. Instead, you need to focus on major events that link the various themes together as well as those that show the relationship between various regions of the world during the historical periods discussed. It also specifically limits coverage of Europe to no more than 30 percent of the overall course (the booklet is written for teachers teaching AP World History, but you need to understand this as meaning no more than 30 percent of the questions will include Europe, and *many* of those will involve some comparison to a non-European society). Also, the United States is covered only concerning its interactions with the larger world; you will not get questions about internal U.S. politics, like those that occur on the AP U.S. History Exam.

Finally, before moving on to content, the AP World History Exam requires students to demonstrate an ability to think like a historian; in the booklet, the College Board calls this Historical Thinking Skills and asks the student specifically to

- develop historical arguments from historical evidence based on their ability to shape a historical question and then identify appropriate evidence after analysis for bias.
- develop chronological reasoning by identifying and analyzing cause-effect relationships, recognizing patterns of continuity and change over time, and developing a thorough knowledge of historical periods.
- develop the ability to compare historical developments within a single society, between related societies, or during different

chronological periods, while also being able to relate historical events to larger regional, national, or global processes.

- develop the ability to interpret the past through the analysis and evaluation of primary and secondary sources and then reach a meaningful and persuasive understanding of the past by the application of historical thinking skills along with information from other fields as well as evaluate all relevant (even if contradictory) information and apply this insight to other historical periods and the present.

There are also five main themes that the exam will emphasize.

COURSE THEMES*

THEME 1: Interaction between Humans and the Environment	Demography and Disease
	Migration
	Patterns of Settlement
	Technology
THEME 2: Development and Interaction of Cultures	Religions
	Belief Systems, Philosophies, and Ideologies
	Science and Technology
	Arts and Architecture
THEME 3: State-Building, Expansion, and Conflict	Political Structures and Forms of Government
	Empires
	Nations and Nationalism
	Revolts and Revolutions
	Regional, Transregional, and Global Structures and Organizations
THEME 4: Creation, Expansion, and Interaction of Economic Systems	Agricultural and Pastoral Production
	Trade and Commerce
	Labor Systems
	Industrialization
	Capitalism and Socialism

THEME 5:	Gender Roles and Relations
Development and Transformation of Social Structures	Family and Kinship
	Racial and Ethnic Constructions
	Social and Economic Classes

From AP World History Course and Exam Description Effective Fall 2011, College Board

These historical thinking skills and themes can also help you frame your answers to essay questions or narrow down your choices on the multiple-choice questions. Don't just glance over them. Throughout the content review section, the information emphasizes these points.

Defining a Society: PERSIAN

Many texts and teachers will quickly throw out terms like *culture* and *society*, expecting you to know exactly what they mean. Often they are wrong or they lack a coherent definition. The most common definitions often don't provide much of a framework for understanding. To help, start by defining a society as a large (*no* specific minimum number) group of people with a common culture. Culture defines the basic systems of the society, everything from family structure to government. To allow you to better analyze and compare cultures, use the following seven areas to break down culture into its component parts: Politics, Economics, Religion (beliefs), Social order, Innovations, Arts, and Nearby influences. Together, they spell out PERSIAN. Each is further explained in the chart on the next page.

PERSIAN

| POLITICS | How members of a society govern themselves. Refers to forms of government and the laws that manage society. May include discussions of types of government (republic, monarchy, dictatorship), individual rights and responsibilities, leaders and how leaders are chosen, and relations between societies. |

ECONOMICS	How members of a society use their resources to meet their needs. Includes discussions of trade, jobs, wealth, natural resources, and industrialization.
RELIGION (BELIEFS)	The common beliefs of a society (most often religion) but including philosophy and basic ideas about individual rights and responsibilities. For example, the U.S. Constitution provides a political framework of the United States but also acts as a core document for the beliefs of the American society. (The mnemonic uses the word *religion* because the *b* in *beliefs* would not spell anything.)
SOCIAL ORDER	How members of a society are organized into class and gender roles. Includes discussions of family structure, caste and class, slavery, gender bias, and the demographics of settlements (rich and poor neighborhoods, house size, and other mixes of economics and class).
INNOVATIONS	The technology available to a society and how the people use it.
ART	How a society expresses itself and its culture. Literature, painting, dance, music, and architecture all fall into this category.
NEARBY INFLUENCES	What other societies, because of geographic proximity, influence and/or are influenced by this society. In essence, the sources of cultural diffusion for a society and how that society affects others.

Society vs. Civilization: In the study of world history, many hesitate to provide a concrete definition of the words *civilization* and *civilized*. While the debate might fascinate some in the field, jumping into it does not improve your World History AP score a single point. For the sake of discussion, I will refer to a society as a civilization *if* it has built a city. From the "Levels of Society" chart that follows, you can infer what the society must have achieved by that point. Referring to civilization does not indicate moral superiority, just the development of a food surplus, a high degree of specialization or division of labor, written records, etc. (Refer to the chart on page 13 for more details.)

For the AP World History Exam, you must demonstrate an ability to compare various societies at different points in history, trace the development of societies over a period of time, and identify the elements of a society that establish its unique point of view, or bias, when describing its world. You will find that the questions on the AP World History Exam often reference the various PERSIAN categories, asking you to explain changes within them or to compare them among different societies.

The earliest societies formed around extended family units, often referred to as tribes, or more properly, nomadic tribes. From this starting point, a society may potentially grow larger in size and influence. The "Levels of Society" chart (page 13) provides an overview of the growth of a society and the external and internal factors shaping this growth. This chart should help you to understand the basics of how a society develops and interacts with its neighbors and to better understand how to compare diverse societies over time.

20 Things to Know

1. Human Society

The basic unit of study for the AP World History Exam is society—a group of people tied together by a common culture. What is culture? In short, culture is a group's way of life that is passed down from one generation to another. The following chart breaks culture down into seven areas, allowing you to better construct comparisons and develop analysis when explaining cultural difference. Together the seven areas spell out PERSIAN.

PERSIAN

POLITICS	How a society governs itself. Includes: • Government • Laws and rights • Constitutions • Monarchs, kings, emperors, sultans • Democracy, oligarchy, dictatorship, absolutism, totalitarianism • Political boundaries and military conquest
ECONOMICS	How a society uses its resources to meet its needs. Includes: • Wealth • Resources • Trade • Labor

RELIGION (BELIEFS)	What members of a society generally believe as a group, including metaphysical as well as philosophical ideas. Includes: • Religions • Philosophies • Fundamental beliefs • Human nature
SOCIAL ORDER	How members of a society order themselves. Includes: • Class • Gender • Family structure
INNOVATION	The technology available in a society and how it is used. Includes: • Inventions • Cultural diffusion of technology • Science • Literacy
ARTS	How members of a society express themselves. Includes: • Types of art • Artistic themes • Censorship • Patronage and control of the arts and expression
NEARBY INFLUENCES	The neighboring societies and their possible influences. Includes: • Political and physical maps • Geography • Trade routes • Cultural diffusion

Using PERSIAN as a Tool

Case one, the essay. When writing your essays, you will often find one of the PERSIAN words included in the question or you will find it useful to use one to establish a grouping for your document-based question or an area for comparison in the compare-and-contrast essay. For your brainstorming, use the categories to provide some structure for your writing. For example:

Analyze the economic and social changes forced on Africa by European colonization from the mid-nineteenth century until the end of World War II.

BRAINSTORMING

POLITICAL CHANGE	ECONOMIC CHANGE
• Europeans limited the power of many local chiefs	• African labor was used to produce raw materials for Europe
• Military might brought almost all areas of Africa under European rule	• Trade benefited the Europeans, not African societies
• Boundaries reflected European needs, not ethnic or cultural division	

Remember the key terms for the categories, and then build the specific historical information you recall into the outline. Politics includes rights. Europeans did not make the peoples of Africa full citizens of the empire and therefore did not guarantee them the rights they gave their own people. This last statement should seem obvious, but many students fail to earn points because they forget to include the obvious.

Case two, the multiple-choice questions. A question might show an image of the Shanghai waterfront in 1920 and ask you to explain what accounts for the fact that all of the buildings are obviously Western or European in design. Cultural diffusion involves both transference of innovations and artistic style, and your answer should include a reference to one or both. Look to associate answer choices to the categories introduced in the question to make a better guess at a correct answer, or at least to eliminate obvious false choices.

2. The Levels of Society

The earliest societies formed around extended family units, often referred to as tribes or, specifically, nomadic tribes. From this starting point, a society may potentially grow larger in size and influence. The next chart, "Levels of Society," provides an overview of the growth of a society and the external and internal factors that shape this growth. This chart should help you to understand the basics of how a society develops and interacts with its neighbors and to better understand how to compare diverse societies over time.

Key Terms

Domesticate: tame to fit human needs.

Complex Government: a government that must rule a society beyond the traditional family, clan, and tribal ties.

Surplus: an extra supply; a surplus of food develops as those engaged in agriculture regularly begin to produce more than they require.

Division of Labor, or Specialization: the process where individuals choose to perform jobs or tasks they do well and, in return, trade what they produce (such as food or pottery) for items they cannot produce themselves. Specialization allows for the more rapid development of tools and techniques in any field, resulting in better products and greater efficiency.

Written Records: complex economic and governmental systems require detailed record keeping; most languages develop as a means of establishing and recording ownership.

City-State: a city and the surrounding lands (including farming villages) necessary for its continued existence, that administrates itself independently.

Empire: a political system in which a society brings other societies under its direct rule but does not merge or integrate the conquered societies into its own. Historical experience suggests that empires eventually fail.

Global Society (?): trends like globalization and international organizations from the European Union to the United Nations hint at the new paths societies might take, but they do not yet offer any concrete steps in the process.

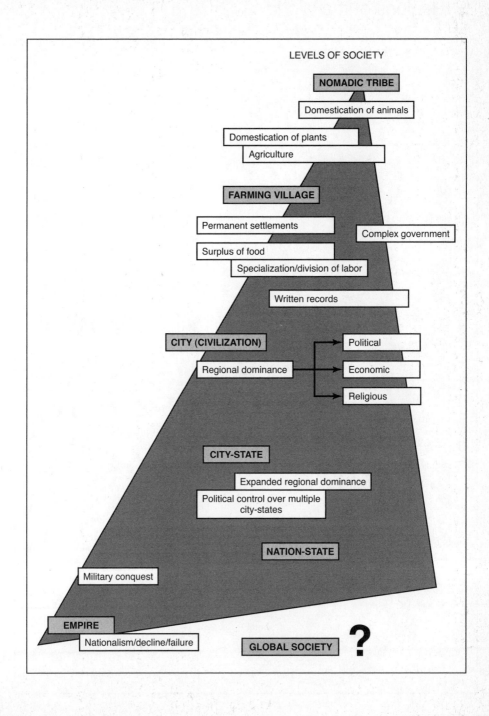

LEVELS OF SOCIETY

NOMADIC TRIBE

Domestication of animals

Domestication of plants

Agriculture

FARMING VILLAGE

Permanent settlements

Complex government

Surplus of food

Specialization/division of labor

Written records

CITY (CIVILIZATION)

Political

Regional dominance

Economic

Religious

CITY-STATE

Expanded regional dominance

Political control over multiple city-states

NATION-STATE

Military conquest

EMPIRE

Nationalism/decline/failure

GLOBAL SOCIETY ?

My Max Score AP WORLD HISTORY

3. Regions of the World

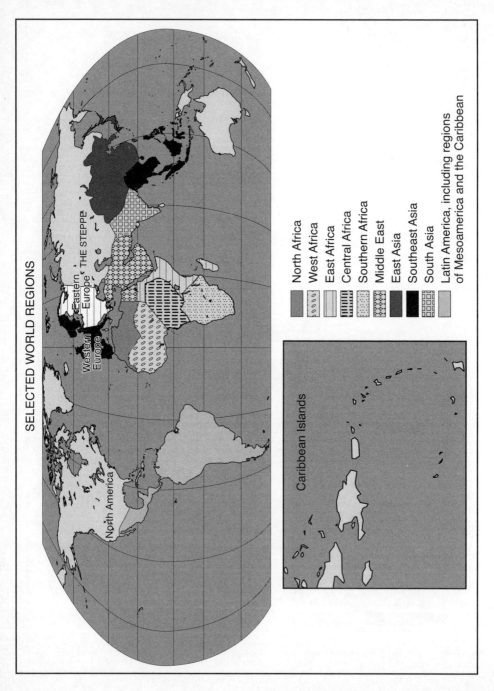

World Regions and the AP Exam

Make sure you remember the various regional names used on the exam. Also, the table below highlights some of the key intersections of regions and relevant world historical context during various time periods.

	FOUNDATION	600–1450	1450–1750	1750–1914	1914–PRESENT
NORTH AFRICA	Egyptian civilization	Islamic caliphate		Imperialism	World Wars Decolonization
WEST AFRICA	Bantu migrations	Islamic expansion	Slave/ Triangular trade	Imperialism	
EAST AFRICA	Bantu migrations	Islamic expansion Indian Ocean trade	Europe and Indian Ocean trade	Imperialism	World Wars Decolonization
CENTRAL AFRICA	Bantu migrations			Imperialism	Decolonization
SOUTH-ERN AFRICA	Bantu migrations		European Colonialism	Imperialism	World Wars Decolonization
EAST ASIA	Chinese civilization Confucianism	Islamic expansion Mongol conquest	European exploration	Imperialism	World Wars Cold War Globalization
SOUTH ASIA	Indian Civilization Spread of Buddhism	Islamic expansion Indian Ocean trade	Europe and Indian Ocean trade	Imperialism	Decolonization Globalization

	FOUNDATION	600–1450	1450–1750	1750–1914	1914–PRESENT
SOUTH-EAST ASIA	Spread of Buddhism	Islamic expansion Indian Ocean trade	Europe and Indian Ocean trade	Imperialism	World Wars Cold War Decoloni-zation
LATIN AMERICA			European explora-tion European coloniza-tion Triangular trade	Decoloni-zation New Imperialism	Cold War

4. Gender

Hunting/gathering societies required both men and women to produce food (the key economic output needed by a society to survive). After agriculture allowed for a division of labor, or specialization, societies almost universally regulated women to a secondary role. Societies then established social rules to enforce this status.

Typically, societies made women dependent on males: fathers, then husbands, and then sons, if they were widowed. By removing most avenues of economic support such as property ownership or the right to work outside of the family home, society left women with no alternatives but to remain subservient to family males.

On questions dealing with gender, you need first to establish the lack of economic opportunity and its source.

EXAMPLES

CHINA	Confucius denied women any role outside of wife and mother. Women remained dependent on males (fathers, husbands, sons) throughout their lifetime.

ISLAM	Arabic influences favored keeping women confined to the family and did not allow them any freedom in public. This included limiting public access, restrictive clothing (veiling), and not allowing them to travel unaccompanied. Some Islamic states today do not allow women to operate vehicles.
MEDIEVAL AND RENAISSANCE EUROPE	Culture demanded that women restrict themselves to the household and offered only the church (becoming a nun) as an alternative to marriage. Many noble daughters found themselves forced into church life when their family could not produce a dowry. Women who sought education and a life without marriage were sometimes accused and even convicted of witchcraft.
INDUSTRIAL REVOLUTION	Unmarried women found work during the Industrial Revolution, but they worked for less pay, often were required to live in dormitories and follow the rules of the factory owner (which was done to assure families of the girls' safety), which permitted owners to withhold even more money from the girls' wages for room and board. When a woman married, she quit her job in order to raise children.
LATIN AMERICA	Here and in other areas, the Roman Catholic Church supported the traditional role of males as the head of the house and breadwinner (money earner). For women, divorce or living independently was contrary to very strong cultural norms. This also occurred in many other areas of the world with strong religious beliefs or cultural taboos.

Force for Change

During the nineteenth century, women in Western Europe and the United States became involved in a number of social movements. These included areas such as education, public health, and prison reform. The largest social movement demanded the abolition of slavery. The success of the abolitionist cause inspired a generation of women to push for greater political opportunities. By the late nineteenth century, many women wanted the right to vote. Protest brought these women notice, but an economic need caused by World War I eventually granted many of them the vote. The unprecedented need for manpower on the western front during World War I (see review part 5, "1914 to the Present," on page 261 for more information) allowed many women to work in factories so the men could go to war. As a result, grateful nations and politicians gave women the right to vote.

Many things remained unequal: wages, opportunities for promotion, educational opportunities, and opportunities in certain fields of work. World War II again intervened, requiring even more women to work so that men could go to war. Postwar political pressure grew internationally to improve the circumstances of women. In Japan, Americans forced the Japanese to include women's equality in the new constitution. In the 1920s, communists in the Soviet Union enforced more rights for women. After the war, communist parties in China, Eastern Europe, and even Fidel Castro's Cuba continued to champion greater women's rights. Though no woman achieved a top political position, equal rights challenged the traditional gender biases of all these regions, notably Confucian China.

In the newly freed colonies, international organizations like the United Nations pushed for women's equality. First, they made the economic argument that the developing nations needed all of their human resources to advance. Second, women who make money spend it on their families: better food, better shelter, better life. Putting more money in the hands of women improved the basic social unit: the family.

On the Essays

If asked about gender inequality, cover both the source of the policy (religion/philosophy, cultural tradition) and how it is enforced: denial of economic opportunity and political rights to force change.

If asked about changes in gender relations, go over the "Levels of Society" chart (page 13) and point out how specialization allowed men to move into the public sphere while keeping women restricted to the family. Specialization created greater economic opportunities that were denied to women.

On the Multiple-Choice Questions

Questions may ask about the role of women at a particular time in history. More often than not, the role is restricted to the family and controlled by a male in the woman's life.

If asked about achieving equality, the forces for expanding women's opportunities came out of the West. Women took the ideas of the Enlightenment and demanded them for themselves. As they gained a degree of economic importance, they achieved political power and used laws to protect themselves. Many men and women in non-Western societies today still do not favor a pure equality of the sexes, so don't assume that the move to greater gender equality is universal or even means the same to everyone.

5. The Great Traditions Comparison: Hinduism and Buddhism

The following table compares the major components of the religious/philosophical traditions that arose in India.

	HINDUISM	BUDDHISM
FOUNDING	No clear founder; evolved from original Indus civilization beliefs mixed with those of the Aryan invaders Northern India About 1500 BCE	Founded by Siddhartha Gautama who became the Buddha (the Enlightened One) Founded in India about 500 BCE
HOLY TEXT	The Vedas The Upanishads Epic Poems (the *Ramayana*)	Basic teachings are explained in his first sermon Each Buddhist tradition has a number of scriptures/stories of the Buddha and his teachings
DOCTRINE	Belief in reincarnation of the soul into another living being Souls seek to escape the cycle of reincarnation, but not all do	Belief in reincarnation of the soul Through enlightenment, the soul can escape this cycle of reincarnation and reach Nirvana (a break with the material world and union with the supreme being)

	HINDUISM	BUDDHISM
DOCTRINE (CONT.)	A soul's karma explains and justifies its current life Caste system: highly structured social order Many individual gods/ goddesses developed over time Women received some degree of status by caste but were not equal to the men of their station	Key teachings are the Four Noble Truths (life was full of suffering caused by desire) Following the Eightfold, or Middle, Path will lead to enlightenment and Nirvana No divine being or god (supreme being is not worshiped or described as a god) Two main traditions: Theravada Buddhist (little raft) requires men and women to seek monastic life to reach the degree of meditation for enlightenment Mahayana Buddhist (big raft) can live a lay life yet still pursue enlighten-ment, often with the help of monks and nuns in their communities
LOCATION	Dominant tradition in India Challenged early by Buddhism, but the upper caste preserved the Hindu dominance Islamic invaders and mis-sionaries established domi-nance in some areas of India Outside of India, Hinduism is found in communities of Indians living in mostly former British colonies or in the United Kingdom While some Hindu political parties exist in India, the government is more secular, having had an elected Muslim prime minister	Theravada Buddhism failed to establish itself as the dominant tradition in India Moving along the Silk Road, Buddhist missionaries established a strong base of support in China (developed the Mahayana school) Chen or Zen Buddhism spread from China to Korea and Japan, becoming a major influence in both regions Theravada Buddhism is a dominant faith in Sri Lanka, Burma, Thailand, and Cambodia

On the Essays

When comparing these two faiths, you should focus on the caste system being the dominant cultural force in India until very recently (British India in the nineteenth century). Caste determined the ruling class, the economic activity allowed Hindus, and defined the social order more strictly than any other system devised. Buddhism, on the other hand, did not deal with these areas in East Asia. In China, Buddhism provided a brief counter to Confucian bureaucrats, but ultimately, Neo-Confucianism and political pressure by the bureaucracy drove Buddhist influence out of the political mainstream. In Japan, monasteries also sought to exercise political influence, but were eventually put down after a militant revolt in the late sixteenth century. Buddhism also did not push one economic system over another. Monasteries might gain wealth from donations of money and land from followers and thus have some economic influence.

Socially, Buddhism provided an escape from the caste system in India, one reason for Hindu objections against it. Particularly, it was attractive to the lower caste and those called "untouchables" because it promoted egalitarianism in monastic life. It also offered a role for women different from that allowed under the caste system. Buddhist nuns had more responsibilities than a Hindu woman could under the caste structure.

On the Multiple-Choice Questions

Recognize that Hinduism resides in India and questions about Hinduism might relate to what you know about India. Also, note that Hindu images of their deities often have multiple sets of arms and faces looking in each direction. Questions on Buddhism will often be about China or Japan, so remember key elements of these cultures when making your answer choices.

6. The Great Traditions: Confucianism and Western Philosophy (Socrates, Plato, and Aristotle)

The following table compares the major components of Confucianism and Western philosophy as defined by Socrates, Plato, and Aristotle.

	CONFUCIANISM	WESTERN PHILOSOPHY
FOUNDING	Founded by Confucius in China during the Warring States period, about 500 BCE	Socrates' student Plato wrote his dialogues after 400 BCE (just after the loss of Athens to Sparta in the Peloponnesian War and the death of Socrates) Aristotle, Plato's student
HOLY TEXT	*The Analects* by Confucius's disciples *The Five Classics*	*The Republic* by Plato *Physics* and *Politics* by Aristotle
DOCTRINE/ BELIEFS	Sought to bring order to society (lived during a time of conflicts between numerous states in China) Believed people were good but needed a proper model of virtue and education in order to follow a moral life Focus on social–family relationships (defined in the Five Relationships) Social class order based on utility to society Emperor first as the model of virtue Confucian bureaucrats as the governors of society Peasants and urban artisans Mean (unskilled workers) group included merchants who materially might be very wealthy	Aristotle established the Western mode of thought: empirical thinking (knowledge based on thought and observation) Reason exercised with virtue produces good, which leads to human happiness, the ultimate end of existence Strong emphasis on collection and categorization of data Politically, Plato argued for philosopher rulers and rejected democracy, because not all people were capable of ruling Strong emphasis on individualism and individual levels of talent and ability

	CONFUCIANISM	WESTERN PHILOSOPHY
DOCTRINE/ BELIEFS (CONT.)	Great emphasis on roles of father and son (filial piety: loyalty and obedience of son to father) Women were relegated to roles of wife and mother (Neo-Confucian tradition further limited the position of women)	Aristotle did not believe women had the cognitive ability of men, thus women should not be involved in government
INFLUENCE	Since its founding, Confucianism has held an importance in Chinese civilization The Han dynasty established Confucianism as the main philosophy of government Communist Party rejects Confucianism, which still dominates much of the social structure of China; more so in Korea and Japan	Aristotle dominated Renaissance thought when Greek learning was restored to Europe during the Renaissance (referred to as humanist philosophy at that time) Discoveries by Galileo, Newton, and others disproved many of Aristotle's theories, but his methods continued Western thought, especially the dependency on empiri-cal thinking and reasoning, influences many regions outside of Western Europe

On the Essays

Confucianism's influence on China's history lasted through each of the dynasties, so any question concerning a dynasty should involve a discussion of Confucianism. Politically, Confucianism provides for a meritocracy, which means that all people, especially candidates for the bureaucracy, were evaluated on their merits for the purposes of advancement. Confucianism also serves as a guide for the administration of government, bureaucrats were expected to make decisions based on their knowledge of what actions Confucius might take in a situation. Economically, Confucianism resulted in the lowering of the social status of merchants and government policies that favored landowners and ignored the potential of international trade, although the Song and especially the Mongol Yuan dynasties encouraged mercantile connections.

Social order also falls under Confucianism, especially the status given to women and the importance of hierarchy in all relationships. A woman's only role, defined in the Five Relationships, is that of wife (maintaining her husband's household) and mother (bearing her husband a son for the security of the family's future). Also, the Five Relationships establish a hierarchy of duty, honor, and respect: those above must provide for and guide while those below must follow their obligations and honor those above them. Above all, the family is seen as the key to social stability. If the family is correct, then all else can be made correct.

Western philosophy establishes a greater emphasis on individuals rather than the group. Democracy (a Greek innovation) is not championed by Plato but was accepted by Aristotle. These ideas gradually spread to nearby Rome. Later, Roman thinkers created the republic: a society ruled by elected representatives, in the spirit of Greek democracy. Humanism, the Enlightenment, Romanticism, and individualism remain key concepts. Even in the debate over socialism and communism, the importance of the individual versus the group remains a key area of contention.

On the Multiple-Choice Questions

Do not forget the importance of Confucianism in all East Asian societies: China, Korea, and Japan. Also, do not ignore the fact that as the Americas gain their freedom from colonization and the issue of slavery is debated, Western ideas drive the discussion. These Greco-Roman ideas of individual liberty also become a source of the independence movements in the twentieth century as the colonial empires across the world declined.

7. The Great Traditions: Judaism, Christianity, and Islam

Common Characteristics

- Monotheistic religion (one god)
- Traditionally founded by Abraham (first follower of God)
- Emphasis on an individual's relation with God
- The Old Testament/Torah is accepted by all, including the instructions given to Moses (the Ten Commandments)

Judaism

- Philosophical and historical foundation of both Christianity and Islam
- Founded about 2000 BCE
- Religion of the Hebrew people (a nomadic tribe from northern Arabia)
- Moses led the Jews out of captivity in Egypt and gave them the Ten Commandments, which is the basis for their laws
- Prophets argued for greater ethical and moral behavior; this was more important than religious ceremony
- Jewish state was formed but split and was then conquered
  - A Jewish state reformed under the Persian emperor Cyrus the Great and the temple was rebuilt
  - Alexander the Great conquered the region and it went to his generals upon his death
  - Pompey the Great of Rome entered the region in 68 BCE
- Rebellion against Rome in 66 CE resulted in the destruction of the temple and the expulsion of the Jews from Palestine
- Judaism spread through the diaspora of the Jewish people who fled conquerors or were banished
- Followers of the Jewish faith often faced severe persecution; legal discrimination was instituted in most West European countries during the Medieval period and continued to the early twentieth century

- Today fewer than 20 million followers
  - ◦ Many different sects; specific differences evolved between Eastern European Jews and those in Spain, North Africa, and the Middle East
  - ◦ Israel, the Jewish state, established after World War II, now has a population just over 7 million, mostly Jewish

Christianity

- Founded during the first century in Roman Judea
- Originally seen as a sect of Judaism but would add a number of books (the New Testament) to the Jewish holy writings, creating the Bible
- Based on the belief in salvation offered by the sacrifice of God's son, Jesus; basic teachings: love thy neighbor and do unto others (Golden Rule; Confucius offered the same advice, referred to as the Silver Rule)
- Apostles spread the word to Jewish and non-Jewish populations in the Roman Empire (using the road network and the security of the empire to travel across Europe and around the Mediterranean)
- Egalitarian message of salvation for all appealed to the lower classes as well as the slave populations of the empire
- By the fourth century, the upper classes were converting
  - ◦ Emperor Constantine legalized Christianity in the empire, and it soon became the official religion
  - ◦ With the fall of Rome in the West, Christianity survived as the unifying force of Europe
- Egalitarian in belief, Christianity nevertheless developed a hierarchy; the bishop of Rome asserted control over the church in the West, leading to the first major split in Christianity between the Roman Catholic and the Eastern Orthodox Church
- The Reformation saw a further split in the church with the development of Protestant sects

- Today, Christianity is the largest single religion, with over 2.3 billion followers of all denominations; its influence is exceptionally strong in the Americas and sub-Saharan Africa

Islam

- Founded by Muhammad during the seventh century
- Muhammad encountered monotheistic beliefs (Judaism and Christianity) during his travels as a caravan merchant
- The teachings of Muhammad were revealed to him; eventually recorded in the Quran, the holy book of Islam
- Basic teaching require a submission to God's (Allah's) will

  - The Five Pillars of Islam
  - Acceptance of one God (Allah) and of Muhammad as his prophet
  - Prayer five times a day facing Mecca
  - Fasting during the holy month of Ramadan
  - Paying the zakat, a tax for the poor
  - Making a pilgrimage to Mecca once during one's life if possible

- Muhammad referred to Jews and Christians as "people of the book" and encouraged his followers to treat the religions with respect
- Muhammad called for a community of all Muslims, the *umma*, hoping to break the tribal customs of Arabia that led to constant warfare among the nomadic Bedouin
- A detailed set of laws (the sharia) arose out of the Quran and Arabic tradition
- Islam placed political power in the hands of Muhammad's successors, the Caliphs
- An early succession dispute led to a split in Islam, creating Shiite and Sunni branches
- Sufism is a third but much smaller branch of Islam

- Women were important in the early formation of Islam, because Muhammad had no sons, but Arabic traditions limited the role of women outside of the family
- Strict interpretation of sharia law can limit a woman's contact with people outside of her family and require the wearing of various head coverings in public
- Islam did not define specific social classes and has allowed slavery (although in theory Muslims are prohibited from enslaving other Muslims), encouraged the merchant and warrior classes, and held men of learning of both a religious and/or scientific nature in high esteem
- Like Christianity, Islam promotes an egalitarian idea and opens heaven to all who follow the religion
- Over 1.1 billion people currently follow Islam; it is one of the fastest growing religions in the world
- Sunnism is practiced among most of the Arab countries (Iraq having a large Shiite population) in the Middle East and North Africa; the Ottoman and Mughal Empires also were Sunni, and the region's Muslim populations remain Sunni
- Shiism includes a strong majority in Iran (historical Persia) and minority populations in many Persian Gulf states

On the Essays

When asked about any of these religious traditions, do not forget their ties to politics (the authority of the pope through the Middle Ages and the Renaissance and the joining of religious and secular authority in the caliphs) and the use of religious themes in the art of each society. Comparison questions will also likely focus on conflicts between the three traditions. Muslims drove the Byzantines (Orthodox Christians) out of the Middle East and eventually destroyed the last remnant of the Roman Empire. The Crusades not only sent Christian armies of both knights and peasants to the Holy Land to rid it of Muslims, but

Crusaders also killed many Jews in Europe as they marched toward the east. Throughout history, the Jewish people faced social and legal discrimination. Muslim lands were repeatedly colonized by European states during the nineteenth century, due to rich economic and cultural resources. One result of the decolonization process was the artificial creation of the states of Israel and Palestine by the United Nations, which has led to more than 60 years of violence in the Middle East.

Also, the traditions of each religion face serious challenges from international economic forces. Societies created through the colonial economic policies of Europe and America are often less religious and more tolerant, while oil wealth in Saudi Arabia and Iran allow the theocratic governments to impose a strict form of Islam with tight controls over dissent to religious authority. Israel, a Jewish state, finds itself also with large parts of its population professing only weak ties to their faith. If asked about social influences, be sure to review the question to find the right time period. During the height of Islam, its society was far more secular than today, because international trade brought great prosperity and cosmopolitanism to the empire. At the same time, in Europe, the Roman Catholic Church demanded absolute obedience to its doctrine and established special tribunals to identify and punish heretics who disagreed with the Church.

On the Multiple-Choice Questions

Remember the commonalities: monotheism has its origins in the Middle East and the Old Testament. Also, questions will often tie religion to a political state. Review these:

- Judaism—Rome, Israel
- Christianity—Rome, eastern and western Europe, the Crusader states, the Spanish Empire, the imperial powers of the nineteenth century
- Islam—the caliphates, the Ottoman, Safavid, and Mughal Empires, Mamluks from Egypt, Iran (especially the 1979 revolution)

8. Converts: The Spreading of Religions

BUDDHISM	Egalitarian appeal to the lower caste in India
	Missionaries followed the Silk Road, bringing the religion to China
	China's cultural influence over Korea and Japan helped spread the religion to those areas
CHRISTIANITY	Missionaries carried the word of Jesus into the Roman Empire
	Egalitarian beliefs (the meek shall inherit the earth) created many converts among the enslaved and poor of the empire
	Conversion of Constantine and recognition by Emperor Theodosius I of Christianity as the official religion of the empire cemented its position in Europe
	Missionaries in the Middle Ages converted the Germanic tribes, the Vikings, the Slavs, and the Russians to Christianity
	European exploration, especially the discovery of the New World, spread the word with a mix of missionary work and weapons
	Nineteenth-century evangelical movements brought missionaries to all corners of the world; many in Africa and significant minorities in other regions converted
CONFUCIANISM	Korea, Japan, and Vietnam all had elites in their society who adopted Chinese customs to establish their position of authority; this included Confucianism
ISLAM	Initially, the Arab conquerors were able to convert many, because they were perceived as liberators by some, and the egalitarian message of Islam (the concept of the *umma*) was appealing
	Economic advantages, specifically the exemption from taxes charged to non-Muslims and the ability to join the conquering armies, also encouraged conversions
	Trade routes allowed merchants to disseminate Islam; their piety and the scientific advances of Islamic civilization influenced many in distant areas to convert to Islam
	Migrations within colonial nations spread Islamic communities into some regions of Africa and Europe

ISLAM (cont.)	Economic migrations into Europe and the United States in the second half of the twentieth century have created growing minority Muslim populations in the West
JUDAISM	Not an evangelical religion
	Spread by diasporas caused by conquest, especially during the time of the Roman Empire
	Later spread by pogroms in eastern Europe that encouraged Jews to flee to the West, particularly the United States
	The Zionist movement encouraged a return of Jews to Palestine in the twentieth century

On the Essays

Make sure to cover both the method (missionaries, conquest, trade) and the reason (egalitarianism, social or political advantage, threat of force) for the movement of a religion.

9. Democracy

Taken for granted by many in the twenty-first century, democratic government seems to hold the dominant position in international politics. Even states such as China, with authoritarian governments, are seen as having to adopt measures to gain more popular approval or risk losing power. However, democratic governments are relatively new, and they were slow to rise, and even when they did form, they often did not enfranchise everyone.

First, Ancient Greece

- Only free adult male citizens could participate in most assemblies.
- Citizenship was very restricted: one must have been born in a city-state to parents who were already citizens. Of the roughly 300,000 people in Attica, the Athenian state, only an estimated 30,000 (10 percent) could actually participate in the democratic government—and Athens was one of the *most* democratic states.

- Many of the assemblies were limited to debate topics selected by a smaller council mostly consisting of aristocratic families; laws from an assembly could be nullified by a smaller council of aristocrats.
- States like Athens did not incorporate individuals from other areas into their government, even when they were allied or conquered.

Ancient Rome

- Necessity required a republic (a body of elected representatives because of the size of the overall population).
- Citizens were initially of two classes: patricians (the landowning elite) and plebeians (the commoners of the city and countryside).
- Patricians enjoyed special privileges in government, although over time the plebeians worked to limit these. One way to limit patrician power was the veto power of the tribune (an elected plebeian).
- Over time, wealth (mostly generated by trade) allowed more plebeians into the senate and other government offices.
- The wealth of Rome gained from conquest brought slaves, who took jobs from the poorer classes and even did some skilled work, like tutoring.
  - The poverty of unemployed Romans allowed some to manipulate and exploit them by providing basic needs; Julius Caesar was one of the most famous to do so.
  - Public entertainments (or games) and the distribution of food won over the masses and cost Rome its republic (the practice became known as "bread and circuses").

Venetian Republic

- A popular revolt created a limited republic in Venice in the seventh century.
- As the wealthiest state in Western Europe, Venice had a large

middle class of merchant families that used the revolt to limit the power of the older, established noble families.

- The Venetian trade empire allowed them to remain an independent republic for four centuries.
- Venice declined as trade shifted from the Mediterranean to new routes around Africa and across the Atlantic to the New World riches, and the republic fell because the nobles allied with more powerful states (Austria-Hungary, France, Spain).
- Wealth equals democracy, and economic decline causes it to falter.

The British-American Model

- Britain's tradition of limited government began in 1215 with the Magna Carta.
- The English civil war temporarily gave England a ruling Parliament, although it fell to the dictatorial rule of Oliver Cromwell.
- The restoration of the monarchy and the Glorious Revolution of 1688 produced a limited monarchy and a limited republican government.
- Industrialization created a large middle class.
- As the gentry class's advantage in wealth faded, more and more people were enfranchised (given the vote).
- By the mid-nineteenth century, both the liberal and conservative parties in England saw an advantage in giving voting rights to more male citizens, eventually enfranchising all of them (women would have to wait for the end of the First World War).
- Americans during the Revolution wanted only what they believed their British cousins had, that is, a very limited form of a republic.
- America limited enfranchisement to protect the power of the wealthy and middle classes.
- Over time, all would be enfranchised in the United States through the passage of amendments to the Constitution.

Modern Democratic Principles

- After decolonization, the European powers hoped that their colonies would adopt democratic governments.

  ○ Colonies with large European populations did so (for example, Canada, Australia, and New Zealand).

  ○ Some (for example, South Africa) refused to enfranchise native groups.

  ○ Non-European populations faced a number of issues.

    · Many former colonies, especially in Africa, were populated by multiple ethnic groups that turned on each other in order to secure their own positions.

    · In general, poverty allowed a small elite to establish control over populations through patronage (a system as old as Rome, where wealthy families largely supported a pool of poor families who did as they were told).

    · The Cold War meant that an elite that was willing to work with the Soviet or Western alliance would have the military force to do as they wished within their own country.

  ○ Even though India suffered from crippling poverty, it created a true democracy in the 1960s and 1970s. But India is the exception.

- The end of the Cold War and globalization produced a climate that increased the size of the middle class and promoted democratic ideas championed by many of the major powers (the United States and the European Union), resulting in many more democracies today.

On the Essays

Democracy as a political idea originated in the West. When discussing democracy in societies outside of the West, you must make the connection between Western culture and the introduction of democratic ideas into the region. Often this occurred during the colonial period, with independence bringing at least temporarily democratic regimes. The spread of capitalism and the fall of the Soviet Union also contributed to greater adoption of democratic principles.

On the Multiple-Choice Questions

When looking for causes for political change, democracy is popular, but often economic change and political conflict occur first. Make sure not to pick an answer just because it plays on the popularity of democracies. More often, economic reforms and a growing middle class precede democracy.

10. It's the Economy

When analyzing change over time or the similarities and differences between two cultures, often economics will provide an answer. Psychologists describe people as operating based on their needs (Maslow's hierarchy of needs). The basic needs include food and shelter, and the fundamentals of economics include these as well. Until basic needs are met, not much else will occur.

In times of wealth, societies will advance on a variety of fronts. Politically, they must adapt to new groups with economic influence that want to protect what they have. Emperors, kings, governors, senates, and parliaments must all incorporate new social groups into the political system, because if they fail to enfranchise them, the new groups will use their economic power. Examples include

- Adjustments in the Roman republic for greater participation by plebeians.
- The Magna Carta granting legal protections over private property for the nobles of England.
- The institution of civil service exams in China that allowed educated individuals—including the children of wealthy merchants who could afford tutors—to enter the government.
- As the Middle Ages came to a close, Western European leaders began granting royal charters to cities to protect the growing middle

class (merchants and artisans) from local nobles in exchange for the payment of taxes that kings could use to raise their own armies and eventually equip them with firearms.

- The Ottoman Turks' bureaucratic administration of merchant and labor guilds allowed protection of jobs and wages by favoring the guilds' control over how many could enter a profession and the quality of production to protect trade income.

- The inclusion of Enlightenment ideas into England's Glorious Revolution and the American and French Revolutions in the late eighteenth century all enfranchised the middle class that grew out of industrialization.

  ○ Even the failed European revolutions of 1830 and 1848 forced monarchs to accept greater participation by the middle class in government and to offer them protections (property and civil rights).

Economics also allows for social change. When given economic opportunities outside of traditional family roles, women gain greater status. The West experienced this between the two world wars of the twentieth century, giving women the right to vote but also accepting more women in the workplace in nontraditional jobs. The decline in the serf population in Europe after the Black Death increased the value of serfs (actually their labor) and forced the nobles to raise wages and abandon some feudal duties, even changing laws to allow serfs to flee their lands in search of work. In India, the caste system, although outlawed, still exists, but the closer one is to multinational corporations and modern call centers, the less influence caste has and the more education and skills determine one's path in life.

One sign of economic prosperity you should not overlook is the increasing importance of art. Artists are specialists. Only a surplus of wealth allows individuals to make careers out of works of art. Wealthy patrons buy works of culture, and governments engage in public building projects that promote architecture. Economics also favors literature, because wealthy societies are more educated, creating a market for more works with words.

On the Essays

Be sure to include economics in any analysis of your argument. How do the ups and downs of wealth shape changes or allow for differences between societies? Make note also of the constant conflict between the haves and the have-nots in a society and how changes in economic activity affect that balance. For example, the development of better oceangoing vessels transferred trade from the Turkish-dominated overland Silk Road to the European-controlled Indian Ocean trade routes. Initially this aided European kings, but as it made rich men out of both merchants and manufacturers, the balance of power shifted to the middle class. For example, in Portugal the kings resisted change, and their government fell from its previous eminence.

On the Multiple-Choice Questions

Remember to consider how economic changes free up an individual's potential actions, or how negative changes can restrict those options. If you are trying to narrow down your choices in a cause-and-effect question, go with the money.

11. Plagues

Plagues introduce a devastatingly force for change in societies. They affect most areas of culture. Economically, they introduce several changes. First, plagues disrupt trade, because population centers, even before real scientific understanding of what causes a disease to spread, close themselves to outsiders, fearing that outsiders bring disease. The disease itself also may reduce the population of urban areas so much that the urban areas are no longer attractive destinations for goods. Without wealth in the cities, surrounding rural communities lose markets for their goods, thus putting a strain on their incomes. Without the need of workers, the poorest of the rural populations face starvation because they can no longer earn wages with which to buy food. Economic disruptions may touch off political change. Tax revenues decrease as economic activities decline. Governments that try to collect taxes at the previous levels often face desperation among the poor, which may evolve into revolution.

People do not turn only on their governments. Religions—a primary source of stability in a society—may face challenges when the people lose faith in their beliefs or in their religious leadership, even when religion may offer hope of stability by providing care for the sick and a meaning for all about the losses a plague might bring. Either way, do not forget to discuss the effects of plagues on religious stability in a society. The indiscriminate nature of death brought on by plagues may also weaken the elite of a society. The general failure of any social group to escape the plague calls into question the accepted beliefs about the social hierarchy. It can also leave a vacuum in the social order, because deaths among the elite and economic decline remove some of the key controls the elites hold over the masses in a society. As new patterns of economic activity arise, new groups can seize greater social status to match their increased economic importance.

Even art may take on new expressions as people try to cope with their loss. Images of death occur more frequently. Written works and plays address more issues around death and may even mock it as it overwhelms the people's ability to process what is going on around them. Many of the paintings during the Black Death in Europe included images of death itself, often depicted as a skeletal figure. Works of literature like *The Decameron* by Italian Giovanni Boccaccio, which includes numerous tales that once might have offended readers, are set during the time of the plague and use the plague as a literary device—the cause for the storytellers to share their experiences—thus the Black Death freed up people to express themselves more openly.

MAJOR HISTORICAL PLAGUES

LOCATION	TIME PERIOD	CHANGE
Athens	5th century BCE	Weakened Athens, contributing to its loss during the Peloponnesian War and the failure of Greece to unite into a larger state
		Macedonia under Philip II and then Alexander the Great would unite Greece a decade later
Rome	3rd century CE	Possibly caused by mumps or smallpox
		Caused shortage of men in the legions and reduced agricultural output
		Contributed to overall decline in the empire
Spread from Central Asia and China to Egypt and Byzantine Empire	6th century	Probably bubonic plague
		Prevented Emperor Justinian's attempts to reconquer the western Roman Empire
		Allowed the Germanic tribes to extend their control over more of Europe
Black Death: Asia and Europe	14th century	Worst pandemic in history
		Spread along trade routes (Silk Road) between China and Europe
		Weakened Mongol Empire and Islamic states in the Middle East
		Depopulated Western Europe (killing about a third of the population) and altered the social, economic, and political structure of feudalism
The Columbian Exchange: The Americas	16th–17th centuries	Triggered by the introduction of diseases by the Europeans into the New World
		Devastated the population of the Americas
		Wrecked whole societies before Europeans even encountered them
		Lack of indigenous labor led to increased importation of slaves from Africa

LOCATION	TIME PERIOD	CHANGE
China and India	mid-19th century	Bubonic plague Further devastated Qing China, which was already torn apart by revolution and European intervention
Spanish Flu Pandemic	1919	Influenza Spread around the world as soldiers returned home from the First World War in Europe China, spared from much of the fighting of the First World War, still suffered huge casualties from the flu Demonstrated the danger of modern, rapid global transportation
SARS	2002–2003	Started in China and spread to Vietnam Identified but kept secret initially by the Chinese About 8,000 cases with nearly 800 deaths Spread rapidly via airline traffic Forced nations and the World Health Organization to develop contingencies for monitoring and quarantining passengers

12. Elites and the Masses

Historically, most societies find themselves dominated by small elites. Elites use a variety of methods to control the larger masses. Political authority must be backed up with any of a variety of forces. In many early civilizations, the elite mixed politics and religion, taking on the position of a god on earth or of being appointed by the heavens. This enabled the elite to threaten the masses in life and in death.

Economically, elites use wealth to fragment the masses, building patron-client relations with parts of the population. Many in the masses saw their livelihoods dependent on keeping the elites in control. The use of money to buy segments of the masses also allowed elites to apply force to the remainder of the population. State police, security forces, and secret police all received high wages for oppressing larger segments of society. These high wages and the fear of what might happen to them should the elites lose power made security forces a powerful tool.

Military force also separated the elites from the masses. In feudal Europe and Japan, the nobles monopolized military training. The invention of simple, deadly weapons like the crossbow and then firearms, however, limited the ability of any small group to control deadly force. In the twentieth century, military coups became a common occurrence in developing nations when the elites found themselves unable to manage the economic demands of their people and control the powerful militaries that were supplied by the Cold War superpowers: the United States or the Soviet Union.

Other methods elites used to control the masses of people include

- access to education
- control of media (especially in the era of radio and television)
- restrictions on technology
- limited legal rights to the masses
- control of the justice system

On the Multiple-Choice Questions

On questions about political control and power, make sure to consider how those in power maintained control.

On the Essays

A document-based question could include groupings based on elites and masses. This can also be used to establish point of view: someone in the elite would definitely perceive something differently than a member of the masses. Change-over-time questions will often consider the shifting balance of power between elites in a society and the masses. Changing economics (new sources of income, the Industrial Revolution) and new technologies (firearms) will alter the balance.

13. Slavery

No period of history is without slavery. You need to identify the origins of the slaves in major civilizations and how these individuals were used. Classical civilizations generally used conquered peoples as slave laborers. Most found their way into mining or agricultural work, both of which were very labor intensive and often very dangerous.

SLAVERY

CLASSICAL CIVILIZATIONS	Slaves originated as conquered peoples
	Used most often in mines (very hazardous work) or in agriculture
	Some skilled slaves were employed in business and as tutors
POSTCLASSICAL— ISLAMIC CALIPHATE	In Europe, slavery was largely replaced by serfdom
	In the caliphates, slaves were mostly agricultural workers and servants
	Turks were captured and enslaved by Arabs, only to overthrow them in the eleventh century
	Turks, Slavs, and other peoples purchased along the Black Sea coast were used as slave soldiers in Egypt and by the Abbasid caliphate's elites
	East African slave trade was an important part of the Indian Ocean trade routes
OTTOMAN EMPIRE	Janissaries formed a military elite of slave soldiers; they would dominate Ottoman politics until the nineteenth century
	A plantation system of agricultural workers was developed from East Africa (prisoners of war and convicts taken by African states and sold to merchants in trade city-states along the coast)
RENAISSANCE EUROPE	Slavery was abolished in some areas, but some slaves were kept, and serfdom continued through the period

THE NEW WORLD	The plantation system required massive amounts of labor, especially for sugar production
	Natives worked on plantations and in mines, but they died very quickly, and their numbers after the initial deaths from exposure to European diseases never provided enough labor
	Africans first imported from East Africa initially provided labor for colonies like Brazil
	Demand exceeded supply, and European traders offered bounties for slaves along the West Coast of Africa
NINETEENTH CENTURY	Slavery was eventually abolished by the Europeans and the New World colonies and nations
	Slavery continued to exist in the Ottoman Empire and some areas of Central and Southeast Asia and Africa
	The imperial powers eliminated slavery in the areas under their rule, but many slaves remained virtual slaves because they were forced to work for the imperial governments or companies as a form of taxation
TWENTIETH CENTURY	Legal slavery ended, but many nations failed to prevent the selling of children as workers, women as sex slaves, and sweatshops in developing nations
	At the start of the twenty-first century, the U.S. government reported between 700,000 and 4 million individuals were "trafficked" or sold as slaves annually

On the Multiple-Choice Questions

Do not isolate slavery as an American issue or slaves as coming solely from Africa. All civilizations used or were subject to enslavement prior to the twentieth century. Many slaves also performed professional and even military duties, depending on their talents.

On the Essays

Be sure to discuss the slaves' origins, their economic activity, and their position in the social order of the civilization in question. In a document-based question, look at groupings based on those that benefit economically from slavery and those who work with enslaved populations and wish to improve their conditions (such as missionaries in early Spanish America). For a change-over-time question, discuss the economic situations that made slavery less profitable or politically useful. For example, industrialization and better agricultural techniques make slave labor on plantations less economically viable.

14. Mercantilism and Free Market Capitalism

The age of exploration and subsequent colonization allowed for an evolution of European economies into one based on the private ownership of capital. Initially, European nations sought to control markets and resources through colonization and protective trade practices. The belief that the world's wealth was limited and that economic wealth now defined a state's political power encouraged confrontation between the European powers.

Eventually, economists argued for less protectionism and open trade. One of the most significant economists, a Scotsman named Adam Smith, published *The Wealth of Nations*, which argued for free trade. He described an "invisible hand" that represented the individual interests of each person and drove the economy. He also made a strong argument to end government interference in the economy, to allow market forces and individuals to manage the overall economy and to control production, distribution, and wages.

Capitalism became the dominant economic system in the nineteenth century and remained so throughout the twentieth century. Globalization in the late twentieth century used markets and reduced protectionist practices to further integrate national markets into a larger global market. While no nation operates a completely free market system, the vast majority of nations do allow market forces to control much of the production and distribution of goods.

On the Multiple-Choice Questions

Remember to associate mercantilism and free markets both with the idea of private property, individual rights, and the Enlightenment. Do not forget that, under mercantilism, economic interest demanded political action toward colonial conquest and often required wars, because mercantilism relies on colonies for markets for raw and finished goods. Free market systems did not depend on taking wealth from other nations by force, but free trade creates internal conflicts between business interests and labor, because it allows for the movement of jobs to other countries, that is, outsourcing.

On the Essays

Use the term *capitalism* correctly. It is not a "good" or "bad" system; it is simply an economic system that bases production, distribution, and wages on private ownership and private property. On a document-based question, economics can easily be the focus of a group of documents, so a discussion of capitalism or markets or mercantilism might be used to form a group. Comparison essays often require economic comparisons. Use the vocabulary correctly; mercantilism describes the system of the seventeenth and eighteenth centuries. Free trade or free market economics takes center stage in the late nineteenth century and is championed by the United States and Great Britain. In a change-over-time essay, connect mercantilism to the growing efforts of European nations to colonize the globe (imperialism) while free market systems encourage competition and allow powerful economies like the United States to grow into political powers.

15. Socialism

Nineteenth-century political and economic thought created a number of systems that blended both areas and rejected the growing dominance of capitalism, especially free-market capitalism. The most lasting is socialism. Basically, socialism calls for extensive government involvement in the economy. Government, not the individual or market, controls the means of production, supply, price, and distribution. One of the most prominent proponents of this system was Karl Marx, who argued against the inequalities in society allowed by capitalism.

Many historians date socialist ideas much earlier than the nineteenth century, but the mix of the Industrial Revolution and the French Revolution drove the ideas to the forefront of political thought. The Industrial Revolution dramatically altered social and economic systems in Europe. The promise of cheaper material goods and a better standard of living failed to materialize, however. Instead, a seemingly permanent underclass developed. The French Revolution reflected some of the frustration and aspirations of this underclass, known as the working poor.

European democratic governments developed policies that adopted more socialist ideas when they were forced to enfranchise (give the right to vote) to more and more people. Some extreme proponents of socialism called for the complete restructuring of society; people would live in self-sustaining communities and relinquish their private property and family status. More realistically, socialist politicians pushed for greater protection of worker's rights:

- universal male suffrage
- elimination of all property qualifications so that anyone could hold elected office
- salaries for the elected members of government
- equal electoral districts (one man, one vote)
- secret ballot
- elimination of class privileges
- limited workdays
- the right to form unions

Many European governments adopted some of these programs, but none became a full-blown socialist state. Even conservative-dominated governments, in order to prevent a working-class revolution, instituted some socialist programs such as unemployment benefits, old-age pensions, and expanded labor protections.

In the twentieth century, socialism received greater public support in many European nations when political parties formed to promote socialist ideas. By the end of World War II, most developed nations, especially in Europe, employed many socialist ideas and were dominated by socialist political parties. High taxation pays for a number of programs to free them from market forces: public education, health care, social welfare programs, unemployment insurance, subsidized public transportation, and energy. Many developing nations also have generated socialist political parties that demand greater government involvement in their economies.

Communism, a form of socialism, called for even greater change. Karl Marx predicted the violent overthrow of capitalist governments by the proletariat (urban factory workers), in order to achieve a truly equal society. The communist governments of the twentieth century managed to enforce many socialist ideas on their populations, but none were able to produce the material goods to allow for the long-term sustainability of their economies. Most were forced to mix market capitalism with socialism.

On the Multiple-Choice Questions

Remember, socialism is a nineteenth-century idea that finds great support in the democracies of the twentieth century. Socialist ideas focus on greater government control of the economy and on securing economic freedoms for the classes newly gaining political rights.

On the Essays

Socialism might show up on an essay to compare some of the twentieth-century revolutions. Remember, the basic focus of socialism is on politics and the economy. Also, do not forget that communism is a radical form of socialism. Socialism will not likely be the main focus of an essay, but you can use it to explain some of the political and economic changes of the last century, including labor movements, women's rights, mass demonstrations and strikes, the European Union, and Cold War politics.

16. Totalitarianism

The twentieth century saw the rise of totalitarian states. Previously, many absolute governments existed, such as the monarchs of seventeenth-century Europe, Chinese emperors, the Mongol Khans, the pharaohs of Egypt. However, a totalitarian state mixes different cultural forces. Previous absolute monarchs ruled with full political control with backing by military force and religious ideology (pharaoh as god, the "Mandate of Heaven" in China, and the European divine right of kings).

Totalitarian states seek to dominate all areas of culture and require that an individual exists to serve the state. A single political party, often with a charismatic leader, establishes complete control over the government. They mix an authoritarian form of government with a new ideology that replaces previous beliefs. Technological innovations like mass media allow the state to control all sources of information, and social institutions (such as schools) become messengers of the state's ideology. No dissent is tolerated.

The first regime to be identified as totalitarian was Benito Mussolini's fascist Italy. Mussolini was elected to office, then he altered the constitution to gain complete power and then used the press and radio to vilify the opposition, create a national sense of emergency, and promote the fascist salvation of the Italian state. The Nazi Party in Germany did the same. Communists—who were politically opposed to fascists—did the same in the Soviet Union (under Joseph Stalin) and in the People's Republic of China (under Mao Tse-tung).

The control of information appears to be the cornerstone of a successful totalitarian state. During the Cold War era, most uprisings against governments in lesser-developed nations almost always began with the seizure of a single radio or television station by the rebels. However, technology in the early twenty-first century offers a real challenge to the totalitarian state. The Internet, satellite television, cellular phones, texting, Twitter, and social networking all challenge a state's ability to control information. Regimes such as the one in China depend upon modern communication to integrate their economies with the world, but these same connections allow information to flow back into the totalitarian regimes and challenge their view of reality.

On the Multiple-Choice Questions

Take into account the complete control over an individual's life inherent in a totalitarian regime and how that control must be maintained. Questions might touch upon how a totalitarian state mobilizes its people and how outside influences are vilified by the state so that individuals influenced by them become the enemy. Also, nationalism may play a role in totalitarian control, because often the state identifies an external enemy that seeks to destroy the people and their culture.

On the Essays

For document-based questions, review documents for how they both might demonstrate a totalitarian state's control of its people. Don't forget that anyone writing from within such a state clearly must be writing under pressure from the government to state the information as the government sees it, or they are risking punishment by defying the state. Comparison questions should include the ways in which totalitarian regimes shape public opinion via media and the arts (even to the point of rewriting history in textbooks and presenting it in the media). A comparison question could ask you to discuss economic development, something that totalitarian states, anxious to industrialize and protect their military power, often cast as nationalistic or patriotic duties of their citizens. Fascist Italy and Nazi Germany made advanced industrialization a matter of survival for the culture of their nations. The Soviet Union and North Korea identified outside enemies as forcing them to develop heavy industries and vast militaries so their people could survive.

17. Revolutions

When discussing revolutions, focus on the real changes involved in the culture. Use the PERSIAN categories: Politics, Economics, Religion/Beliefs, Social Order, Innovations/Technology, and Arts. For instance, with the Industrial Revolution, the real changes include

- Economics: a new system of production that required changes in
  - financing (because businesses needed to raise capital and borrow funds in much greater amounts)
  - wages paid to workers
  - marketing (to increase consumer purchasing at home)
- Social Order: a new class (the working poor or proletariat) became a key component of industrial and urban societies
  - the middle class expanded greatly as professional skills (accountants, lawyers, engineers, scientists) were required in greater numbers and professionals could demand greater pay due to their specialized skills
- Innovation/Technology: success depended on innovation, and better manufacturing techniques, machines, and chemistry all started to play a role in a nation's power and success

The French Revolution and the revolutions of 1830 and 1848 must include a discussion of class, because middle-class beliefs, the collapse of traditional rural peasant life, and the introduction of the working poor into urban areas all affected the political goals and outcomes of these revolutions.

Do not describe revolutions as a series of events without identifying the underlying pressures for change and the cultural areas affected.

WHAT'S IN A REVOLUTION

AMERICAN	Politics: ideas of a republic vs. a monarchy (even a limited one)
	Economics: limits imposed by mercantilist policies on an aspiring middle class in the colonies

AMERICAN (CONT.)	Social Order: the new colonies were gradually developing a new social identity based on their unique circumstances (like contact with Native Americans, need for self-reliance, and mixed ethnic identity of settlers) that was more socially equal than England
MEXICAN	Economics: many indigenous people and *mestizos* suffered under foreign investors in Mexico, so they supported a change in the elites who ruled prior to 1910
	Social Order: indigenous groups rose in revolt against a government that did not include them, and forced subsequent governments to consider their demands (populism)
	Social Order: managed to maintain a small elite, although its makeup changed, that became very wealthy and stabilized Mexican society by monopolizing many of Mexico's natural resources
RUSSIAN/ BOLSHEVIK	Politics: a failing absolutist monarchy against a new charismatic elite with promises of relief for the destitute masses
	Religion/Beliefs: an entirely untried political–economic system (communism–socialism) replaces a feudal system that was outlawed but still dominated many peasants alongside a failing attempt at rapid industrialization
	Social Order: promises of relief for the working poor and peasants who were on the verge of starvation and had nothing to lose
CUBAN	Politics: U.S. support for the dictator Batista created a resentment among many in Cuba and led to Castro's turning to the USSR after the revolution
	Politics: the Cold War pushed aside several revolutionary goals held by many common people because Cuba immediately became a battleground for the two superpowers and Cuba's leadership could not afford dissent from within
	Economics: American money supported many of the elites in Cuba prior to the revolution and fed general distrust of American motives during the revolution

IRAN'S ISLAMIC REVOLUTION	Economics and Innovation: Westernization programs initiated by the Shah (an autocratic leader backed by the United States) created a wide division between those who benefited and those who did not, notably landlords, small merchants, and religious scholars
	Religion/Beliefs: religious students started the revolution and were instrumental in the ouster of the Shah and the rise to prominence of the Ayatollah Ruhollah Khomeini

On the Multiple-Choice Questions

Be sure to consider the underlying cultural causes for the revolutions and—if asked about changes from a revolution—to consider cultural areas as well. Don't look for questions that simply ask you to order the events of a revolution without considering the cultural pressures for change. You need to understand events based on cultural impacts.

On the Essays

On document-based questions, look to group documents based on cultural areas. On the comparison essay, you can use cultural areas to structure your body paragraphs. For example, comparing the French and Russian Revolutions, have a body paragraph on social forces, political ideas, and economic challenges. The change-over-time essay must begin with a discussion of the cultural areas affected by the revolution. What were they like before revolutionary change? How did that change affect them? What does the culture look like after the revolution?

18. Independence

Two separate waves of independence movements occurred during the modern era. The first began with the American Revolution and ran through the mid-nineteenth century. The second began after the end of the Second World War and peaked in the 1960s.

The first colonies to seek independence followed two distinct paths. For the 13 American colonies, independence meant achieving the freedoms already guaranteed to Englishmen, along with several expanded freedoms put forward by Enlightenment philosophers. The American Revolution pitted an established middle class of landowners and merchants against the economic limitations imposed by the British Crown and its agents, such as the British East India Company. Other colonial revolts in the Americas did not include the same factors.

In Haiti (1804) and Mexico (1810), the lower classes played the significant role in overthrowing the colonial masters. Haiti stands as the only slave revolt to produce an independent nation run by former slaves. The Haitians were inspired by promises of the French Revolution that remained unfulfilled. The slaves were able to win their independence, but they did not enjoy the diverse and globally connected economy found in the American colonies. Sugar produced income for some Haitians, but the Haitian economy failed to lead to a broader middle class or representative government. In Mexico, the original revolt came out of the *mestizos*, the mixed race of peasants. However, the successful overthrow of Spanish rule came when conservative Creoles (those of European descent) overthrew the Spanish authorities and established their own government over Mexico. This government protected the powers of the Creoles and did not pass on the freedoms and ideas of the Enlightenment.

In the other Spanish colonies, Creoles fought to take control from the Spanish authorities and used the Napoleonic Wars as cover for their revolt. Even though many would discuss the ideas of the Enlightenment, they did not create Enlightenment governments, as in the United States. The small Creole class monopolized power and generally sought to appease certain segments of the masses in order to maintain political and economic control.

Generally, the first wave of independence created only European states outside of Europe—with the exception of Haiti. The second wave was very different.

After World War II the promises of self-determination combined with the economic collapse of Europe to open the door for many colonies to demand their independence. The United States and Great Britain both made good on previous promises to their major colonial territories. The United States granted the Philippines full independence and offered it the protection of American military power. In South Asia, the British created Muslim Pakistan and predominantly Hindu India. This rewarded Indians for their participation in both world wars, fulfilled the widely supported goal of Mohandas Gandhi, and recognized the inability of the British to maintain a far-flung empire, especially in areas of active opposition. In the Middle East, Arab and Persian states gained full independence. The United Nations also used its new charter to create the nation of Israel.

Toward the end of the 1950s, independence picked up in the remaining colonial domains; those in Southeast Asia, North Africa, and sub-Saharan Africa. Violence went along with many of these movements, first against the colonial oppressors, then in the form of civil wars (tribe against tribe and often Soviet- vs. Western-backed movements). The United Nations sought to expedite the independence process and encourage the formation of stable governments, but few of these independence movements produced lasting institutions, and many of the newly independent nations found themselves with autocratic governments supported or even sustained by armies supplied by one of the superpowers.

Only toward the end of the Cold War did some of the independent nations truly begin to remove themselves from foreign dominance. In the early twentieth century many already independent nations in Latin America were so dependent on foreign investment, especially from the United States and Great Britain, they were often characterized as colonies of the greater economic powers. The Cold War continued this tradition as the Western policy of containment collided head on with the Soviets' attempt to extend their influence through communist revolutions.

Globalization initially freed many in Eastern Europe from Soviet domination, and the former massive military expenditures that maintained many of the oppressive military dictatorships dwindled away. Nations like South Korea became true democracies through civil protest.

INDEPENDENCE MOVEMENTS BY ETHNIC ORIGIN

BY COLONIST	MIXED	BY INDIGENOUS GROUPS
United States	Mexico	India
South Africa	Philippines	Pakistan
Canada	Cuba	Sub-Saharan Africa
Australia–New Zealand	Rhodesia–Zimbabwe	Indonesia
South America (19th century)		Indochina
Haiti (by African slaves)		

On the Multiple-Choice Questions

Most multiple-choice questions will deal with actual revolutions and not the mix of insurgency and decolonization found after World War II. Remember to take into account the efforts by both the United States and the Soviet Union to influence independence movements and newly independent governments during the Cold War.

On the Essays

When comparing independence movements, look at both philosophies (Enlightenment, communism) and the origins of the movements (colonist or indigenous peoples) when making comparisons or trying to place the independence movement into the larger global framework (the Enlightenment at the end of the eighteenth century or the Cold War during the twentieth century).

19. Ethnic Cleansing–Genocide

Although not new to history, genocide became a far too common part of the twentieth century. Most often, the killings were the result of nationalist feelings in regions with ethnic groups seeking or having just gained independence. In other instances, governments or political parties targeted specific ethnicities long discriminated against as a means of gaining political or economic benefits.

After World War II, the newly created United Nations, in response to the Holocaust, created the Convention on the Prevention and Punishment of the Crime of Genocide. Article 2 of the convention states:

> In the present Convention, genocide means any of the following acts committed with intent to destroy, in whole or in part, a national, ethnical, racial, or religious group, as such:

1. Killing members of the group;
2. Causing serious bodily or mental harm to members of the group;
3. Deliberately inflicting on the group conditions of life calculated to bring about its physical destruction in whole or in part;
4. Imposing measures intended to prevent births within the group;
5. Forcibly transferring children of the group to another group.

MAJOR INCIDENCES OF GENOCIDE IN THE TWENTIETH CENTURY

ARMENIAN	1915–1916 (during World War I)
	Initiated by the Ottoman Empire (although this is denied by modern Turkey) against the Armenian minority living in the empire
	As many as 1.5 million died and another 2 million lost their homes through deportation
KULAKS IN THE USSR	Kulaks were more of an economic class than ethnicity; they were prosperous peasants during the early years of the Soviet Union
	Stalin, to secure power, began seizing land belonging to kulaks in the late 1920s
	Many were relocated to the East or arrested
HOLOCAUST	Initiated in Germany when the Nazi Party came to power in the early 1930s
	Initially the Nazis attacked Jewish businesses and synagogues in order to force the Jews out of Germany
	After the war began, Jews in Germany and the conquered territories were relocated to concentration camps for forced labor or execution

HOLOCAUST (CONT.)	Gradually Hitler's final solution targeted populations of Jewish, Polish, and Gypsy origins as well as physically disabled, mentally disabled, and homosexual individuals
	6 million Jews, mostly Eastern Europeans, died in the camps
	200,000 were liberated from the camps at the end of the war
	The Allies held the German leadership responsible for the genocide and held a war crimes tribunal at Nuremberg
KHMER ROUGE (CAMBODIA)	Initiated by the Khmer Rouge (the Communist Party that took over in Cambodia in 1975)
	The Khmer Rouge attacked all segments of society it viewed as subversive, especially intellectuals, professionals, minorities, and urban dwellers
	About 1.5 million died
	Vietnam invaded Cambodia and replaced the regime in 1979
	Some members of the Khmer Rouge were tried for crimes against humanity
YUGOSLAVIA	From 1992 to 1995 (when a U.S.-brokered peace plan went into effect)
	The disintegration of Yugoslavia after the collapse of the Soviet Union created ethnic violence between Serbs, Bosnian Muslims, and Croats
	Serbs sought to gain territory by driving other ethnic groups off of their lands
	The term "ethnic cleansing" was used to describe Serbian attempts to drive out the other groups
	NATO intervened to isolate the fighting but failed to stop the destruction of the civil war
	Fighting ended in 1998 after NATO forces secured Kosovo from Serbians
	Slobodan Milosevic (the Serbian president) was ousted and put on trial for crimes against humanity (he died in prison before the trial was complete)

RWANDA	Hutus (the majority) attacked Tutsis (the minority) in April 1994
	Hutus were afraid of Tutsi attempts to regain control of the government
	UN response failed to stop the violence or protect refugees
	2 million fled the country into Zaire (now the Democratic Republic of the Congo)
	About 500,000 were murdered
	Heightened international awareness about genocide
DARFUR	Oil-rich region in western Sudan
	Northern Arab population attacked villages in the region to force them off the land
	At least 200,000 have died since 2003

On the Essays

The question would most likely only involve genocide as part of larger world events (change over time). If the question involves the fall of the Soviet Union or the globalization of the 1990s, connect the break-up of authoritarian regimes in Eastern Europe and the pullback of both the United States and the Soviet Union from developing nations as contributing factors to the violence in Yugoslavia and the hostilities in Africa.

On the Multiple-Choice Questions

On the multiple-choice questions, make sure you pay attention to the influence of nationalism on internal occurrences of genocide. Questions may refer to specific instances by location and the ethnic groups involved.

20. Globalization

It is the inexorable [impossible to stop] integration of markets, nation-states and technologies to a degree never witnessed before—in a way that is enabling individuals, corporations and nation-states to reach around the world farther, faster, and deeper and cheaper than ever before, and in a way that is enabling the world to reach into individuals, corporations and nation-states farther, faster, deeper, cheaper than ever before.

—Thomas Friedman, author and *New York Times*
foreign affairs columnist

After the collapse of the Soviet Union and the communist countries of Eastern Europe, the world entered another era of globalization. The first had occurred when the nations of Europe initially established their colonial empires during the sixteenth and seventeenth centuries. A second wave occurred as industrialization in the late eighteenth century pushed nations (again mostly European) to look for greater access to global resources and markets. This period culminated with the imperial scramble for colonies in the nineteenth century. Free-trade movements before and after the First World War further integrated international markets, although this fell apart with protectionism due to the Great Depression. After the Second World War, the United States and Western Europe engaged in extensive market integration, but the political realities of the Cold War limited the flow of goods and capital. The collapse of the Soviet Union removed this barrier to greater world trade, and global trade took off beyond anyone's expectations.

Tools of Globalization

Several technological innovations allowed for greater and "deeper" integration during the recent period of globalization.

- Electronic flow of capital: Electronic banking allows for the immediate movement of funds from almost any location to investments in any other location. Anyone may invest or seek investors anywhere in the world, allowing entrepreneurs in even the poorest nations to attach themselves to the most lucrative markets.

- Mass communication: The delivery of media content, from music to news, occurs almost instantly and provides for extensive cultural diffusion as well as greater market information.

- The Internet facilitates all of this.
- Cellular phones allow for even remote locations to actively connect to global markets at a very low cost.

The Impact of Global Diffusion

The key impact of globalization has been the diffusion of culture on a scale never before witnessed in history. Often called Americanization, much of this diffusion does flow from the West, especially the United States, into other regions. Western clothing, music, food, movies, work hours, consumerism, gender roles, and many other influences seep into almost all societies in the twenty-first century. While many (like Japan and South Korea) have embraced these influences and built democratic, capitalist societies, other nations (like the People's Republic of China) reject this exposure, and a few even attempt to ignore the influences completely. Many of the elites in nations like North Korea, Iran, and Burma (Myanmar) see the changes as challenging their traditional roles and influence over their governments. Those with wealth, power, or influence, in order to protect their status, seek to close their societies to these changes and create the greatest challenge for civilizations today.

At one time, walls and distance might isolate those who would attack a civilization, but this is no longer the case. Global societies are just that: worldwide and exposed. The technologies that allow this to happen (for example, air travel, electronic banking, and cell phones) provide some of the most dangerous weapons to those who reject the changes brought by globalization. Even during the height of imperialism, many locals were able to maintain their own cultures and traditions. They also found unity by rejecting the imperials. However, the forces of globalization are different.

The economic consequences of globalization go far deeper into society than imperial rulers. Since the early 1990s, if not earlier, a middle class has taken shape in many nations. This class exists due to the economic consequences of a global consumer society. Like those before them, the new members of the middle class seek economic advancement, political power to protect what they have achieved, and education and security for their children so they may have a better life. Women in this group especially find themselves capable of challenging the previous limits placed on them. Some nations, like many of the former Eastern Bloc nations have been able to embrace a democratic response to these new forces. Nations like Poland and the Czech Republic enjoy generally positive economic growth and political stability.

Other nations find their social and political systems in great turmoil. Nations that deny the changes see their best and brightest people emigrate to the West, and meanwhile their country falls further behind economically and technologically. Pakistan and, for many years, India saw a general "brain drain" of talent as their societies failed to offer educated and ambitious citizens the security, political rights, and standard of living that the West promised. Other societies that encouraged their people to deny globalization found themselves isolated by the West, because their policies bred violent revolutionaries or terrorists. Oil wealth like that in Saudi Arabia and Iraq supported a minority elite while denying many citizens access to economic and political advancement. Although promised in the media, the failure of the system to employ and advance many members of society created hundreds who resort to violence to attack their governments and the West. The 9/11 attacks in the United States related directly to many of the social upheavals generated by a decade of rapid globalization.

THE MAIN COURSE: COMPREHENSIVE STRATEGIES AND REVIEW

If you have several weeks to go before the exam, there's plenty of time to brush up on your skills using the following section of the book. More detailed than the **20 Things to Know** section, the Comprehensive Review presents additional, more in-depth information about the highlights of world history. A good way to maximize the value of this section is to use the following checklist as a guide.

- Read the **strategies for answering multiple-choice and free-response questions** discussed in the next few chapters to become familiar with the exam.

- Try out the strategies by taking a **practice exam** (page 325). Compare your answers with the answers and explanations provided and note any areas of weakness. If you missed a question, try to identify why so you can avoid doing so in the future. Did you miss a question because you didn't read it carefully? Or was your knowledge of the content covered incomplete?

- Study the **content review chapters** in this section, and devote special attention to the areas of weakness you identified in the practice exam.

- Take at least one more **practice exam** before test day. You can download an additional practice test for free at www.mymaxscore.com.

- A few nights before the exam, go back over the **Last-Minute Essentials** section (page 1) for a refresher on test-taking tips and the **20 Things to Know** about world history.

- Follow the **tips** in this book for the night before the exam and test day. Get a good night's sleep and have a positive mind-set, and you'll be ready to earn a top score.

The Multiple-Choice Questions

If you have to guess, do it intelligently.

Don't Get Stuck: It is more important to read all of the questions than to spend too much time trying to guess at a few. If you read through a question and the answer choices and cannot immediately narrow your choices to one or two, move on. You can mark the question in the test booklet and come back to it later. Points are awarded for what you know; you do not want to miss opportunities because you do not get to a question you know.

Look at *All* of the Choices: The AP World History Exam instructs you to mark the *best* answer. More than one answer choice may be a correct statement; you need to mark the best one. So read each of the answer choices completely before making your decision. A few of the questions will involve basic recall with one- or two-word answers. So if the question asks, "What empire used slave soldiers called Janissaries," and you know the answer to be the Ottoman Turks, mark it when you see the choice. However, most answer choices involve more than one or two words. The test provides answers to many questions in the form of sentences or sentence fragments that must be carefully read in order to understand them. Many choices will also include some of the same terms, so a quick scan will not actually convey the meaning of the choice.

The test makers do *not* design the questions or choices to trick you, but they do intentionally design the questions to check your understanding. So you need to read carefully to make sure you understand the question and the answers provided.

Eliminate a Choice: The key for the questions you cannot answer immediately is to eliminate a choice. The multiple-choice section of the test awards points based on correct answers, with each correct answer getting one point. Starting with the 2011 AP World History Exam, incorrect answers will *no longer* cost you points. So you should answer every question on the exam, hoping to improve your score by eliminating choices before you make your guess.

How do you eliminate a choice? First, do not expect a distracter, that is, a choice that is clearly incorrect. All the answers will appear to be plausible; it is the historical information that will be incorrect. You need to start with the facts. Do the facts fall in the proper time period? Feudalism goes with Europe in the Middle Ages or Japan between 1450 and 1750, but not in the twentieth century. A discussion of capitalism as an economic system could fit into the 1750–1914 period, especially if it is matched with Europe and European colonial empires, but it would not fit the Islamic caliphates between 600 and 1450. Next, are the locations geographically correct? If it is a question about the Mongol Empire, an answer involving East Africa does not make geographic sense.

If the question asks, "Which of the following statements best describes the trading system found in the Indian Ocean between 1000 and 1400," you could eliminate choices that mention the following:

- **Capitalism** (this economic system is not dominant during the time period)
- **The Gupta Empire** (even though geographically correct, this empire occupied much of northern India during the classical period that ended around 600)
- **The New World** (it was not yet connected to overseas trade networks; Columbus did not sail until 1492)

- **Europe** (during the Middle Ages, Europeans did not engage in significant long-distance trade)

Better yet, can you establish a direct causal relationship? For example, industrialization causes urbanization, but does it cause population growth? The answer is "not really." Industrialization will lead to larger urban centers and will allow many innovations, especially in agricultural machinery that, in the long term, will lead to larger populations, but there should be a better, more immediate answer to the question.

Avoid "Absolute" Answers: As you read the choices, look out for absolute statements like *always* or *never*. Look over the following question:

All of the following statements about Buddhism are accurate EXCEPT

A. Buddhism spread along the Silk Road from India to China.
B. Buddhism gained many followers because of its egalitarianism.
C. Buddhism never allows its followers to engage in violence.
D. Buddhism gained followers in China, Korea, and Japan.

The "never" in choice C makes it incorrect. While many Buddhist beliefs are against violence, the statement ignores the fact that martial arts found a home in Buddhist monasteries across East Asia and that, at times, Buddhist monks have left their monasteries to lead violent revolts, such as the Ikko-Ikki revolt in sixteenth-century Japan.

***Don't* Leave It Blank:** If you cannot eliminate a choice using these strategies, you still need to make a guess and move on to the next question. Again, don't get stuck spending too much time on a question that you do not recall any information about. The test covers at least 10,000 years of history. Don't expect to know something about all of the questions. You can make a mark in the test booklet to come back to the question, but do not make this your habit. The test makers pay close attention to all 70 of the questions so that they do not offer clues or answers to other questions, as often happens in a typical classroom chapter or unit test where the information covered is limited. Take a guess. You may make a change if you have time left after you have gone through all 70 questions. Looking at every question must take precedence over trying to rack your brain for information that just may not be available.

Types of Questions
Basic Knowledge-Level Questions

These require you to answer the question based on your knowledge of history. Some are very straightforward:

The dominant political philosophy of the Han dynasty in China was

A.　Legalism
B.　Daoism
C.　Buddhism
D.　Confucianism

The answer is D, Confucianism. Starting with the Han dynasty until the fall of the last dynasty in 1912, Confucianism was the main political and social philosophy of China.

Other knowledge-level questions may appear more difficult, but still require only your knowledge of a historical fact.

Which of the following statements best explains the European mercantilist policies of the eighteenth century?

A.　European nations sought to establish colonies to control resources and markets.
B.　European nations engaged in free trade to expand their markets and reduce prices through competition.
C.　European nations sought to isolate themselves from international alliances.
D.　European nations engaged in government reforms designed to give greater political representation to the lower classes.

If you remember that mercantilism was a form of capitalism that viewed wealth (measured in bullion or hard currency, for example, gold and silver) as finite and that a nation's power depended on its control over as much wealth as possible, you could conclude the following: nations would establish colonies to seize control over bullion and other resources they would need to avoid giving their limited supply of bullion to others, and they would want to protect the markets for their products so that other nations would not be able to sell there and gain more bullion and therefore power (choice A). This requires more thought than just remembering a single fact, but that is the goal of the test. You need to understand historical processes, appreciate how history works, and draw conclusions based on your knowledge and the evidence given in the questions.

Comparisons: The "Both" Questions

Many of the multiple-choice questions require a comparison. Some will ask specifically for a difference or a similarity between two regions, cultures, religions, etc. Others will include the word *both* and ask you to choose a statement that is true for two different things.

Buddhism and Christianity share which of the following beliefs?

A. Monotheism
B. Forgiveness of sins
C. An afterlife
D. The Four Noble Truths

The answer is C; both believe in an afterlife. You should eliminate choices you know to be false for one or the other as you look over the answer. Or you could mark B for the Buddhist beliefs and C for Christian, ending up with one answer with both a B and C marking. For a simple question like this, do not get too complicated in your marking system, because time is important. However, for a question like the one below that requires more reading and analysis, you may want to use notations.

Which of the following best describes both the Mongol (Yuan) and Manchu (Qing) dynasties in China?

A. The invaders sought to completely alter the Chinese governmental system based on Confucianism.
B. The dynasties allowed the Chinese self-rule and only imposed an annual tax on the Chinese people.
C. The dynasties continued to follow Confucian governing and social traditions, although the invaders were placed above the conquered Chinese.
D. The nomadic invaders ruled only for a brief period (less than a century) before being overthrown by the more numerous Chinese populations.

The correct answer is C; both invaders depended on Chinese officials and traditions to maintain order among the Chinese people, who greatly outnumbered them. China remained predominantly Confucian under both invaders, the annual tax was used by the Mongols on the Russians, neither wanted China to break apart, and while the Mongols ruled for less than a century, the Qing dynasty lasted from 1644 until 1912.

The EXCEPT or NOT Questions

These questions include the word EXCEPT or NOT (in capitals) within the question itself. You need to be careful with your answer, because the wording of the question can mislead you. In the EXCEPT question, three of the four choices will be true, but you are looking for the false information.

Buddhism became a major religion in all of the following nations EXCEPT

A. Japan
B. Mongolia
C. China
D. Pakistan

The answer is D, Pakistan. In all of the other nations, Buddhism became and remains a major religion. The problem for you to avoid is reading the question too quickly; only picking up on Buddhism is a major religion, then immediately marking A because you know Buddhism is a major religion in Japan.

The NOT question is very similar.

Which of the following was most clearly NOT a result of Cold War tensions?

A. The 1979 Iranian Revolution
B. The Vietnam War
C. The 1979 Soviet invasion of Afghanistan
D. The Berlin Wall

Again, if you read the question carefully, you will understand that you should eliminate the choices that were a result of the Cold War, leaving you with one answer, A, the Iranian Revolution. Note: there is an argument to be made that the Shah was in power due to Cold War politics, but his 1953 coup is far removed from 1979, and the causes of the revolution were the oppressive policies of his government, not U.S. or Soviet intervention. Choice A is the best choice available.

Image Questions

You will encounter some questions on the AP World History Exam that use images, about one in ten. A few will include text, either as part of a magazine ad, a newspaper story, or a political cartoon, but it must include a picture that you have to interpret. First, read the question so you will know what to look for in the illustration.

The statue in the image above most likely represents a deity from which of the following religions?

A.   Buddhism
B.   Judaism
C.   Confucianism
D.   Hinduism

Since the question asks you to identify a god, you should immediately start by looking for religious icons. Also, since the statue appears feminine, you can immediately eliminate Judaism, Confucianism, and Islam; none has a female deity. You should recognize the many arms of the deity as a symbol of a Hindu god, making choice D, Hinduism, the correct answer. While looking at the question, you know to look for religious symbols or icons to help you determine the origins of the statue. The question could also have asked its origin, requiring you to place it in India.

The image above is most likely an example of art from which of the following areas and time periods?

A. Communist China
B. Gupta India
C. The Persian Empire
D. The Ming dynasty

For this image you need to notice several little clues to determine the origin. Most important are the small square stamps along the top and at the bottom right of the image. This indicates a Chinese painting. Also, you may recognize the plant as bamboo, again indicating only China from your list. Now you have two choices: the Ming dynasty or modern China. As a communist state, many of the modern images of Chinese art use Socialist Realism, representing the peasants or Mao moving the nation forward, most often in large propaganda posters. This image does not do that at all, which makes answer D the best choice.

Map Questions

Very much like image questions, map questions require you to make use of all the little details on and around the map to make your answer choice. Also, like image questions, read the question to narrow what the test expects you to find on the map. Then check for a title that identifies the geographic region, nation, and/or time period for the map. Next, check the legend, or key, for specifics about what the map shows: the countries, trade, wars, exploration. In some cases, you will find that the map has neither a title nor a legend. In this case, the question expects you to recall a specific piece of information shown on the map, most often the boundaries of an empire or culture. Approach this like any other question; eliminate choices, then pick your final answer. Look at the following example and take your best guess.

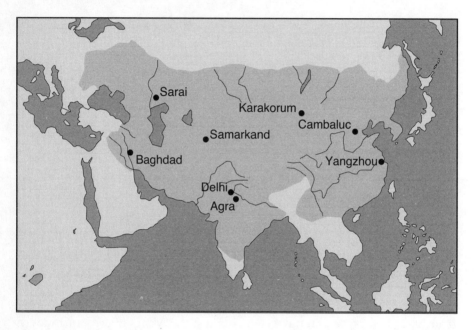

What is represented by the dark shaded area on the map above?

A.   The Byzantine Empire
B.   The Mongol Empire
C.   The Ming dynasty
D.   The Russian Empire

The answer is choice B, the Mongol Empire. This is the largest land empire ever and the only to connect areas of China, the Middle East, and Russia.

If the map includes a title and a legend, use this information along with the map itself to eliminate choices that do not fit the information shown, then make your final choice. Answer the next question using the map below.

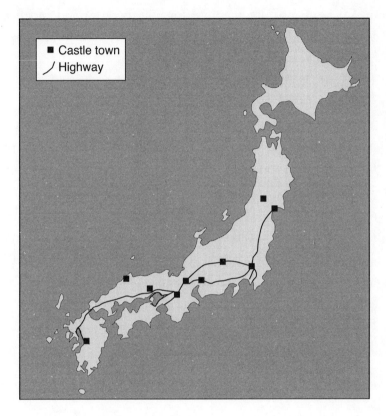

Using the map above, which of the following conclusions could you make based on the evidence provided?

A. Castle towns became the center of internal trade routes in Japan.
B. Castle towns contributed to the continuation of the feudal system in Japan.
C. Castles were constructed to control key mountain passes and waterways.
D. Castle towns were controlled directly by the shogun.

The best answer is A, because the map indicates that castle towns were connected by major roadways, and many of the products traded internally in Japan were produced near certain castle towns. Since the map does not indicate mountainous terrain, you cannot pick choice C, even if it is historically accurate for many castles and fortifications around the world. Also, nothing on the legend gives any indication of the feudal system in Japan at the time.

Charts and Graphs

The key to these questions is understanding what is and *is not* shown on the chart. Be sure to carefully look at the title of the chart or graph and then the headings on the graph or labels on the rows and columns of a chart. If the chart shows numbers in millions, don't expect an answer to contain the term *percent*. If the title of the graph is "Cotton Shipments to Europe," the chart will not likely show other commodities and may not even indicate the price of cotton. Don't assume information that is not apparent when you make your answer choice. However, you will have to make conclusions for your answer. The question will not ask "how much cotton was sold during a specific year," but it will require you to draw conclusions from the information given.

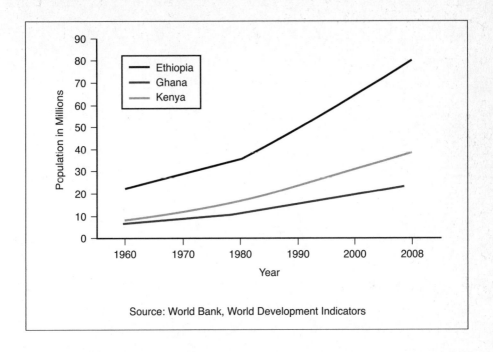

Source: World Bank, World Development Indicators

Based on the graph above, which conclusion is most supported by the evidence available?

A. Some African nations have seen substantial population growth over the last five decades.
B. Despite war, drought, famine, and disease, Ethiopia has seen positive population growth for the last five decades.
C. Since Africa gained independence in the 1960s, wars and famine have caused internal migrations, increasing populations in successful nations like Ethiopia and Kenya.
D. Over the last five decades, even with wars, droughts, disease, and famine, improvements in medicine and foreign aid have led to population growth in some African nations.

Both B and D are correct, but you do not get all of the information they depend upon from the graph. The only conclusion supported by the evidence is A. There is no evidence given that the population increase was due to migration, making C unsupported.

The Free-Response Questions

The essay portion of the AP World History Exam requires 130 minutes and includes three essay questions. The first question is the *document-based question*, or DBQ for short. Second is the *continuity* or *change-over-time question*, followed by the *comparison essay*. You will have a 10-minute reading and organizational period before you begin writing. During that time, you should carefully read over the documents for the DBQ and begin organizing your answer. After 10 minutes, you may begin answering the three questions in any order. But because you want the documents fresh in your mind, and many students feel more confident in writing with the help of the information from the documents, you should answer this question first. You should then answer the essay you feel most comfortable with, either the continuity and change over time or the comparison. The order does not matter, but since the score is based mostly on what you know, the essay you know the most about should get the greatest consideration.

The following advice applies to all three of the free-response questions. First, read the question carefully. Many students answer a question, but not necessarily the question being asked. Famously, the 2007 document-based question asked students to "analyze Han and Roman attitudes toward technology," but most responses compared Han and

Roman technology and ignored the attitudes of the document authors and the people they were writing about. Take your time and underline the keywords in the essay so you understand what is being asked. Most often, the first word to consider will be the verb. What is the essay asking you to do? The College Board suggests that essays will ask you to do one or two of the following:

ANALYZE	Determine and separate the component parts to examine relationships between them and the whole. So if asked to analyze European feudalism, you would need to discuss the role of hierarchy, nobility, the church, manorialism, and fiefs and how they related to each other; military service to a noble in return for land; the role of the church in supporting the authority of the king.
ASSESS– EVALUATE	Judge the value of something; review positive and negative points; provide your opinion about the value of something; discuss the advantages and disadvantages of something. Here, you could be asked to assess the impact of something on a region; for example, assess the impact of trade on the Middle East during the period from 1450 to 1750.
COMPARE	Note similarities and differences. Often you will be asked to analyze, describe, or discuss the similarities and differences. Note that you must do *both*, even if the question does not specifically state both similarities and differences. The term *compare* requires *both* in the answer.
CONTRAST	Note differences. Like compare, it will often be paired with *analyze, describe*, or *discuss*.
DESCRIBE	Tell about or give a detailed description of something. For instance, describe the continuities and changes in Japan between 1750 and 1914. For a question like this, you must focus on as much historical detail as possible. Also, expect it to be paired with something else like *analyze*. If that is the case, make sure you answer the whole question.
DISCUSS	This is a very broad question that allows you to explore points of view or debate various sides of a topic. If the question asks you to *discuss* a topic like gender roles, be sure to include all sides of the issue you have available; for instance in a DBQ, you would want each group to present a view of gender roles.

EXPLAIN	Make clear, in detail, the topic. This can include talking about cause and effect or interpretation of evidence, like you would for a DBQ.

Second, your first statement should be the beginning of your thesis, which can be several sentences long. Do not try to find a hook or some other device to attract the reader. The grader has to read the essay, so get on with it. Also, the thesis statement *must* be in the first or last paragraph. The reader (what the College Board calls the people who grade the essays) can only give a point for the thesis if it is in the first or last paragraph. If you try writing an introduction, you could cost yourself at least one point or as many as five. Make sure that your thesis answers the question and does not just restate it. In each of the examples given later, note how the first few sentences answer the question rather than just introduce the topic of the essay—or worse, just restate the key terms in the essay prompt.

Third, use a proper essay format. Do not write a single, long paragraph. This will prevent the reader from awarding you all of the Basic Core points and will make it more difficult for you and the reader to clearly create document groups for the DBQ or direct comparisons for the comparison essay. A typical good essay will include a thesis paragraph at the beginning, followed by three detail paragraphs, each of which explores one of the key arguments or points of the answer. Finally, a conclusion paragraph can be included at the end. None of the three rubrics include a conclusion, but if possible, you should include one that restates your thesis and main arguments. If pressed for time, you can recopy the main points from the first paragraph. The reasoning behind this originates with the method used to score the essay. If the reader gives you a point for your thesis in the first paragraph, the reader cannot award additional Basic Core credit for information in that paragraph; it is all treated as the thesis. Therefore, if you include some historical detail in the thesis paragraph that you then did not mention in any of the detail paragraphs (you may have just forgotten or thought it redundant to mention again), you would not receive credit for that information. If, though, you wrap up your essay by restating this information, you then could get that credit. Also, should you not get credit for the thesis in the first paragraph, it is possible that by making yourself restate it again in the final paragraph you may fix the wording enough to earn the thesis point; there is often a fine line between restating the question and writing an actual thesis.

Note: unlike the other AP history exams (United States and European), there is no choice of question for the continuity and change or the comparison essay; each student answers the same question. However, often one or even both of the questions will allow some degree of choice, letting you choose to answer the question for one of three or four regions given or to pick one of two or three choices to compare with something given in the question. For example, the comparison essay might ask you to compare the political and economic changes in Cuba after the communist revolution to political and economic changes caused by revolutions in one of the following: Mexico in 1910, Iran in 1979, or Russia in 1917. You should make this choice very quickly. Generally, one of the options will immediately stand out in your mind. Pick it and get writing. There is no perfect choice. Each of the options is valid; you cannot choose wrong. If none immediately stand out, begin brainstorming and see which choice you recall the most information about. *Do not* get bogged down in making your choice. The grade is based on what you write on the paper in essay form. If you take 20 minutes to make your choice, that is 20 minutes of writing that you will not have. I am not suggesting that you not take time to brainstorm; in fact, as you will see later, brainstorming is where you can spend your most productive time. But taking 10 minutes to decide between Russia or Iran in the example above because you remember three good facts about Iran but think you should do Russia because you do remember the revolution there involved communism does not earn you anything for the essay. If you quickly remember three things about Iran that match with the information you have about Cuba, *start writing*. For example, the Iranian Revolution involved religion (Islam) in politics, while the Cuban Revolution did not emphasis religion in politics; the Cuban Revolution overthrew a dictatorship supported by the United States just as the Iranian Revolution did; and both came under severe economic sanctions by the United States after the revolution. This is enough to form the basis for your essay. Spending time trying to remember something about Russia when you have enough to get started with Iran does not generally pay off in a higher score.

The Document-Based Question

For the DBQ, you will be given a set of primary source materials that you are to use to answer the question. You are expected to analyze the documents individually then develop an answer to the question based on your understanding of the documents, the authors' point of view, and historical processes. Prior specific content knowledge is not critical to a complete answer, but an understanding of broader historical trends is important. For instance, if the DBQ question asks "based on the following documents, analyze the changing roles of women brought about by the twentieth-century communist revolutions in Russia and China," you would not be expected to identify specific women or even men involved in either revolutions. But you would need to have an understanding of the general political, economic, and social status of women and the issues confronted by women seeking a greater role in society. This would help you then to better examine the documents for the exceptional opportunities offered to women and traditional reluctances for societies to treat women on an equal basis in these areas. The documents would provide specifics for each civilization on women's roles and opportunities created by the revolutions, but you would need an initial understanding of gender roles to make an informed answer to the question.

When writing the DBQ, like all the essays, you must first write a thesis statement. This can only be in the first or last paragraph. You should use the thesis to establish both your answer to the question and the specific groups you will use. You do not need to mention any of the documents specifically. Wait to do this in each paragraph as you introduce the groups. Each of the detail paragraphs that follow will focus on one of your groups. In the topic sentence of each paragraph, explain your group and how it supports the answer to the thesis. Then, begin explaining the group and how it supports your answer by introducing the first document and tying it to the group theme. Do not just repeat what the document says, but paraphrase it, using it to make your point. You can refer to documents by author or source and document number. I would recommend that the first time you use a document, you mention the author or source and follow it, in parentheses if you like, with the phrase "Doc. #." After this, just use Doc. # to reference the document, even if it is being used in a second group. In the conclusion, you should make a point of stating what additional document you need to complete the essay. Make sure to explain the point of view or critical information that is missing that the document would provide. Do not spend too much time trying to figure out the type of document (that is, newspaper, diary, government statistic, map, or graph), as the explanation for the need of the additional viewpoint or information is what will earn you the Basic Core point you need. To provide additional assurance that you receive this point, you can close each detail paragraph by explaining what additional document would fit in the group and why you would need it. This helps in case one of your additional document suggestions is incorrect or if you get all of the Basic Core points, it can earn you an Expanded Core point.

Knowing the Rubric

The College Board provides a generic rubric for the document-based question in their World History Course Description booklet (available online at apcentral.collegeboard.com/apc/public/repository/ap-world-history-course-description.pdf). While each individual question may set slightly different requirements for meeting each part of the rubric, all of the DBQs require the same basic elements described in the rubric. The rubric is explained below in two parts. Part one, the Basic Core, includes 7 of the possible 9 points available from the document-based question.

You *must* receive all of the Basic Core points to get any points in the Expanded Core section.

THE DOCUMENT-BASED QUESTION CORE POINTS (0–7)

Has acceptable thesis (addresses the global issues and the time period(s) specified).	1 Point	The thesis must do more than just restate the question. It must make your specific answer to the DBQ prompt and should establish the groups that you will use to analyze the documents and explain your answer.
Addresses all of the documents and demonstrates understanding of all or all but one.	1 Point	You must make an attempt to use *all* of the documents when answering the question. To use a document, you must do more than quote it or mention it as part of a group. You need to demonstrate that you understand the meaning of the document. You may misinterpret *one* but still receive the point. If you make no attempt to interpret a document because you are not sure of your understanding, you *have not* addressed all of the documents and cannot get the point; a misinterpretation still counts as addressing the document.
Supports thesis with appropriate evidence from all or all but one document.	2 Points	You now use the evidence from the document to make the argument you started in your thesis. In your own words, you need to link the evidence from each of the documents to your answer (you can still misinterpret one document and get both points). If you simply quote the documents or just summarize them, you will not get credit, as the intent is for you to demonstrate a link between the evidence and your conclusions reached in the thesis.
		If you do not use *two* of the documents to support your thesis, you can still receive *one* point, but you will not be able to score higher than a 6 as you must have all of the Basic Core points to receive any of the Expanded Core points.

Analyzes point of view in at least two documents.	1 Point	Based on the source of the document and the text itself, you should be able to identify a bias or point of view and explain it and how it affects the evidence for your conclusions, based on the prompt. You must specifically do this for two of the documents, but you should include it for as many of the documents as you can.
Analyzes documents by grouping them in two or three ways, depending on the question.	1 Point	All documents must be grouped with other documents based on criteria you establish after reading the documents. Groups can include many different organizational principles established by you and can include gender, class, positive and negative viewpoints, ethnicity, time period, age, source, and many others. Also, a document may be in more than one group.
Identifies and explains the need for one type of appropriate additional document or source.	1 Point	You must finally include an additional document that would help complete the argument you have made in the essay. The additional document does not need to be a specific document (for example, the U.S. Constitution), but instead should be a generic document that would include a point of view not given in the documents already under consideration or provide missing information. For example, you could ask for a worker's diary, because the sources had all come from government officials or upper-class individuals. You could also ask for statistics from a source outside the government and possibly involved in the question because of potential bias. To get the point, you must explain the need for the additional document, not just say what document is needed.

If you receive all 7 of the Basic Core Points, you may then possibly receive 0, 1, or 2 Expanded Core Points. The chart below offers suggestions on how to receive those points. Note: the reader can give 1 or even 2 points for any of these criteria; you could write an extended thesis and receive 2 Expanded Core because of its quality.

THE DOCUMENT-BASED QUESTION EXPANDED CORE POINTS (0–2)

You can only receive these points if *all* 7 Basic Core Points are earned. Examples of expanded core areas include:	2 Points maximum	
Has a clear, analytical, and comprehensive thesis.		In your thesis, after you give your initial answer or argument to the question, you should then use the thesis to outline the paper, introducing your groupings, not by naming documents, but by identifying the point each group makes.
Shows careful and insightful analysis of the documents.		In general, you show the reader some understanding of the documents that most others have missed.
Uses documents persuasively as evidence.		As you make your argument to prove your answer to the question, the reader must see you actively using the document to make your point. You go beyond just saying this document proves this fact and instead make the documents do the arguing for you; name the author and use active verbs to have them (the author and the document) make the point. Refer to the example essay following this rubric.
Analyzes point of view in most or all documents.		If you can offer an analysis of most of the documents based on their point of view, you can receive points here. As many students do not include any point of view, it is very likely that the reader would give expanded points here if you can do this. Note: grouping several documents and saying they all have the same point of view will not always give you credit; address point of view for each individual document.

Analyzes the documents in additional ways—groupings, comparisons, syntheses.		You can earn points by having more than three groups or by using documents in more than one. Also, original but accurate groupings can earn you this Expanded Core point. Be careful not to try too many groups as you could run out of time for the other essays or you may end up with groups that do not really support your thesis or are only one document, which does not count as a group.
Brings in relevant "outside" historical content.		If you get a question where you know some outside (that is, not mentioned in the documents) information, great! Use it to strengthen your argument. However, be careful. If you focus on the information you already knew and do not use all of the documents to make the argument, you will not get points here, because you will not have received all of the Basic Core points.
Explains why additional types of document(s) or sources are needed.		Much like the Expanded Core for point of view, if you can think of multiple viewpoints left out of the question and/or the documents and explain why they should be included, you can receive Expanded Points here.

The following sample DBQ will walk you through the process and break down the component parts of one possible answer to the question.

The Free Response booklet (the green booklet labeled AP World History Exam Section II that you write your free-response answers in when taking the exam) will give the following instructions for the document-based question.

WORLD HISTORY
SECTION II
Part A
(Suggested writing time–40 minutes)
Percent of Section II score–33 1/3

Directions: The following question is based on the accompanying Documents 1–10. (The documents have been edited for the purpose of this exercise.)

This question is designed to test your ability to work with and understand historical documents.

Write an essay that:

- Has a relevant thesis and supports that thesis with evidence from the documents.

- Uses all of the documents.

- Analyzes the documents by grouping them in as many appropriate ways as possible. Does not simply summarize the documents individually.

- Takes into account the sources of the documents and analyzes the authors' point of view.

- Identifies and explains the need for at least one additional type of document.

You may refer to relevant historical information not mentioned in the documents.

1. Based on the following documents, analyze the effect on the traditional roles played by women brought about by the twentieth-century communist revolutions in Russia and China. Identify an additional type of document and explain how it would help analyze the effects on women in Russia and/or China after the revolutions.

Historical Background: The communist revolutions in Russia in 1917 and China (1946–1949) occurred in societies that had very limited roles for women. Communism promised greater gender equality as part of broader social change.

Document 1

Source: The Situation of Chinese Women, Information Office of the State Council of the People's Republic of China, June 1994, Beijing

In semi-colonial and semi-feudal old China, women were for a long time kept at the bottom of society. It was not until the first half of this century that the Chinese Communist Party led the Chinese people to wage a great and profound national democratic revolution on this ancient land. At the same time, a large-scale women's emancipation movement was launched, resulting in the historic liberation of Chinese women that won worldwide attention.

Document 2

Source: The Situation of Chinese Women, Information Office of the State Council of the People's Republic of China, June 1994, Beijing

The Marriage Law of the People's Republic of China, promulgated in 1950, was the first statute enacted by New China. It clearly declared the abolition of the feudal marriage system characterized by arranged and forced marriage, male superiority and female inferiority, and disregard for the interests of children. Implementation of the new system was marked by freedom for both men and women in marriage, monogamy, sexual equality and protection of the legitimate rights of women and children. This signified a profound revolution in the patterns of wedded and family life that had prevailed for several thousand years in Chinese society.

Document 3

> *Source: Constitution of the People's Republic of China, 1982*
>
> Article 48. Women in the People's Republic of China enjoy equal rights with men in all spheres of life, political, economic, cultural and social, and family life. The state protects the rights and interests of women, applies the principle of equal pay for equal work for men and women alike and trains and selects cadres from among women.

Document 4

> *Source: "On Widening the Scope of Women's Work in the Agricultural Co-operative Movement," Mao Tse-tung, Founder and Premier of the People's Republic of China, 1955*
>
> Enable every woman who can work to take her place on the labor front, under the principle of equal pay for equal work. This should be done as quickly as possible.

Document 5

> *Source: Theses on Communist Morality in the Sphere of Marital Relations, 1921, by Alexandra Kollontai, Russian noble who defied her family and joined the Bolshevik Party, leader of the woman's branch of the Communist Party*
>
> There are two grounds on which, in the interests of the workers' collective, the relationships between the sexes ought to be the subject to legislative regulations: A. the health and hygiene of the nation and the race, and B. the increase or decrease of the population required by the national economic collective. In the period of the dictatorship of the proletariat, the regulation of relationships enters a new phase. Instead of laws and the threat of legal proceedings, the workers' collective must rely on agitational and educational influences, and on social measures to improve the relationships between the sexes and to guarantee the health of the children born from these relationships.

Document 6

Soviet Factory Workers, 1930s

Document 7

Source: Protection of Women and Children in Soviet Russia, 1932, by Alice Withrow Field, sociologist

Both the maternity clinics and the Museums of Mother and Child hold regular meetings for pregnant women where they and their husbands are given general instruction in the biological processes of pregnancy and their practical applications to everyday life. In case the employment of a pregnant woman would endanger the life of her child she is released from it when she presents a disability card signed by her doctor. In any event she is not allowed to go to work for about two months preceding and two more months succeeding the giving of birth. Her release from work because of her pregnancy does not involve any financial hardship for she continues to receive her regular wages and is always allowed to go back to work as soon as her doctor gives her a bill of good health. In case of a miscarriage, the woman is given careful treatment and ample time to recuperate in order that such an accident may be avoided in the future.

Document 8

Source: U.N. Deliberations on Draft Convention on the Political Rights of Women, Eleanor Roosevelt, U.S. representative to the United Nations, 1953

I have been glad to hear that Soviet women hold many public offices and participate widely in public life. I have been glad to note this year that the Soviet Union, the Ukraine, and Byelorussia have included women on their delegations to the General Assembly. There have been very few women on these delegations in the past—in fact, I do not recall any since the first General Assembly in 1946. I hope that this convention may lead to greater participation by women in the true organs of power in the Soviet Union, such as the Presidium and the Secretariat of the Central Committee of the Communist Party, in which I understand no women are now included. The experience women have achieved in the more formal and subsidiary bodies throughout the Soviet Union should entitle them to recognition also in bodies which determine the major policies of their Government.

The Soviet Union has brought in a number of amendments, and I want also to discuss these briefly. I understand those on the first three articles of the convention are similar to those presented in sessions of the Commission on the Status of Women and in the Economic Council. Both the Commission and the Council rejected the changes and additions in these proposals on the ground that they are unnecessary in so simple a convention as this one. I would like to point out, however, that the language proposed by the Soviet Union, presumably to assure application of this convention "without discrimination," is in fact very discriminatory, because it enumerates only a few grounds and omits others. The most notable omission is in regard to political opinion. The Soviet amendment also omits the phrase "without discrimination of any kind," which might otherwise cover "political opinion." It seems to me that in a convention on political rights, if you are going to provide any guaranties against discrimination, the most important one would be freedom for all types of political opinion. But, as I said before, the intent of this convention to apply to all women is entirely clear, and we believe any such additional clause would be confusing and might in fact have the result—as the Soviet proposal does—of limiting its effect.

Document 9

Source: The Soviet Code on Marriage and Divorce, the Family, and Guardianship, decrees of the All-Russian Central Executive Committee, November 19, 1926

Rights and Duties of Husband and Wife

7. On registering a marriage the contracting parties may declare it to be their wish to have a common surname, either that of the husband or of the wife, or to retain their antenuptial surnames....

9. Both husband and wife enjoy full liberty in the choice of their respective trades and occupations. The manner in which their joint household is conducted is determined by the mutual agreement of the two contracting parties. A change of residence by either husband or wife does not oblige the other marriage partner to follow [the] former.

Document 10

Source: The Soviet Family Law of 8 July 1944

Section 1, Article 3

To establish state assistance to single (unmarried) mothers for support and upbringing of children born after the publication of the present Decree, in the following amounts:

100 rubles monthly for	1 child
150 rubles monthly for	2 children
200 rubles monthly for	3 or more children

State assistance to unmarried mothers is paid until the children reach 12 years of age.

Step-by-Step Answer

GROUPING

The following groups can be used for the essay.

Group 1: Chinese Views, Document 1, 2, 3, and 4. This grouping may seem obvious, but don't forget the obvious. Determine a general statement that explains the basis for the group. For example, in China, the communists saw the revolution as liberating women from the control of males in society and guaranteeing them greater rights. A good essay will then provide evidence of each document and how it attaches to this theme. Document 1, for instance,

expresses both the idea that prior to the Chinese Communist Party, women were for centuries treated as the lowest rank in society and that the party "emancipated" women as they freed all of Chinese society. Though the claim that the world recognized this achievement must be met with skepticism at the source, the Chinese Communist government may be overstating the result to make itself appear beneficial to women and a champion of democratic ideas.

The last statement brings into question the point of view of the author or source of the document. Part of the purpose of the document-based question is to make you judge the accuracy and honesty of a document based on the source's bias, available information, and intent.

Group 2: Like group 1, you can use national focus, so group 2 includes all of the documents from or about the Soviet Union: documents 5, 6, 7, 8, 9, and 10. This group may be explained by the following statement:

> A number of documents, when describing the condition of women in Soviet Russia, also emphasize the need for improvements in the lives of women, but they do not all agree as to what constitutes an improvement and what actual changes are taking place. Document 5 wishes to place government regulations on relations between men and women and believes that the relations must serve the interest of the state. Documents 9 and 10, both from the government of the Soviet Union, aim more at protecting the rights of women and children by providing protections in marriage and for assistance to single mothers. Both of these reforms represent a real change from the previous systems that made the man dominant in the relationship.

With this group, you must take care to discuss how each of the documents differs in their discussion of Soviet changes.

Group 3: You have used all of the documents so far, but it is possible to use a document in more than one group. For the third group, you could use documents that specifically address the issue of providing economic independence to women: documents 3, 4, 6, 7, and 10.

> A key factor in improving the lives of women would be securing their economic independence from men: their fathers, husbands, and even sons. Several pieces of evidence from both China and the Soviet Union discuss this. Document 3 offers constitutional guarantees to Chinese women for equal pay for equal work. Document 4 by Mao, the founder of the People's Republic of China, echoes this as well. Both documents would serve to build support

from women for the Communist Party in China, but might at the same time alienate some men who preferred the more traditional role for their wives. The documents demonstrate a commitment by the Chinese communist to the broader communist ideology and a break from traditional Chinese thought. Document 7 and 10 also demonstrate on the part of the Soviet government that women must have the economic means to support themselves and a family. Document 6 also indicates at least a realization that women must be allowed to work alongside men in the same jobs, though it does not indicate if the pay is equal. Unfortunately, no source is available from women in either China or the Soviet Union that indicates these laws are actually followed. The picture in document 6 could be posed for propaganda's sake, and the Soviet Family Law might make the government look as if it cares for women, but they could be ignored in reality. A document from a woman working in a Soviet factory or on a Chinese collective farm might offer better proof as to whether the laws are simply propaganda or actually enforced for the benefit of women.

The last statement introduces the idea that some viewpoints are missing from the available evidence and must be considered for a more accurate answer to the question. The DBQ requires you to name at least one additional document and explain why it should be included to arrive at a more complete and accurate answer to the question.

Although not the complete essay, the example sections above demonstrate the key requirements of the DBQ:

- At least *three* groups
- The use of *all* documents
- Discussion of point of view in at least *two* documents (point of view in document 1 is addressed as is point of view in documents 6 and 10 in group 3)
- At least *one* additional document or point of view missing from the information provided and why it is important to include it

Continuity and Change Over Time

The continuity and change-over-time (CCOT) essay requires you to analyze causes for change or stability or continuity in a region over one or more of the periods the AP World History course covers. When answering this essay, you need to make sure that you cover several important areas.

First, you must include both continuities and changes during the period. Continuity refers to practices that remain continuous over a substantial period of time, typically through one of the time periods covered by the AP World History Exam. Continuities can address any aspects that run through all or most of the time period. For example, most questions dealing with Chinese dynasties could incorporate Confucianism as a continuity in politics, economics, social order, and/or philosophy and religion through any time period. If the question asks you to "analyze continuities and changes in China's attitude toward foreign contacts between 1750 and 1914," Confucianism would prove very helpful in addressing the question. You could argue that Confucian attitudes toward merchants and trade kept the Chinese government from actively seeking foreign trade agreements and allowed Europeans, Americans, and even Japanese to take advantage of China's wealth. Also, Confucian scholars tried to protect their own positions, and thus generally wanted China to avoid bringing in new technology and ideas from the West. This prevented China from modernizing its military and caused the government to actively fight political reforms based on republican ideas from Europe. You just need to explain to the reader how, throughout most or all of the period, Confucianism played an important role in the way China handled foreign contacts.

The second task is to identify changes and, more critically, the causes for these changes. In the previous example, Confucianism provides the root cause for continuity. Your answer must identify it as the cause of continuity: What makes the Chinese continue to follow the same policy even as it clearly fails them? For change, you must also identify causes.

Continuing the example, one cause for change in Chinese attitudes could be China's defeat in the Opium War. After the Chinese government finally attempted to resist the opium trade, which was dominated by the British, war broke out. The immediate cause was the action of a Chinese official, Lin Zexu, also known as Commissioner Lin. The resulting defeat caused China's government to sign the Treaty of Nanjing and officially open more of China to European trade and influence. This was an attempt by the Chinese to pit Europeans against each other; the Chinese offered most-favored-nation status to other countries besides the British in order to achieve this goal. The military defeat caused Confucian bureaucrats to rethink their policy toward Europeans, and some changed their attitude, accepting the need for European weapons and other technology if they were to continue to be independent. So the military defeat convinced some in China that they should adopt European technology in order to survive. Later, in 1861, some Chinese, under the leadership of Prince Gong, began the Self-Strengthening movement after continued military defeats at European hands and the failure of the Chinese government to modernize or limit European spheres of influence within the nation.

As a rule, and demonstrated above, when looking for continuities, identify the core beliefs and traditions of a region or culture. If the question is between 1450 and 1750 and involves the Middle East, North Africa, or East Africa, then Islam is likely a source of continuity. For Europe between 600 and 1450, both feudalism and Christianity represent the forces of continuity. For change, you want to identify key global movements by time period and the regions they affect. During the 600–1450 period, the expansion of Islam acts as a force of change on three continents. During the same period, the Mongol invasion and the European Crusades also act as causes for change in Europe and Asia. Each of the topic review sections will include a table discussing forces of continuity and change during specific time periods.

Once you establish continuities and changes and their causes, you need to write a thesis that directly answers the question. What you *never* want to write is, *There were continuities and changes...* The question already makes that statement obvious, and you are simply repeating the prompt instead of answering the question, which is not an effective way of making or earning you point. A good start, based on our example, might begin as follows:

> While Confucianism remained the guiding force behind China's attitudes toward foreign contacts between 1750 and 1914, several factors forced some in China to change their views. The Confucian scholars in China's government wanted to ignore the "Southern Barbarians," as they called the Europeans, and refused to negotiate trade and diplomatic agreements with them. However, the military victories of the Europeans over China beginning with the Opium War caused some to use negotiations to try and get the Europeans to fight each other, ignoring China in the process. Others sought to adopt European technology, economics, and politics, seeing them as superior to the Chinese versions and now necessary for China's survival.

The first sentence does several things. First, it establishes Confucianism as the continuity behind Chinese attitudes toward foreigners, completing the first part of the question. It also sets the time period. If a date is given in the question, you *must* include it in the thesis; do *not* write with the assumption that the question is in front of the reader. They can only give you credit for what you write on paper, not what they assume you know. Finally, the first sentence includes the keyword *attitudes*. If you were to write about how the Chinese and European acted toward each other during this time period, you could possibly receive no credit, because the question asks about attitudes, not actions. Since the beginning of the AP World History Exam, several questions included a key term that many students missed, causing them to write an answer to the wrong question. In this example, Confucian teachings always shaped the attitude of many Chinese, but the initial indifference is replaced by trying to get the Europeans to fight and eliminate each other—a traditional Chinese technique when dealing with outsiders or barbarians. Finally, some Chinese began a self-strengthening movement based on traditional Confucian morality alongside modern Western technology. This was a much more practical attitude toward the foreigners, because it recognized that China could not survive without joining the modern world. Always make sure you are answering the question asked.

For the detail paragraphs, you should attempt to follow this pattern:

- Detail Paragraph 1: establish what things were like at the beginning of the period and introduce the main continuity.
- Detail Paragraph 2 and possibly 3: introduce the broad forces of change and explain the changes that occurred.
- Final Detail Paragraph: discuss what things are like at the end of the period, being sure to refer to both continuities and changes that occurred.

In each of the paragraphs, use as many historical details as possible. Typically, to get the points available, you will need to have *five* specific, factual details. Use your brainstorming to generate as many historical details as possible to work into the essay as you write it. Names of people, places and regions, specific events, religions, philosophies, specific holy books or texts, trade routes, trade items, even dates can count as historical evidence. Do not write as if the reader knows all of the basic information. Write so that everything you know about the topic gets on the paper. If the question concerns cultural diffusion, and you mention the Silk Road, mention that—in addition to silk—porcelains, teas, carpets, Chinese technology, and even Buddhism traveled along the route. Also mention that the route connected China with the Middle East and markets in North Africa and Europe. Mention that Islam traveled along its route to China. Mention that camels carried most of the goods. Let the reader know what you know about the topic. The grade is based on *what you know*.

Knowing the Rubric

The College Board provides a generic rubric for the continuity and change-over-time essay questions in its World History Course Description booklet (available online at apcentral.collegeboard.com/apc/public/repository/ap-world-history-course-description.pdf). While each question may set slightly different requirements for meeting each part of the rubric, all of the continuity and change-over-time essays require the same basic elements described in the rubric. The rubric is explained below in two parts. Part one, the Basic Core, includes 7 of the possible 9 points available from the CCOT essay. You *must* receive all of the Basic Core points to get any points in the Expanded Core section.

THE CONTINUITY AND CHANGE-OVER-TIME CORE POINTS (0–7)

Has acceptable thesis (addresses the global issues and the time period(s) specified).	1 Point	The thesis must do more than restate the question. It must make your specific answer to the CCOT prompt and identify at least one continuity and one change you will explain and analyze in the essay.
Addresses all parts of the question, though not necessarily evenly or thoroughly. (Addresses most parts of the question: for example, addresses change but not continuity.)	2 Points (1 Point)	You must include at least one continuity and one change. If the prompt asks for continuity and changes in two areas (such as politics and economics), you must do a continuity for each and a change for each.

Substantiates thesis with appropriate historical evidence. (Partially substantiates thesis with appropriate historical evidence.)	2 Points (1 Point)	You must include at least *five* (this number varies, but five should guarantee you credit) historical facts that go with your thesis. Of the five, you must have at least one for continuity and one for change. If all five are continuity, you will only receive 1 point instead of the 2 available. If you are asked about political *and* social areas, you must provide evidence from both in order to receive the full 2 points. It is very important that you establish this in your brainstorming so that you make sure to provide the evidence you need in each area. See the sample below for ideas on how to set up your brainstorming.
Uses relevant world historical context effectively to explain continuity and change over time.	1 Point	For each of the time periods, there are major world events that can affect the area. You must include a mention of these. For instance, if you are discussing continuity and change in China between 1000 and 1450, you must mention the Mongol conquest and the Black Death. If the question was from the same period but asked about the Aztecs, you could point out that the major factors shaping European and Asian cultures (such as the Black Death) were not yet experienced by the Aztec because the Americas were isolated from other civilizations.
Analyzes the process of continuity and change over time.	1 Point	You need to make a direct connection between what you state is a cause for continuity or change and exactly what continuity or change results from it. For example, if you argue that the Ottoman Empire gained influence in Europe around 1450, you would need to explain that this was because they were able to use gunpowder, which allowed them to use massive cannons to break down the wall of Constantinople and destroy the Byzantine Empire.

If, you receive all 7 of the Basic Core Points, you may possibly receive 0, 1, or 2 Expanded Core Points. The chart below offers suggestions on how to receive those points. Note: the reader can give 1 or even 2 points for any of these criteria; you could write an extended thesis and receive 2 Expanded Core Points because of its quality.

THE CONTINUITY AND CHANGE-OVER-TIME EXPANDED CORE POINTS (0–2)

You can only receive these points if *all* 7 Basic Core Points are earned. Examples of expanded core areas include:	2 Points maximum	
Has a clear, analytical, and comprehensive thesis.		In your thesis, after your initial answer/argument to the question, you should use the thesis to outline the paper, establishing what the situation was at the beginning of the period, continuities, forces for change, and the final situation at the end of the time period.
Analyzes all issues of the question (as relevant): global context, chronology, causation, change, continuity, effects, content.		The purpose of the exam is for you to demonstrate your understanding of history. Here, by offering a detailed analysis of the points or arguments you make during the essay, the reader can reward you.
Provides ample historical evidence to substantiate thesis.		Go beyond the 5 or 6 detailed pieces of information that you used for the Core Points. The more specific information you can recall, the better.

Provides links with relevant ideas, events, trends in an innovative way.		This is dependent on the question and very subjective on the reader's part. However, if you can bring in information that few other students do or if you make a sound argument that others skip or is especially difficult, the reader can give you a point. Do *not* spend time brainstorming, trying to figure out how to get a point here. Either it will happen or it will not. You do not have the time to force this one. You might get a question on a topic you have a special interest in or your teachers went out of their way to explain in great detail and therefore can provide that relevant link in an innovative way. For example, if the question asks you to discuss Japan's economy in the nineteenth century, and you point out that Japan was able to rapidly change to a more capitalist system because of the unintended consequences of the Tokugawa feudal rules, which created a middle class ready to adopt European economics, that would—provided you explain it in more detail—probably impress the reader and earn you 1 or 2 points.

The following sample continuity and change-over-time question will walk you through the process and break down the component parts of a possible answer to the question.

WORLD HISTORY
SECTION II
Part B
(Suggested planning and writing time—40 minutes)
Percent of Section II score—33 1/3

Directions: You are to answer the following question. You should spend 5 minutes organizing or outlining your essay.

Write an essay that:

- Has a relevant thesis and supports that thesis with appropriate historical evidence.
- Addresses all parts of the question.
- Uses world historical context to show continuities and changes over time.
- Analyzes the process of continuity and change over time.

2. Describe political continuities and changes in one of the regions below during the Cold War (1945–1991).

- Eastern Europe
- Africa
- East Asia

Step-by-Step Answer

Make Your Choice: For some questions, I may want to brainstorm first, but in this case I feel very confident about one area.

EASTERN EUROPE

Brainstorming: I first want to list everything I can recall about the question. But to help me to have a little organization for my writing, I will create a table to fill in with my information and give structure for the essay and to also make sure I include all of the information I need in order to get a high score.

BRAINSTORMING

AT START:

Area overrun by Soviets as Germany retreats

Soviets take control and install puppet governments in most countries— Yugoslavia more independent than others

Marshal Tito, hero of the resistance, in charge there

Germany divided into four occupation zones (U.S., USSR, British, French)

Berlin, in USSR zone, also divided into 4 parts

Stalin promised independence for these areas but will break his promise

Soviets want reparations from Germany (money and industrial equipment)

Soviets want a buffer between them and Western Europe

Soviets want land taken from Poland and Baltic states at the start of the war

U.S. wants independent government and free elections but does not want to fight Stalin, so they accept Soviet dominance

CONTINUITIES:	CHANGES:
Soviet military presence to support governments	Soviet nuclear weapons
Hungary 1956	Marshall Plan
Prague Spring 1968	Death of Stalin
Dependence on Soviets for economic support	Berlin Wall
Communism	Brezhnev
Autocratic rule	Soviet economic decline
Truman Containment Policy	John Paul II, Thatcher, Reagan
	Gorbachev
	Fall of the Berlin Wall

IN THE END:

Entire Soviet system collapses

Communist ousted in mostly bloodless changes

Romania kills dictator/wife on TV

Democracy takes hold

Break up of some states

Fall of the USSR

THESIS

For most of the Cold War, Eastern Europe would remain under the political domination of the Soviet Union. Soviet occupation began in 1945 at the end of World War II, and it would be until 1989 when that military occupation finally began to end and the countries of Eastern Europe began to achieve political independence. For the first few decades, little would change for the Eastern European governments. However, at the end of the 1970s, a Polish pope, John Paul II, would encourage the Polish people to challenge their communist government. A British prime minister, Margaret Thatcher, and an American president, Ronald Reagan, would join the effort to break Soviet control of Eastern Europe. But it would be a Soviet dictator, Mikhail Gorbachev, who finally allowed change, letting the dominance of the USSR and communism come to a mostly peaceful end.

So far this essay should have *one* point because it has a thesis that includes the region selected (Eastern Europe), the period specified, continuities (cued by lines like "would remain" and "little would change") and changes (cued by the word itself).

BODY 1, THE SITUATION IN 1945

As World War II was coming to an end, the Allied leaders held several meetings to discuss the postwar world, including Eastern Europe. By April 1945, the Soviet armies had pushed the Germans back into Germany itself, occupying most of Eastern Europe, including Poland, Hungary, Romania, Bulgaria, and parts of Czechoslovakia and Austria. Stalin, the Soviet leader, wanted to make sure that his nation remained in power over these areas to prevent future invasion, and he also wanted to remain in Germany to collect reparations for the damages done to the USSR during the war. The United States and its Western allies wanted to allow the nations of Eastern Europe to choose their own futures, but they were not willing—even with sole possession of nuclear weapons—to challenge Stalin. So within a few years the Soviets put into place communist-run governments supported by Soviet troops and Soviet economic aid. For the most part, these governments were not responsible to their own people but instead to Stalin. Yugoslavia was different. Josip Tito, the resistance leader against the Nazis during the war, was very popular with the Yugoslavian people, and the Soviets could not force him to accept their military presence. So Yugoslavia was communist but not under Moscow's control. The Americans, not wanting the Soviets to expand their power, were eventually forced to adopt their policy toward Eastern Europe to accept Soviet dominance but not allow its expansion. This began when President Harry S. Truman agreed to support the Greek government against communist rebels. This support soon expanded to any European government wishing to accept it. Truman's secretary of state, George C. Marshall, oversaw the plan, so it took his name: the Marshall Plan. Money from the Marshall Plan allowed democratic governments in Europe to repair their nation's infrastructure and improve their economies. This avoided the rise of strong communist parties in these nations, which was something the United States wanted. However, Stalin would not allow the nations of Eastern Europe to participate. Winston Churchill had already stated that an "iron curtain" had separated the free West from the communist East. Truman would issue a statement that promised the United States would not allow the expansion of communism, but once the Soviets developed an atomic bomb, the Truman administration also said that the United States would not try to overthrow a communist government. Soviet influence and America's containment policy would dominate Eastern European politics for practically all of the Cold War.

More Points: This paragraph expands upon the continuities mentioned in the thesis: Soviet political domination and communist governments in Eastern Europe. It also has some historical details that may earn the essay the historical evidence points. Also, since it begins to address the key reality of the Cold War—United States vs. USSR—it has a global context, which is an additional Core Point.

BODY 2, FAILED ATTEMPTS AT CHANGE

The Eastern European peoples did not always accept their government's domination by the Soviets. Twice during the Cold War, different peoples in Eastern European countries attempted to oust Soviet-controlled governments. First, in 1956, Hungary attempted to replace its Soviet-controlled communist government. This occurred when the Soviets appeared weak, after the death of Stalin. However, the Hungarians were mistaken. The Soviet Union ordered its army into Hungary to put its puppet government back into power. This left many Hungarians dead and forced others in Eastern Europe to accept that the Soviets would not give up political control over their countries. The United States, still operating under the containment policy, did not actively try to stop the invasion. In East Germany, the people did not try to overthrow their communist government, but they did defy it. Many in East Germany crossed the border into West Germany and did not return. Eventually, the communist government of East Germany, trying to avoid continued embarrassment, erected a hash border around their territory, symbolically placing a large concrete wall around West Berlin. The Berlin Wall would become a symbol of the failure of Eastern European communist governments to get the support of their people. In 1968, Czechoslovakia attempted an overthrow of its government, but as it had done in Hungary, the Soviet military invaded and put a loyal Soviet dictator into power. It seemed that nothing could change in Eastern Europe.

Continuing Points: There are more specific historical details in this paragraph that continue to accumulate points, allowing me to receive both of the Core Basic points for substantiating the thesis with historical evidence. Also, I have introduced change—the Berlin Wall—so I should get both points for addressing all parts of the question. Since I explained why the wall was needed, I have also included analysis, which is another Basic Core point.

BODY 3, CHANGE BEGINS

At the end of the 1970s, an Eastern European—specifically a Pole—was elected head of the Roman Catholic Church and took the name John Paul II. His election to the papacy was the beginning of political change in Eastern Europe. Soon after his election, a labor union, called Solidarity, formed in Poland. Although this party was illegal in the one-party communist state, the Polish government found itself unable to crack down on the party and its leader because the pope spoke in favor of it, and the Polish people were listening to him and not their government. When the pope visited Poland, the government feared for its continued existence. They would eventually, under Soviet pressure, suppress the union, but it showed a weakness in the Eastern European communist bloc. At the same time, Margaret Thatcher became the prime minster of the United Kingdom, followed by Ronald Reagan's election as president of the United States. Both leaders hated communism and wanted to end Soviet domination in other parts of the world, including Eastern Europe. **Reagan began to increase the size of the American military, including nuclear forces. This forced the Soviet Union to keep pace. However, the Soviet economy was very weak. They had made money in the 1970s from oil, but now prices had fallen, and they did not have the economic means to build up their military and pay for the communist governments in other countries. Without economic support, the communist governments of Eastern Europe had a hard time maintaining their control.**

More Analysis and Change: The bold area includes analysis as to why the Soviets began to lose control in Eastern Europe. You should always try to offer an explanation as to why events are occurring at a certain time or in a certain way. Analysis is important in each of the three essays, even if the word itself is not in the question.

FINAL BODY, END OF THE COLD WAR

When Mikhail Gorbachev came to power in the Soviet Union, he realized that the Soviet system could not continue as it was. He turned his attention on the USSR, and the governments in Eastern Europe found themselves freer of Soviet influence than they had ever been before. In Poland, Solidarity leaders were free, and the union was allowed to participate in elections. More surprisingly, the elections were not rigged against them and they won. When the Soviets did not reverse the elections, other governments took notice. In 1989, after severe economic problems, many people in East Germany tried to flee by traveling to Hungary, then crossing the border into Czechoslovakia and finally West Germany. The most educated in East Germany were fleeing, and when the East Germans demanded that the USSR order the Hungarians to close their border, the USSR did not respond and the Hungarians tore down the barbed-wire border between them and Czechoslovakia. At first, it looked as if the East Germans, like China, would fire on their people for protesting and defying the government, but when it became clear that Gorbachev wanted the East Germans to solve their own problems and would not authorize military action, the East German government, for the first time, surrendered to the demands of its people. They allowed the Berlin Wall to open and eventually tore it down. With this, other communist governments in Eastern Europe began to turn over power to elected representatives of the people and open their economies to Western trade. Only in Romania did the government use its military to fight

> against the people. It did not work, and on Christmas Day, 1989, dictator Nikolai Chauchesku and his wife were tried and shot. Real political change had finally come to Eastern Europe after over four decades of Soviet domination. The Soviet Union itself would only last another two years.

At this point, you can end the essay. You could do a concluding paragraph that restates the thesis and your key points, and you should do so if you have time. At this point, all of the Core Points should have been scored. This essay can also expect to get an Expanded Core Point for the thesis that outlines the essay and for the amount of historical information.

The Comparative Essay

The Comparative essay asks you to identify similarities and differences between two things and offer analysis for the reasons underlying the similarities and differences. The comparisons must be direct, apples-to-apples comparisons and must include both similarities and differences, unless the question specifically states differently.

For the Comparative essay, you must first establish what you will compare. The question should provide you with a starting point. For instance, the question will not say compare China and Japan, or even compare China and Japan in the seventeenth century. Instead, it will ask you to "compare the political system of the Ming dynasty to the Tokugawa shogunate in Japan." So you need to begin brainstorming by drawing a T chart like the one below.

CHINA	JAPAN
Confucian beliefs gave authority to the emperor and his scholar bureaucrats	
	Feudal government run by shogun (Tokugawa family), emperor just a figurehead

CHINA	JAPAN
Strong central government based on the bureaucracy and its taxing authority	Strong central government based on the military strength of the Tokugawa
Bureaucracy chosen by exam on Confucian teachings	
	Daimyo (large landowning samurai families) were tightly controlled by Tokugawa government
Mandate of Heaven—emperor ruled by will of heaven, natural disasters, wars Economic decline means dynasty's time is up	
Allowed some European advisors, such as Jesuit missionaries, to work in the government	Banned all foreigners from the country except for limited Dutch and Chinese trade

Notice, on the chart, if you recall a fact about China, in the space across from it, for Japan, you only include information that facilitates a direct, relevant comparison, otherwise leave it blank. For example, you remember that China's government was very centralized (second fact on T chart). This triggers your memory that Japan's Tokugawa government, although feudal, was also very centralized, so you include this fact because it is a direct comparison. Once you complete your initial brainstorming, you want to look over the chart to see if you have three or four direct comparisons *and* that you have at least one similarity and one difference. In your review of the chart, you find two direct comparisons, one similarity, and one difference. Now you must go back to brainstorming and try to fill in at least one more relevant comparison. Your easiest solution: adjust the first facts from each column.

China was governed by Confucian bureaucrats with an emperor whom Confucianism said had absolute authority, although most were weak and let the bureaucrats rule	Feudal government run by shogun (Tokugawa family), emperor just a figurehead

By changing the focus from Confucianism on the Chinese side to who really controls the government, you create a direct comparison out of the information already on the chart. With three direct and relevant (*relevant* meaning that it actually addresses the question and is not something unrelated—in this case, to their respective governments or something obvious [they have a government] or unimportant [the royal color in China was yellow while in Japan it was not]) comparisons, go back to your brainstorming and try to fill in more details for the comparisons. Then start your thesis.

When writing the thesis for the comparison essay, you must avoid a very common pitfall. Most students write a thesis for this essay that basically says, *There are similarities and differences between these two things.* (This also should go down as another line you *never* use if you want to make your point.) This just restates the prompt, which made it obvious that the two shared similar traits as well as differences. You must take a different approach. To get the thesis point, you need to make an argument or evaluation of the comparisons. The easiest tactic is to quantify your answer: *While both Ming China and Tokugawa Japan developed centralized governments, the people in power and the means of control the governments used were quite different.* You state a similarity but then emphasize that the two governments are mostly different. Now, go back to the essay and cover each of your relevant comparisons in detail, one per body paragraph. You want to make sure you follow this structure. Some students try to write one body paragraph all about the first subject (for example, China in this example), then a second body paragraph about the second subject. You do not want to do this. Often, in this format, direct comparisons get lost among the facts you attempt to bring into the essay. Also, as you will see in the rubric, you must offer some analysis to explain the similarities and differences, and this format makes that difficult to do without a lot of needless and confusing repetition.

Knowing the Rubric

The College Board provides a generic rubric for the Comparative essay in its World History Course Description booklet (available online at apcentral.collegeboard.com/apc/public/repository/ap-world-history-course-description.pdf). Like the previous free-response essays, the rubric is divided into two parts. Part one, the Basic Core, includes 7 of the possible 9 points available from the Comparative essay. You *must* receive all of the Basic Core points in order to get any points in the Expanded Core section. While each question may set slightly different requirements for meeting each part of the rubric, all of the Comparative essays require the same basic elements described in the rubric.

THE COMPARATIVE CORE POINTS (0–7)

Has acceptable thesis (addresses comparison of the issues or themes specified).	1 Point	The thesis must do more than just restate the question. It must make your specific answer to the Comparative prompt and identify at least one similarity and one difference you will explain and analyze in the essay.
Addresses all parts of the question, though not necessarily evenly or thoroughly. (Addresses most parts of the question: for example, deals with differences but not similarities.)	2 Points (1 Point)	You must include at least one similarity and one difference for each of the areas included in the prompt. If the prompt asks for a comparison of revolutions *and* their effect on social classes, you must find a similarity between the revolutions discussed, a difference between the revolutions, a similarity on their effect on social classes, and finally, a difference.

Substantiates thesis with appropriate historical evidence. (Partially substantiates thesis with appropriate historical evidence.)	2 Points (1 Point)	You must include at least *five* (this number varies, but five should guarantee you credit) historical facts that go with your thesis. Of the five, you must have at least one for similarities and one for difference. *Also*, if you are asked to compare two sets of things, you must include historical information for a similarity and a difference in *each* comparison. If all five are similarities, you would only get 1 point instead of the 2 available.
Makes at least one relevant, direct comparison between/among societies.	1 Point	Each comparison, similarity, or difference must address the question (relevance) and must include a discussion of both things being compared (direct).
Analyzes at least one reason for a similarity or difference identified in a direct comparison.	1 Point	For analysis, you need to look for a cause for the difference or similarity. Between societies, look at religion, economic activity, gender and ethnic policies, and government system for possible areas of analysis. Within a society, social class, economic activity, gender, and ethnicity all provide good starting points for analysis.

If you receive all 7 of the Basic Core Points, you may possibly receive 0, 1, or 2 Expanded Core Points. The chart below offers suggestions on how to receive those points. Note: the reader can give 1 or even 2 points for any of these criteria. You could write an extended thesis and receive 2 Expanded Core Points because of its quality.

THE COMPARATIVE EXPANDED CORE POINTS (0–2)

You can only receive these points if all 7 Basic Core Points are earned. Examples of expanded core areas include:	2 Points maxi-mum	

Has a clear, analytical, and comprehensive thesis.		In your thesis, after you give your initial answer/argument to the question, you should use the thesis to outline the paper, introducing your direct comparisons in the order you will make them.
Addresses all parts of the question thoroughly (as relevant): comparisons, chronology, causation, connections, themes, interactions, content.		Very subjective and completely in the hands of the reader as to how to award points here. Make sure that key elements to the society or societies mentioned get included. For example, you should not discuss a Chinese dynasty without mention of Confucianism or the twentieth-century Middle East without mentioning Islam and oil. Make sure in your brainstorming that you identify key cultural forces and, in your analysis, discuss their impact on society.
Provides ample historical evidence to substantiate thesis.		Go beyond the 5 or 6 detailed pieces of information that you used for the Core Points. The more specific information you can recall, the better.
Relates comparisons to larger global context.		In your analysis, consider forces that affect the society or societies from beyond their borders: the plague, foreign invasion, or new technologies. If any seem to make an impact, include a discussion of these forces and impact in your essay.
Makes several direct comparisons consistently between or among societies.		*Every* comparison needs to be direct *and* relevant to the question.
Consistently analyzes the causes and effects of relevant similarities and differences.		For each relative, direct comparison, offer some explanation for the similarity or difference, just as you did for one of the Basic Core Points.

Content Review Part 1: Transformations

Prehistory to 600 BCE

The Paleolithic and Neolithic Ages

Prior to the beginning of history (the point where written records could be maintained), the earliest human societies lead a nomadic existence that remained relatively unchanged for tens of thousands of years. The period, called the Paleolithic or Old Stone Age, began with the first use of stone tools by hominids, about 2 million years ago, and ended as late as 10,000 years ago. This was followed by a relatively short Mesolithic, or Middle Stone Age. This ended with the beginnings of agriculture during the Neolithic, or New Stone Age. Through all of this time, humans lived in small nomadic groups and followed their food supply: migrating animals and seasonal plants. During this era, human populations expanded to settle over most of the continents. Archaeological evidence suggests change occurred very slowly in human societies and was mostly caused by geological and climate factors. Significantly, the last ice age ended about 10,000 years ago, freeing up large parts of the planet for easier habitation and isolating the Americas as the land bridge across the Bering Strait disappeared under the rising oceans.

Domestication and Agriculture

The retreating ice ushered in a new era of human development. Societies began to develop new and more specialized tools, mostly designed for greater production of food. Humans also domesticated several animal species—including dogs, pigs, sheep, and goats—and adopted a pastoral lifestyle, moving herds from pasture to pasture instead of depending solely on hunting. More critically, some societies—first in the Middle East but later in northern China, Africa, and Mesoamerica—developed agriculture, which changed their whole pattern of living. The earliest crops to be domesticated were cereal crops, such as peas, wheat, and rye. Agriculture touched off the Neolithic Revolution, the period during which some societies transformed from hunting and gathering to small, permanent agricultural settlements. This slow revolution created the conditions in which civilizations could develop, beginning with the growth of cities out of small agricultural communities along the Tigris and Euphrates Rivers in modern Iraq.

The River Valley Civilizations

Agriculture spread out from the Middle East and most likely developed independently in China and possibly in some areas of Africa. Eventually, several societies were able to establish large cities. After spreading their influence through religion, trade, and military strength, they became the foundations for four great civilizations: Egypt along the Nile, the Sumerians in Mesopotamia between the Tigris and Euphrates Rivers, the Harappans along the Indus River, and the Chinese along the Yellow River. The rivers provided long-term stability for the agricultural settlements along their banks, not only by supplying abundant water, but also by flooding on a regular basis, replenishing the topsoil used by the farmers.

Mesopotamia/Sumer

Mesopotamia, the "land between the waters," saw the development of the first true civilization, the Sumerians, between 3500 and 2350 BCE. By 5000 BCE, extensive agriculture already dominated the lands between the Tigris and Euphrates Rivers. Over time, the cities that developed here adopted, via trade, a common religious pantheon and language. Eventually, several large city-states arose and dominated the irrigated lands both politically and economically. By 3300 BCE, these people developed the first written language, primarily to keep records of financial transactions. The cuneiform system of writing was created using a small stick to press simple characters into clay tablets. Over time a class of scribes rose to prominence for their ability to record not just financial records but also laws, poems, stories, and histories. They also left accounts of day-to-day activities, providing extensive information about the lives of people in many different social classes, not just priests and kings.

A STRUGGLE FOR CONTROL

The economic success of the Sumerians attracted many other societies to Mesopotamia. None of the Sumerian city-states ever achieved dominance over the whole region. Instead, successive invaders conquered existing cities or built new ones. The newer societies built on the culture of the Sumerians, including their written language, religion, and agriculture. The table below lists the various empires to arise in Mesopotamia over this time period. The AP World History Exam will not ask you to identify each, but the names could be used in connection with the river valley civilizations or with various cultural developments, which are also included on the table.

MESOPOTAMIAN EMPIRES

CIVILIZATION	DEVELOPMENTS
Akkadians	Founded by Sargon of Akkad
	First historical empire
	Language became most common in Mesopotamia/Middle East after 3000 BCE
Assyrians	Language was a mix of Akkadian and Sumerian
	First true cavalry army
	Conquered Israel, Judah, and Egypt
Babylonians	Used almost interchangeably with Mesopotamia
	Hammurabi, a Babylonian king, developed the first system of written laws: Hammurabi's Code
	Created a complex bureaucracy and regular taxation instead of forced tribute
Hittites	First to smelt iron; iron weapons were the main reason for their military successes
	Occupied areas along the Mediterranean coast and upper Mesopotamia
	Main military rival to the Egyptian Empire
	Famous for the introduction of chariots to Middle Eastern warfare
Persians	Achaemenid dynasty in Iran would conquer most of the Middle East beginning about 550 BCE
	First great conquering emperor was Cyrus the Great
	Used satraps (local governors) to collect taxes and send them to the capital
	Practiced Zoroastrianism, founded about 1000 BCE
	Constructed an extensive road network from Iran to the Aegean coast to move and supply its army

SUMERIAN SOCIETY

Like those in other early civilizations, the Sumerian religion mixed a large pantheon of gods with a king who was partially divine and who acted as a connection between humans and the gods. To display their economic power, Sumerians built cities with massive brick temples (ziggurats) that rose in the center like artificial stepped hills. Priests presided over ceremonies that attracted farmers and merchants from nearby cities at various times during the year. This increased trade within the city and added to its power. Sumerian temple carvings, the epic of Gilgamesh, and clay tablets make it clear that the main city-states—35 in all—fought each other constantly for political and economic dominance.

In the cities, archaeological and written evidence suggest that social classes developed based on jobs. Skill determined income, with scribes and priest living in many of the best dwellings. The ruling king and nobles also enjoyed great luxuries. In Babylon, one of the seven wonders of the ancient world—the Hanging Gardens—formed part of a palace complex for the ruling king. Family played an important part in one's social placement. In Hammurabi's Code, the largest section is devoted to the family. Within family law, the code allows women some freedom, but it clearly places them below men in society, either their husbands or their fathers.

EXCERPTS: HAMMURABI'S CODE AND WOMEN
If a seignior [free man of some rank but not a noble] wishes to divorce his wife who did not bear him children, he shall give her money to the full amount of her marriage-price and he shall also make good to her the dowry which she brought from her father's house and then he may divorce her.
If a seignior's wife has made up her mind to leave in order that she may engage in business, thus neglecting her husband…he may divorce her with nothing to be given her as her divorce settlement.
If a woman so hated her husband that she has declared "you may not have me," her record shall be investigated at her city-council, and if she was careful and not at fault,…that woman may take her dowry and go off to her father's house.… If she was not careful, but was a gadabout, they shall throw that woman into the water to be drowned.

So a woman received some rights, such as divorce, but her economic rights were at the control of her husband. Should she leave the marriage, the economic property (her dowry) would return with her to her father's house.

Egypt

Egypt developed into a large civilization at about the same time as the Sumerians. Neolithic culture developed in the grasslands near the Nile by 5000 BCE. Eventually, as the grasslands dried up, the people were forced to concentrate their settlements along the Nile. In 3100 BCE, the landed elites of these settlements united Upper Egypt (the area south of the Nile delta) and Lower Egypt (the delta) into a unified state under the control of Pharaoh Menes. The pharaoh combined the economic power of the landowners (who controlled important resources like copper) and religious power, taking on the role of a god on earth. The early pharaohs established dynasties to rule over Egypt. They also introduced many of the markers of a pharaonic lifestyle that would dominate Egyptian culture in the years to come, including luxury for the royalty and widespread use of sacrifice in religious worship.

AGES OF EGYPT

PERIOD	DEVELOPMENTS
Old Kingdom (2575–2134 BCE)	Pyramid building; hieroglyphics Irrigation system Trade routes develop toward the south and into the Middle East
First Intermediate Period (2134–2040 BCE)	Failure of the Nile floods causes famine and brings about political collapse
Middle Kingdom (2040–1640 BCE)	Capital moved to Thebes Conquered by the Hyksos, who wielded bronze weapons and rode in horse-drawn chariots—both previously unknown to the Egyptians

PERIOD	DEVELOPMENTS
Second Intermediate Period (1630–1540 BCE)	The Hyksos dominate a fragmented Egypt
New Kingdom (1539–1075 BCE)	Egypt expands in North Africa and the Middle East under pharaohs such as Ramses II, known as Ramses the Great
	Extensive building projects completed, including temple building at Karnak
	Declined due to internal strife, weak pharaohs, and outside invaders
Third Intermediate and Late Period (1070–332 BCE)	Egypt remains politically fragmented and many areas fall under foreign domination, especially the Persian Empire
	In 332, Alexander the Great conquers Egypt; Egypt would not gain complete independence until the twentieth century

Note: Do not get too concerned with dates. Questions will *not* ask when the New Kingdom ended, although they may ask why the New Kingdom declined by ca. 1100 BCE.

Economically, the Egyptians remained an agrarian society, with the overwhelming majority of the people living in small farming communities along the banks of the Nile, especially in the delta. Grain surpluses allowed the Egyptians to engage in trade with people in the eastern Mediterranean and southern kingdoms, especially Kush, which is in modern Sudan. This brought in luxury goods such as olive oil, wine, and gold. Egypt also exported some of its culture, including the Egyptian polytheistic form of religion to Kush and spreading the use of papyrus (a reed paper used for writing) into the Mediterranean.

Egyptians maintained the polytheistic beliefs of the earliest societies that settled the region. They worshiped a pantheon of gods that was dominated by the sun god Ra. They believed the pharaoh was a divine being descended from their gods and that the pharaoh's role was to maintain the order of the universe. Pyramids were constructed to ensure that the pharaohs would proceed to the afterlife and become gods to protect their people. These massive tombs became a symbol for Egypt, both of its wealth and power and of its technological ability. Most Egyptians believed that the afterlife would be a continuation of life on earth and therefore buried the deceased with everyday implements, such as cooking equipment and household goods, that would be needed in their next life. The strong belief in the afterlife also prompted the Egyptians to develop elaborate and technical means of embalming the body. Their most important religious writings, popularly called the Book of the Dead, dealt almost exclusively with the afterlife. Because of the religious significance of the pharaoh and of the importance of the after-life to Egyptians, the priestly class wielded great political and economic power. At various times, they ruled Egypt as a theocracy.

Egyptian society was dominated by a small elite: pharaoh's family, priests, and warriors. The majority of Egyptians were poor subsistence farmers, not slaves as is often depicted. Women, as in other civiliza-tions of the period, were secondary to men. They managed the house-hold and were responsible for their children's education and training. Upper-class women could join the priesthood, and at least one woman—Hatshepsut—became a pharaoh. You need to remember that this was the exception, not the rule.

Technologically, Egyptian civilization was among the more advanced of its time. Like others, it developed a pictograph system of writing (hiero-glyphics), which was later expanded to include some phonetic characters. Its people were the first to use papyrus. They also developed some of the most advanced architectural and construction techniques in the ancient world. Through trade, they gained the knowledge of bronze making and created some of the most advanced bronze tools and weapons. Their soci-ety excelled in developing medicines, mathematics, and astronomy.

Egyptian art included political and religious themes, most famously in the pyramids. Many of their temples, tombs, and palaces are decorated with massive sculptures of political figures and gods. Egyptian architects also developed the obelisk as a monument device, using hieroglyphics to record the histories of the pharaohs and other important individuals along the sides or depicting the leaders' making offerings to the sun god Ra. Paintings of religious and common scenes adorn many of their tombs.

The Indus Civilization

Sometime around 2600 BCE, a civilization arose along the Indus River in modern Pakistan and India. The civilization—called the Harappan after their major city, which was first excavated in the 1920s—covered an area larger than the Egyptian or the Mesopotamian Empires, with more than 70 cities stretching from the Himalayan foothills to the Arabian Sea. Archaeological evidence suggests (we must rely on archaeology because their written language has not been translated) a highly centralized government, possibly controlled by a priest, that provided stability over the region for a long period of time. The largest public buildings include temples and public baths, possibly for cleansing rituals like those found in India today, further indicating a connection between religion and government.

The cities' structures also included large, presumably public granaries for food storage. Extensive agricultural communities were required to feed the large city populations that totaled as many as 50,000 in some. The main crops were wheat and barley, but rice, peas, lentils, and dates were also staples. All of these (except rice) came by trade and social migration from the Middle East. Sheep and goats also arrived as domestic animals from the Middle East. The Harappans domesticated cattle, used elephants and water buffalo as beasts of burden, and were also the first to produce cotton. Ivory and precious stones were exported from the Indus region to Mesopotamia. This trade is evidence of the first long-distance sea trade, because the items traveled along the shores of the Arabian Sea, through the Strait of Hormuz, and into the Persian Gulf.

Many of the temples in Harappan cities include images of animals, especially humped bulls similar to images later found in Hinduism, a religion founded in this region after the fall of the Harappan civilization. Temples also include images of a man comparable to later images of the Hindu god Shiva. However, Harappan society appears exceptionally egalitarian, with most of the houses uniform in size, suggesting little material difference between the social classes. This contrasts sharply with the Hindu caste system that later dominates this region. The uniformity of images between all of the major sites and the consistency of the language throughout the Harappan period only suggest centralized authority and stability.

Beginning about 2000 BCE, archaeological evidence speculates that the Harappan civilization started to decline, although it is unclear why. Around 1800 BCE, a group of Indo-Europeans identified as Aryans began to move into the region from the steppes. Their horse-drawn chariots gave them a military advantage over the peoples in the region. Around 1500 BCE, the Aryans founded a new civilization in India. This new civilization borrowed heavily from the Indus people, but with some definite Aryan adjustments. The Aryans established a strong social hierarchy that eventually, under the teachings of Hinduism, developed into the caste system; the most elaborate social order ever established by a society. Hinduism used many symbols of the Harappan tradition but integrated Aryan beliefs from their sacred text, the Vedas.

China

Neolithic agricultural settlements existed along the Yellow River by 4000 BCE. People farmed millet and cabbage and domesticated the pig. Later farmers added rice and soybeans to their crops and began using sheep, cattle, and chickens. By 2200 BCE, these agricultural communities became the first cities in China. Oral tradition and written texts suggest that this first civilization joined into the Xia dynasty (a dynasty is the period of rule of one family). The Xia were previously considered mythical, but an archaeological discovery in 1959 found evidence of the dynasty's capital city. The ruler of the Xia, a king, also acted as a religious connection between his people and the chief deity in the heavens. In about 1766 BCE (the Chinese religion stressed cosmology, so the Chinese made detailed observations of the heavens that allowed modern scientist to date events based on comets, planetary positions, and eclipses), the Xia were replaced by the Shang dynasty (also con-sidered semilegendary until excavations in the 1920s revealed several Shang capitals).

Shang kings ruled over a collection of city-states—theirs being the most powerful—that acknowledged the king's authority. As king, the ruler was not considered a deity as in Egypt or Sumer, but instead he was believed to communicate with his ancestors, who would intercede with the supreme deity in heaven on the king's behalf. The king levied taxes and enlisted troops from the city-states. The troops most often fought invading nomadic groups, although evidence and writings from late dynasties mention internal conflict and the king's using his armies against rebellious city-states. Near 1122 BCE, a former vassal peoples of the Shang, the Zhou, allied with many city-states that were dissatisfied with the Shang king. This alliance overthrew the king and started the longest of the Chinese dynasties. The Zhou, making use of the idea of the moral and political failure of the Shang king, claimed that the heav-ens favored them, giving them the Mandate of Heaven. They referred to their emperor as the Son of Heaven.

The Mandate of Heaven is the idea that a dynasty comes to pow-er because the heavens favor it, granting the dynasty legitimacy. However, if China experienced natural disasters, such as floods and earthquakes (both very common events), then it was argued that a dynasty had lost the Mandate of Heaven and should fall. Outside invasions and internal bandits were also signs of a dynas-ty's losing the mandate.

The Dynastic Cycle describes the rise and fall of Chinese dynas-ties. During times of good leadership, Chinese governments made great efforts to ensure that they completed irrigation and flood control projects. They also invented the earliest seismographs to detect earthquakes so that aid could be dispatched quickly to an affected region. Under corrupt governments, tax monies were wasted and important flood control projects were neglected. Taxes also were increased, forcing peasants to sell their land, and many resorted to banditry. When the armies engaged the bandits, nomadic groups found it easy to raid Chinese territory. The floods, the increased suffering of the peasants at the hands of bandits and tax collectors, and invasions created a self-fulfilling prophecy: the dynasty would fall, having lost the mandate, and another would eventually take its place.

Zhou emperors distributed land to families that supported their rule, creating a feudal system in China. By 771 BCE, the feudal vassals of the Zhou realized that the imperial system was weaker than it seemed, and they began to break away from the central authority. This era, dubbed the Spring and Autumn Period by Chinese scholars, saw the fragmenting of China into more than 170 regional powers. By 475 BCE, these independent regions were condensed into seven larger kingdoms that fought continuously until 222 BCE, when the Qing state united China into a new dynasty. The period is called the Era of Warring States.

Like other river valley civilizations, the Chinese depended on agriculture as the basis of their economic system. Prior to the Xia, the Chinese developed silk production, using the cocoons of worms fed mulberry leaves to spin one of the most popular natural threads in history. The Chinese maintained a monopoly on silk production until the fourth century CE. Silk would attract merchants to China for centuries, giving its name to one of the most important ancient trade routes: the Silk Road.

From early times, Chinese society looked to oracles as a way of divination. Pictographs were written on bones and then heated. Priests read omens from the cracks that occurred in the bones. The Chinese also sought help in the present by venerating their ancestors. Many families maintained a central altar or shrine to their ancestors. These shrines served as a detailed family history and a place for the living to make offerings to departed family members and inform them of new family events, such as births and marriages.

At the heart of Chinese families was the father. Women were relegated to the role of wife and mother. They were under the control of their fathers then their husbands. In old age, their sons were responsible for them. Women played an important role in silk production, and Leizu, the wife of the mythical Yellow Emperor, is credited in Chinese lore with the discovery of silk. During the Era of Warring States, the Chinese scholar Confucius further defined women's roles when he identified the Five Relationships in society: the only roles for women were wife and mother.

Classical Civilizations: Organization and Reorganization of Human Societies, 600 BCE–600 CE

Ancient Greece

A Bronze Age civilization developed on the coast and islands of the Aegean Sea about 3000 BCE, reaching its height with the Mycenaean Greeks about 1,500 years later. The civilization formed around small city-states that were dominated by a king and warrior aristocracy. Their cities include Troy, Knossos (capital of the Minoan civilization on the island of Crete), and Mycenae. They produced an abundance of olives and wine for trade, but because of limited farmland, the city-states were forced to develop colonies and trade routes to bring in grain supplies. As the city-states grew, conflict over these routes and the sources of grain led to almost continuous war. Around 1200 BCE, the weakened civilizations were defeated by a combination of natural calamities, migrations into the area by Dorians from the Balkans, and the expansion of the Sea Peoples (a group of unknown origin) throughout the eastern Mediterranean that cut off many of the important trade routes with the grain-producing colonies.

For the next 400 years Greece experienced a dark age in which civilization collapsed and people fell back into small isolated agrarian communities. Writing knowledge was lost, and the memories of civilization became legends. *The Iliad* and *The Odyssey* both originated from the oral traditions of this time. Small farming communities sought to protect themselves by enlisting all able-bodied men into simple militias. Armed with crude spears, some body armor, and a large round shield, these volunteers were known as hoplites (after their shields). They fought in a line formation called a phalanx. This was primarily a defensive position, because they were protecting their homes, not conquering other areas. By giving military power to a community's citizens, the Greek idea of democracy began to develop as those who fought were also granted political power. By about 800, the Greeks were building a new civilization with a new system of writing and a new political model, one that was shaped by assemblies of free men, not a king.

Classical Greek civilization, as the new period became known, followed many of the previous patterns. The city-state, or polis, emerged as the primary political and social unit. The people shared religion, language, technology, and even a social order, all with some local variances. Citizenship was reserved for free adult males who were natives of the city, and this included political and economic rights above those of others. Women, even those born in a city, did not receive the rights of a citizen. By 500 BCE, political power in most of the city-states rested with an assembly that made laws and appointed government officials. This form of government—a direct democracy—played an important part in Western political philosophy. As the wealthiest of the city-states, Athens came to represent all that was successful about democracy. Political freedoms also encouraged greater enterprise and trade. Soon hundreds of Greek colonies sprouted up along the shores of the Black Sea, Sicily, and the southern part of the Italian Peninsula. All of these regions produced grain (which was still very much in short supply in Greece), olives, or wine for trade. The colonies encouraged the Greek powers like Athens to construct large navies to move trade items and to protect their trade routes. The basic Greek galley, the trireme, remained the model for Mediterranean ships until at least 1571, when the last galleys of the Ottoman Turks and the Christians of Spain and Italy fought the battle of Lepanto.

KNOW YOUR GREEKS AND THEIR NEIGHBORS

PERICLES	Popular member of the Athenian assembly
	Leader of the golden age of Athenian art and government
	Died of plague during the early stages of the Peloponnesian War
SOCRATES AND PLATO	Considered the two greatest Greek philosophers
	Rationalists: knowledge arises from the mind of the thinker
ARISTOTLE	Student of Plato, but he eventually rejected Plato's rationalism
	Empirical thinker; knowledge must come through observation
	Greatest classical scientist
	Introduced the importance of classification into the natural sciences
	Taught Alexander the Great
ALEXANDER THE GREAT	Macedonian, civilization north of Greece
	Already a military commander at age 18 when his father conquered the Greeks
	At age 20 became king when his father was assassinated
	Invaded the Persian Empire and conquered everything from Egypt to India
	Spread Greek culture (Hellenism) well into Asia; his most lasting accomplishment
	Died at age 32 as ruler of most of the known world

Persia, Pericles, and the Peloponnesian War

Attracted by the economic success of the Greeks, driven by their own political imperative to conquer others, and motivated to punish Athens for helping conquered Greek city-states try to overthrow them, the Persians invaded Greece in 490 BCE. The initial attack focused on Athens. The Persians, using a massive fleet of ships, landed an army north of the city at a site called Marathon. The Athenian phalanx won the day, destroying the main part of the Persian army and forcing the Persian emperor Darius to give up his plan of conquest.

Ten years later, Darius's son Xerxes I attempted to destroy the Greeks. A massive army moved by land against the Greek city-states. Heading toward Athens, the army met stiff resistance from 300 Spartans at the mountain pass of Thermopylae. Although eventually defeated, the Spartans held back the Persians long enough for the Athenians to evacuate and then turn their fleet against a larger Persian invasion force. At Salamis, the smaller Greek navy, led by Athens, destroyed the Persian navy. This cemented Greece as the foremost power in the eastern Mediterranean and Athens as the greatest of the Greek cities. Athens experienced several decades of cultural and economic growth, referred to as its golden age or the golden age of Pericles.

During the golden age, Pericles and his followers in the assembly encouraged public investment in the arts and architecture as well as an expansion of democracy. He pushed Athens to limit special powers to upper-class citizens and passed several measures to encourage the poor to take a greater part in government, including increasing the pay for jury duty. His construction projects repaired the damage done during the Persian wars and added the Parthenon, dedicated to Athena (the patron goddess of Athens), to the central Acropolis of the city. He also strengthened the defenses of Athens, built up the navy, and established overseas colonies for citizens. The colonies secured grain and other resources for Athens, because the people were allowed to remain citizens of Athens and retain their political and economic privileges. Many of the Greek polis came under the direct influence of Athens either through economic necessity or military coercion.

The success of Athens appeared to be leading Greece toward the formation of a unified state. To avoid domination, however, Sparta began to construct an alliance of cities against Athens. Eventually, war broke out between Athens and her allies and Sparta. The 27-year-long Peloponnesian War (as it was called) resulted in defeat of Athens and the continued independence of the Greek city-states. In 338 BCE, Greece would finally be united, but not by a Greek. Philip II, king of Macedonia, defeated the Greek city-states and established a hegemony, or leadership, over them. He passed this on to his son, Alexander the Great. Alexander eventually spread Greek culture (referred to as Hellenic culture) over the known world during a decade of conquest. This influence over politics, ethics, philosophy, medicine, architecture, and technology lasted into the modern world.

Empire of Alexander the Great

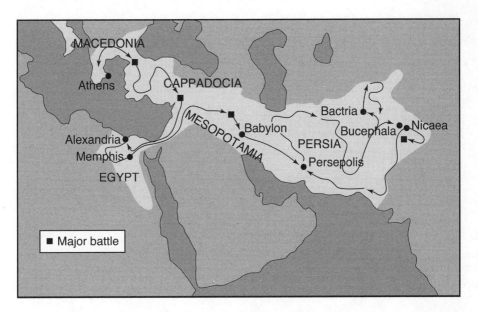

Note: The multiple-choice section may include a map with few or even no labels and require you to identify what it shows. It is important to associate geographic regions with political boundaries (empires and nations), economic activities (resources and trade routes), and religions.

The Roman Republic

In 509 BCE, the people of Rome overthrew their king and established the first republic in the Western world. Citizens of the city, divided into two classes, created a government run by elected representatives that would serve as a model for the modern democracies that would arise in Europe more than 21 centuries later. Patricians (the property-owning class) elected a legislative body, the Senate, to issue decrees and send legislation to the assemblies of citizens and manage the appointments of military commanders, including the two top military commanders, called consuls. The senate also controlled taxation, foreign policy, and the appointments of provincial governors. At first, the patricians also commanded the only assembly that mattered when it came to passing laws, justice, and the military.

Plebeians, the lower-class citizens, enjoyed certain rights under the laws, but they would spend generations fighting for greater political representation. Eventually, as Rome became the center of a great trading civilization, the wealth from commerce earned by many in the plebeian class would gain them the right of veto over the senate's laws and open a path to membership in the senate and other top posts.

In the third century BCE, the city of Rome embarked on the path toward empire. Militarily, it mobilized its citizen-soldiers into legions, a new fighting unit based on open lines of swordsmen. Soon the legions expanded south along the Italian Peninsula and brought the cities and former Greek colonies into the Roman state. As the Romans reached Sicily, they fell into economic confrontation with the greatest maritime power of the day: the North African city-state of Carthage (founded by the Phoenicians).

Rome fought three wars with Carthage over economic dominance of the western Mediterranean. During the Second Punic War (Punic is Latin for Phoenician), the Carthaginian general Hannibal famously and unsuccessfully invaded Italy across the Alps with an army that included elephants. Rome's legions were fed by great resources of manpower (people from the areas added to the state gained citizenship by fighting in the legions) and ultimately wore down Carthage. The Third Punic War ended in 146 BCE with the complete destruction of the already broken Carthaginian state. The Roman army took drastic steps to ensure that Carthage could never again threaten their political power, even going so far as to raze the city of Carthage and sell all the remaining inhabitants into slavery.

By 100 BCE, the tremendous wealth of Rome allowed for the expansion of the republic's empire across the Mediterranean, from Spain to

Asia Minor. The wealth of trade also brought with it internal upheaval. New families, both patrician and plebeian, rose in prosperity while old ones faded from power. Also, the legions created new centers of power as the legionnaires turned their loyalty from the state to the generals who, through victories, won them land to retire on and raise families. Several civil wars broke out, culminating with the rise of Julius Caesar up the military ranks. A brilliant military commander, Caesar recognized the hardships of the poorer citizens of Rome who were denied jobs because of an abundance of slaves gained from the wars. His popularity with the masses and his defeat of Pompey and the senate allowed him to achieve political control of Rome. He was named dictator, not for the standard six months commonly allowed to individuals who rose to power in times of strife, but for ten years and then life. A faction of senators assassinated Caesar in 44 BCE, but Caesar's death did not restore the republic.

ROMAN INNOVATIONS

POLITICS	Republican government
	Written laws; the Twelve Tables
	Veto; right of the lower class to nullify a law
ECONOMICS	Extensive road network facilitated trade (but not the first road network; the Persians also built an extensive road network)
	The imperial navy removed the threat of pirates from the Mediterranean
	Europe was connected to long-distant trade routes (the Silk Road)
SOCIAL STRUCTURE	Patron-client system of social obligations
INNOVATIONS	Cement
	Architecture: arch, dome
	Aqueduct
	Water wheel

The Roman Empire

Even before Caesar's death, the republic faced seemingly insurmountable problems. Lands in Rome were consolidated into massive estates. More and more of the poorer farming families found themselves without land or work. They fled to the cities. In the cities, the slaves working for wealthy landowners or merchants occupied both skilled and unskilled jobs. Public handouts of food kept most from starvation. Also, games were sponsored by the government, and wealthy families provided some distraction from the social disparity. This system of "bread and circuses" depended on stable public revenues and the ability of those in power to continue their support of the games.

In 31 BCE, Octavian, Caesar's heir, consolidated his hold over Rome. He looked like a republican, and the Senate even appointed him to office, but he held full power and became Augustus, the first Roman emperor. His loyal legions and the addition of Egypt (Rome's main source of grain) allowed Augustus to expand the empire and secure greater political power. For the next 200 years, Rome's wealth and power created one of the greatest civilizations in history.

Technology and art flourished. Roads connected all parts of the empire, securing trade in the empire and allowing the legions to keep the peace from Spain to Scotland to Mesopotamia. Conquered territories provided more slaves for the estates of the wealthy and continued to increase the disparity between wealthy and poorer Romans. In the senate, the wealthy families fought for the spoils gained from new territories and for influence with the emperor. The wealthy families established themselves as patrons to tens and even hundreds of poorer client families that worked for them and gave them support in exchange for protection. Women of wealthy families were used in arranged marriages to cement family alliances, but they lacked individual rights. Instead, they were viewed as the property of their fathers and husbands. The client families acted to support their patrons, lived in cramped, overcrowded tenements in the cities or as tenet farmers on their patron's lands, and accepted their lot as long as there was food and protection from their powerful patron. As long as conquests continued and the government could provide food and distraction, the system flourished. About 200 CE, the system changed.

Numerous internal problems doomed the Roman Empire. Economically, the system exhausted the lands of many of the grain-producing regions. This cost many powerful families their wealth and disrupted the internal politics of Rome. As conquests ended, both due to weak emperors not wanting powerful legions or popular commanders and there were fewer territories convenient for the taking, the legions became less attractive to Roman citizens. Once a civic duty of landowners, joining the legions to protect the lands of the wealthy offered little incentive to poor plebeians who could no longer count on lands and money upon retirement. Still, the legions became very political, supporting or deposing emperors at the senate's urging or their own desire for a larger payday. Inflation also created social upheavals, and social upheavals became a reality as food prices rose.

Some attempts were made to fix the system, most notably by Diocletian, who fixed food prices, increased pay to the legions, fortified the frontier borders, reformed the provincial system and tax collecting, and divided the empire into two more manageable states. He also reinforced the worship of the emperor as a divine representative. His attempt to reinstitute a divine emperor clashed with the growing populations of Christians within the Roman Empire. Many of these Christians were unwilling to accept the Roman system of religion and faced severe persecution for their beliefs. Ultimately, the Diocletian reforms failed, the legions revolted, inflation continued as new sources of gold and silver could not be found, taxes hit the small middle-class landowners the most, and the co-emperor system engendered new civil wars. Later, Constantine would reunify the empire, legalize Christianity, and create a stronger center of power in the east at his new capital of Constantinople.

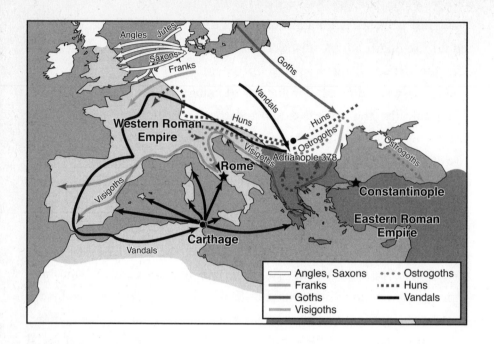

The Han Dynasty

In 221 BCE, China was again united by the Qing and its leader, Shi Huangdi, the first emperor of China. The short-lived Qing dynasty (221–206 BCE) based its rule on military power and a philosophy of legalism that stressed the need for the government to establish order with the threat of severe punishments and the promise of potential rewards. Shi Huangdi ruthlessly controlled his people. He put them to work, and they built the first wall to separate China from the northern nomads. Then they built him a massive tomb at the capital, Xi'an. He forced the nobles to move to his capital, thereby destroying their independent authority. He attacked Confucianism and other philosophies that might question his rule; he ordered the burning of all books of philosophy and history so he could rewrite them according to his own ideas. Many scholars were executed.

High taxation and attacks on the traditional Confucian family structure created resentment among his people. When Shi died and his son became emperor, the new emperor was quickly overthrown and replaced with the Han dynasty (206 BCE–220 CE). The Han dynasty is the most important in China's history; the Chinese population's name for themselves is "people of the Han." This dynasty re-institutionalized Confucianism as the ruling philosophy of the state. The boundaries of the Han also established the heartland of the Chinese people.

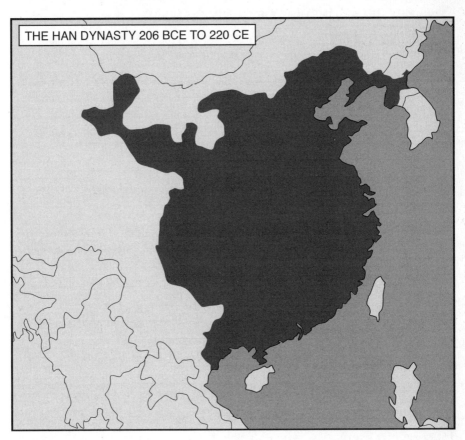

THE HAN DYNASTY 206 BCE TO 220 CE

The Han sought to establish a lasting order in China (see the box on the Mandate of Heaven and the Dynastic Cycle on page 129). Confucianism—a philosophy originating at a time of much upheaval in China—sought to do the same. Confucius had taught that a moral leader, a superior man who practiced all the virtues, would act as a model to develop virtue in his people. Scholars of Confucianism in the Han court strove to establish the emperor as this model.

The cornerstone of Confucian philosophy is that everyone knows his or her place or role in society. To establish this, Confucius defined the

Five Key Relationships possible between in society. They appear below in the traditional order of importance (although Confucius put the greatest emphasis on father to son, the second one listed).

FIVE KEY RELATIONSHIPS OF CONFUCIANISM

RULER TO RULED	A ruler is benevolent and a model of virtue to his subjects; therefore, the subjects are loyal.
FATHER TO SON	A father provides protection and guidance to his son; therefore, the son reveres his parents and cares for them into old age. (Respect for age is also extremely important in the Chinese social order.) This is an expression of *filial piety.*
HUSBAND TO WIFE	A father provides for the family; therefore, the wife and mother cares for the home and raises the children.
ELDER BROTHER TO YOUNGER BROTHER	An elder brother serves as a model and provides guidance for a younger brother; therefore, a younger brother respects an elder brother's instructions, especially when caring for their elderly parents.
ELDER FRIEND TO JUNIOR FRIEND	Age establishes a hierarchy in relations outside the family, but these are less important than family relationships. An elder is considerate and guiding; a younger person is deferential and respectful.

Note: Three of the relationships involve the family; the Chinese consider the family as the basic unit of society and most important for the proper function of society. Also, the *only* role for a woman is wife and mother.

A strong emperor with honest officials could establish order in the large empire. However, after officials isolated the emperor in the capital, making him a symbol of authority, they took over the responsibilities of government themselves, and other forces began to disrupt the imperial rule. The military, wives and the families of the emperor's wives, and even the emperor's eunuch slaves all competed to influence the isolated emperor. This competition bred corruption.

HAN INNOVATIONS

POLITICS	Confucian bureaucracy; most complex of any government
	Centralized government and taxing authority
	Limited use of merit for government appointment; government not completely dominated by upper class
ECONOMICS	Government monopolies over iron and salt
	The government built an extensive canal system for transportation
	Annual labor tax on peasants built many public works
SOCIAL ORDER	Confucian hierarchy dominated the social system
INNOVATIONS	Government sponsorship of astronomical research
	Government actively maintained historical records
	Government promoted Confucian philosophy throughout the country
	First collar to allow draft animals to pull wagons or plows
	Most advanced pottery; lead to development of china
	Paper

Indian Empires

Although South Asia (modern India, Pakistan, and Bangladesh) shares a dominate religion, language, and social order, it has historically resisted political unity. Most states are formed by a conqueror who establishes a short-lived dynasty. Local leaders almost immediately start to resist centralized control, and the empires break apart piece by piece. The Mauryan Empire, founded by Chandragupta Maurya after Alexander the Great left India, survived through much of the classical period. Chandragupta expanded the empire by bloody conquest and then ruled it through a strong bureaucracy and military. The third emperor, Asoka, started his reign in the same way; he eventually tired of bloody military conquest.

Asoka was bothered by the many deaths his armies caused, and he converted to Buddhism and sought to rule by morality rather than the harsh laws of the previous emperors. The peace he brought to his empire encouraged economic growth, and the Mauryans reached a height in wealth and innovation. India benefited from the monsoon winds of the Indian Ocean that made seasonal travel to India by ship from both Southeast Asia and the Middle East relatively simple and safe. The sub-continent was also connected via land trade routes through the Khyber Pass just to the north. Valuable goods from China arrived both by land and sea, making Indian merchants exceptionally wealthy.

Upon Asoka's death after more than 30 years of rule, the empire began to break apart. Many Hindus who had lost power because Asoka favored Buddhism fought back, and the authority of the central government weakened. Eventually, local lords declared independence from the central government, and the Mauryan military was unable to hold the state together.

In 308 CE, about 120 years after the fall of the Mauryan Empire, a new family, the Gupta, began to unify northern India, mostly by marriage between powerful families. By 380, the Gupta Empire ruled all of modern Pakistan, Nepal, and northern India, stretching from the Arabian Sea to the Bay of Bengal. As strong Hindus and members of the Brahman caste (the highest class and the priestly class), the Gupta emperors encouraged construction of Hindu temples and financed many Hindu works of art. They also encouraged artists to come to their court and produce Hindu literature and poetry. At the same time, they tolerated Buddhism and allowed the construction of Buddhist temples as well.

The cultural golden age carried over to economics as well. India became famous for the production of fine cotton textiles. It also produced the best iron tools in the world. Merchants enjoyed high social status, unlike those in China, and benefited from a government that encouraged trade. Technology also improved India's economy, as the use of a lateen (or triangular) sail on oceangoing vessels allowed for more rapid and regular trade. Improved trade methods and high-value goods made India as wealthy as any area of the globe at the time.

Alliances between local nobles and the Gupta worked well at temporarily unifying India, but it left the military fairly weak. In 480, the Huns invaded northern India, and by 550, when the last of the Gupta emperors died, the empire controlled only a small fraction of its former territory.

The Fall of the Roman Empire and the Han Dynasty

After Constantine (272–337), the Huns and many Germanic invaders eventually overwhelmed the Roman Empire. The Germans came into the empire by migration of their whole peoples. When it became impossible for the weakened Roman legions to hold them at the borders, the emperors allowed them to enter Roman territory as allies, employing them to support the legions. In return, the Germans and their families were granted citizenship. When Attila the Hun invaded Gaul, the Romans were able to drive him out only with the help of their German allies. However, the undeniable weakness of the legions and the abundance of Germans looking for land eventually overwhelmed the system. The divided empire could not resist.

In the east, geography helped to preserve the eastern empire, protecting the Byzantines from a large land invasion and allowing them to continue their trade profitably via the Indian Ocean and East Asia. In the west, invading tribes occupied Gaul, Spain, and North Africa, and declared themselves independent kingdoms. In 455, the Vandals sacked Rome. Eventually, the Western Roman Empire fell in 476 to the German tribesmen.

For the Han dynasty it was much the same story. External invaders—the Xiongnu—took advantage of internal difficulties and occupied areas of northern China while the Han collapsed. Like many dynasties after it, the Han followed the basic dynastic pattern. As emperors became more and more insulated from political life, failure of the central government gave local landlords greater authority. They stopped collecting taxes for the emperor and instead created their own states. Peasants faced greater taxes, the loss of their lands, and received no aid from the emperor. They turned toward the mysticism of Daoism for help, because they saw the Confucian government failing. The Yellow Turbans, a Taoist sect, rebelled and weakened the already corrupt dynasty.

With fewer peasants on the tax rolls, the Han generals were forced to depend on professional armies instead of peasant militias to put down the rebels. These armies, some including Xiongnu, just like the Romans had included Germanic tribesmen, added to the breakup of the centralized authority when they refused to disband after the completion of a military campaign. In 220, the last Han emperor relinquished the title, and China entered a period of warring states known as the Three Kingdoms.

China recovered from the collapse, although somewhat changed, with the new influence of Buddhism that entered into the region prior to the dynasty's collapse. Similarly, while the Western Roman Empire had collapsed, the growth of Christianity retained some of Rome's cultural legacy among the new barbarian states, because missionaries spread the religion from Italy to all corners of western and northern Europe.

Africa and the Americas

Both the Americas and sub-Saharan Africa (the region south of the Sahara Desert) were much slower at developing agriculture than the areas already discussed. Many arguments exist as to why the Neolithic Revolution was slow in coming to these regions. For brevity's sake, the easiest explanation involves the specific types of crops that were available (for an expanded answer to this question, read *Guns, Germs, and Steel*, by Jared Diamond; for a completely different answer, read *Carnage and Culture*, by Victor Davis Hanson). In the Americas, the only native grain in Central America was corn, but it would take generations of selective cultivation to produce the modern strain of corn; its natural state was a small husk with only a few kernels of grain. None of the important grain crops were native to North or South America. Agriculture required a great deal more time to develop because of this, leaving most Americans as nomadic societies throughout this period.

In sub-Saharan Africa, a similar problem existed. However, this region had a geographical connection to other areas with agriculture. Well into the Common Era (CE), most sub-Saharan Africans continued to live in hunting-gathering societies. However, beginning in about 1000 BCE, western Africans, called Bantus, started migrating into southern Africa, bringing with them agriculture and metallurgy. Over time, Bantu speakers overwhelmed local cultures, and by the fifth century CE became the dominant group through most of sub-Saharan Africa. As in other areas, Bantu villages began to grow into larger communities. The first city established in sub-Saharan Africa (outside of the influence of Egypt) was Great Zimbabwe, founded about the fourth century.

Multiple-Choice Review Questions

1. A society is almost certainly a civilization if

    A. it has a population over 1,000 people.
    B. it produces works of art.
    C. it has built a city.
    D. it has a government.

2. What change during the Neolithic Revolution impacted human society the most?

    A. The development of agriculture
    B. The development of new tools made of metal
    C. The development of long-distance trade routes
    D. The introduction of domestic animals, like sheep and pigs

3. Which of the following did NOT occur as part of the Neolithic Revolution?

    A. Increased human populations
    B. Improvements in the building of shelters
    C. The introduction of permanent human settlements
    D. The introduction of metal tools to replace stone implements

4. What statement most accurately compares early Sumerian and Egyptian civilizations?

    A. A unified Egypt became a greater political and economic power than the independent city-states of Sumer.
    B. The trade wealth of Sumer overshadowed the agrarian economy of Egypt.
    C. Because of its writing system (cuneiform), Sumer developed a more complex political and social structure than Egypt.
    D. Attempts to unify all of Sumer caused them to develop a political system dominated by the military while Egypt, protected by natural barriers, did not develop a powerful military.

5. What statement best differentiates between a modern democracy like that found in the United States or France and that found in ancient Athens?

    A. In a modern democracy, only citizens can directly participate in government.
    B. In Athens, citizens directly approve laws instead of assigning the task to representatives.
    C. In Athens, representatives of the more powerful families controlled most decision making while modern democracies do not discriminate based on wealth.
    D. In a modern democracy, the government is responsible to its citizens while in Athens the government acted in the interest of the military and empire.

    "When the personal life is cultivated, the family life is regulated; when the family life is regulated, then the national life is orderly; and when the national life is orderly, then there is peace in this world."

6. The quote above most likely comes from which of the following sources?

A. Hammurabi's Code
B. Justinian's Code
C. The works of Confucius
D. The Aryan Vedas

7. What statement best characterizes the Gupta Empire?

A. The Gupta created a feudal system in India in order to govern a culturally diverse society.
B. The Gupta Empire established a large, culturally unified state that survived the fall of the ruling dynasty.
C. The Gupta failed to do more than briefly unify India, an area dominated by many regional, politically independent states.
D. The Gupta Empire used the treat of establishing Buddhism as the national religion to coerce the Hindu nobility into unifying their various states under the Gupta dynasty.

8. What statement about the classical civilizations is most accurate?

A. Classical civilization began in Greece and was spread first by the conquests of Alexander the Great and then by trade routes to Asia and the Mediterranean.
B. By the classical period, religion no longer played a dominant role in society as it had done during the earliest civilizations.
C. Nomadic societies proved a challenge to all of the classical civilizations.
D. While Rome depended on its military to conquer new areas, the Chinese and Indian civilizations used trade.

9. What statement best explains the success of the Germanic tribes when encountering the Romans in the fifth century CE?

A. The Germans had developed a fighting formation superior to the Roman legions.

B. The Romans failed to take the German threat seriously and did not send the legions to defend the borders, but instead used them to settle internal political disputes.

C. The Romans could no longer adequately man the legions, lacking both manpower and the wealth needed to defend all their frontiers.

D. The Germans allied with the Persians, and the Huns were able to overwhelm Rome's defenses.

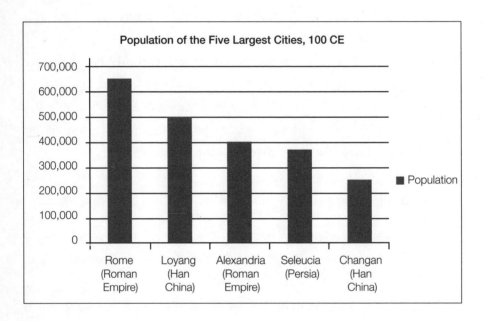

10. What statement is best supported by the information provided on the above chart?

A. By 100 CE, the Roman Empire and the Han dynasty had urbanized a large percentage of their populations.

B. Agricultural production in Rome and China allowed for a great deal of job specialization.

C. The population density of Roman cities was greater than that of their Chinese counterparts.

D. By 100 CE, the Han dynasty was already in decline when compared to the Roman Empire.

Answers to Multiple-Choice Questions

1. **C.** A society that has built a city must have developed many of the prerequisites for a civilization: a surplus of food, a complex government, a division of labor, and record keeping (see the "Levels of Society" chart on page 13 for more information). There is no set population for a society to become a civilization, and all societies produce art and have some type of political system, although it might be very simple in a nomadic group.

2. **A.** Since agriculture allows for the development of permanent settlements, a surplus of food, and a division of labor, it clearly has the greatest impact on how a society develops. In the Neolithic period, societies depended on stone implements, not metal tools (remember the name means New *Stone* Age).

3. **D.** A, B, and C all are results of agriculture. By not needing to move as in a nomadic society, it became practical to develop more specialized tools, because they would not need to be transported. Also, the term Neolithic refers to a period of advanced stone tools.

4. **A.** Because Egypt was able to unify its many cities into a single empire, it developed a much stronger and stable state. B and E are simply false. C fails because it ignores the fact that Egypt also developed a complex writing system: hieroglyphics.

5. **B.** Athens is a direct democracy where the assembly of citizens makes all of the laws. Modern democracies follow a republican model in which elected representatives carry out the task of legislation. A is true, but it is also true for the other system as well. C is true for Athens but not legally true in a modern democracy, although wealth does affect political influence.

6. **C.** Confucianism strongly supports the family as the core structure of society. Stability in the family creates stability in the kingdom.

7. **C.** Until the last century, India, although unified by language and religion, remained politically fragmented. Empires like the Gupta and

those that followed (the Delhi Sultanate and the Mughal Empire) failed to create a permanent unity between the Indian states (making choice B incorrect). D is partially true—the Gupta supported Buddhism—but not as a means of coercion.

8. **C.** Nomadic civilizations were one of the key causes for the fall of each of the classical civilizations. A and B are false. D is partially true: Rome did rely on its military for conquest, but it also used trade, and India defiantly used military might to build the Mauryan Empire.

9. **C.** Previous German tribes failed to break into the Roman Empire, but by the fourth century, the legions were having difficulty finding recruits as well as suffering from internal disputes. Answers A and B are false, and D is only partially true (the Romans did suffer from Persian and Hun attacks, but the Germans were not allied with them—in fact, Germans fighting with the legions saved Gaul from the Huns).

10. **B.** The only argument that follows from the information (based on the "Levels of Society" chart) is that both the Romans and the Han had high degrees of specialization, which is a requirement for building cities. The other choices all make conclusions on information not available on the chart. A and C would require more information on total populations and land area, and for D you need more historical information on Chinese populations (Roman as well).

Free-Response Examples
Continuity and Change over Time

Directions: You are to answer the following question. You should spend 5 minutes organizing or outlining your essay. Write an essay that:

- Has a relevant thesis and supports that thesis with appropriate historical evidence.
- Addresses all parts of the question.

- Uses a world historical context to show continuities and over time.
- Analyzes the process of continuity and change over time.

Analyze political and economic continuity and changes in one of the following regions between 2000 BCE and 500 CE:

- India
- China
- The Middle East

Comparative Essay

Directions: You are to answer the following question. You should spend 5 minutes organizing or outlining your essay. Write an essay that:

- Has a relevant thesis and supports that thesis with appropriate historical evidence.
- Addresses all parts of the question.
- Makes direct, relevant comparisons.
- Analyzes relevant reasons for similarities and differences.

Compare the internal and external causes for the fall of the Han dynasty and the Roman Empire.

Content Review Part 2: Interactions

600 to 1450

Civilization did not end when the classical empires fell. While civilizations in western Europe suffered a near collapse, new civilizations arose in other areas that continued cultural traditions. In eastern Europe, the Byzantines continued the Roman Empire and Hellenistic culture. Persia and China rose again (in the case of China, repeatedly). In South Asia, some areas came under the control of invading Islamic and nomadic societies while others areas remained under the rule of local Hindu princes. Africa, too, saw the advancement of larger civilizations as more areas of the continent actively engaged in international commerce. But this was not simply a period of continuity with the past. The barren deserts and fertile coast would soon serve as a launching point for massive cultural change affecting three continents.

CLASSICAL CIVILIZATIONS AND THEIR FATES

BY 600	NEW INCARNATION
ROMAN EMPIRE	
Western empire falls	The remains of the Western empire were loosely united under the pope and the Roman Catholic Church
Eastern empire centered in Constantinople (now Istanbul)	Eastern empire becomes Byzantine Empire

BY 600	NEW INCARNATION
HAN DYNASTY	
Collapses; China broken into regional dynasties Reunited by the Sui in 581	Tang replaced the short-lived Sui
	Tang culture second only to Han in importance in Chinese history
	Song, Yuan, and Ming dynasties continue, expanding the Han system of centralized bureaucracy during this period
GUPTA	
India returns to regional states that are loosely united culturally	Foreigners (many Islamic) would establish states in northern India; Delhi Sultanate; Mughal Empire
	Parts of southern India come under the control of Hindu kingdoms

Islam

Muhammad founded Islam in 622 when he and his followers left Mecca, a major trade and religious center, for Medina (the event referred to as the *hijra*). Islam impacted societies from western Europe to Tang China. Islam follows the tradition of monotheistic religions found in the Middle East and traces its origins back to Abraham, as do Judaism and Christianity. Islam refers to Jews and Christians as "people of the book" but does not accept their interpretation of God's wishes. Followers of Islam, or Muslims, believe they must follow the instructions God gave to Mohammed, his prophet, through the archangel Gabriel.

According to tradition, Muhammad, a caravan merchant operating out of Mecca, received these revelations and began recording and sharing them with his immediate family, the first Muslims. As his teachings began to spread, the leaders of Mecca, concerned over the impact they might have on trade and the pilgrimages many Arab tribes made to the Kaaba and its many religious idols, started to suppress his message. Fearing attacks on his people, Muhammad moved his followers to Medina, a nearby city that was home to both Arab and Jewish clans.

After negotiating a peace between the two Arab tribes, Muhammad gained prestige and won many converts to Islam. In 630, Muhammad and an army of 10,000 followers returned to Mecca and brought it under his control. This marked the beginning of the rapid growth of Islam during the seventh century.

Building an Islamic Civilization

Arab society based itself on clan loyalties. Muhammad wished to unite all Muslims and end the warfare between the Arab clans. He created the idea of the *umma* (community of all Muslims), which ignored clan and tribal allegiances. Muhammad sought to establish a political system over all of the *umma*. This idea grew into the original Islamic caliphates, or empires.

After dedicating the Kaaba to Allah (the term for God in the Islamic faith) and destroying the idols placed there by the Arab tribes, Muhammad launched his followers on waves of military conquest and religious conversion that rapidly spread up the Arabian Peninsula and into the Fertile Crescent. Here, the Persian Sassanid dynasty and the Byzantine Empire had fought each other to exhaustion. The Arabs found the area ripe for conquest. The Sassanians collapsed completely in 651. Their highly centralized bureaucracy became a model for the Islamic conquerors, who lacked experience in managing a complex government. The Byzantines were forced to retreat to Anatolia (Asia Minor, now modern Turkey), defeated by the skilled and motivated Arab armies. Muhammad's successors, called caliphs, established the first Islamic Empire, the Umayyad caliphate, while the eastern Romans retreated.

Under the Umayyad, Islamic culture spread and diversified. The collected revelations given to Muhammad were bound into the Quran. Islamic architecture took shape, blending elements of Greek, Roman, and Persian traditions. In the literary arts, Arab oral tradition mixed with calligraphy and the poetry of Persia. Many gladly converted to the new religion, finding the Arabs less oppressive than the Romans or the Persians. They were attracted, too, to the egalitarian teachings of Islam.

Others converted in search of advantages; Muslims did not pay certain taxes, they could not be enslaved by other Muslims (although this was not strictly enforced), and as the religion of the conquerors, conversion opened one up to both political and economic opportunities.

While adopting some of the facets of other cultures, the Arabs did not give up their own. Along with the Quran, traditional Arab practices formed the basis of much of Islamic law, the sharia. This included rules on the treatment of women. Muhammad, based on how he treated his first wife and daughters, appeared to grant women some religious, economic, and political roles beyond Arab traditions. However, Islamic law restricted women's activities to the family and made them the responsibility of their father, brothers, and husband. Many other customs concerning the family structure, eating, education, and finances also transferred from Arab to Islamic society. Other cultures, specifically Persian culture, contributed ideas in areas that the Arabs lacked regarding government bureaucracy and the arts.

ISLAMIC SOCIETY

FIVE RELIGIOUS "PILLARS"	FIVE CONTRIBUTIONS
Belief that there is one God, Allah, and Muhammad is his prophet Prayer five times a day facing Mecca Fasting during Ramadan, a monthlong period The zakat, a tax to support the poor of the *umma* The hajj, or pilgrimage to Mecca, once during one's life	Preservation and distribution of Greek and Roman knowledge after the collapse of the Roman Empire Arabic numerals (first decimal system) Algebra (the same mathematician also developed algorithms) Astrolabe for navigation (also a slide rule for computations) Unified trade system from West Africa to China (goods and ideas passed across the known world)

Civil War: Politics and Religion

Because Muhammad had no sons and because there were no clear instructions in the Quran, appointing a successor to Muhammad created the first fracture in Islam. The murder of the third and fourth caliphs permanently split the *umma* along political and then religious lines. Followers of Ali, the murdered fourth caliph, formed the Shia branch of Islam (followers are called Shi'ites). Those who rejected Muhammad's line through his daughter (Ali's wife) became the Sunnis. They were the power behind the new Umayyad dynasty (a dynasty because the title of caliph now passed through the male line of a single family). A third group arose in Islam: the Sufi. Accepting both Sunnis and Shi'ites, Sufism stressed a mystical, spiritual path toward God. Sufi sects became an important missionary movement within Islam as it spread into South and Southeast Asia.

FRACTURES IN ISLAM

RELIGIOUS	POLITICAL
Shi'ites: "the party of Ali," the fourth caliph; found mostly in modern Iran, Iraq, and Bahrain	Umayyad dynasty, 661–750: capital at Damascus; conquered North Africa and Spain; introduced Arabic as the dominant language throughout this region; fell to civil war
Sunnis: "people of custom and the community"; dominant in the rest of the Islamic world	Abbasid dynasty, 750–945: moved capital to Baghdad; expanded into central Asia; lost Spain to a separate caliphate (first political split in Islam; *umma* no longer a single political unit); empire fragmented in 945; the Abbasid were religious leaders until 1258, when Mongols killed the last Abbasid caliph
Sufis: mystical branch of Islam whose followers seek a closer relationship with Allah through meditation and rituals; important in the spread of Islam into South and Southeast Asia	Other caliphates (as the central authority of the Abbasids collapsed): Umayyad in Spain Fatimid in North Africa Almoravid Empire in southern Spain and Morocco (ruler did not take the title of caliph, but was based on a strong, literal Islamic foundation)

The Abbasid Caliphate

The Abbasid caliphate arose out of civil war in 750 CE. The capital was moved to Baghdad, which became a great center for trade, culture, and learning. Trade routes with gold from West Africa, slaves from East Africa, frankincense and myrrh from Yemen, textiles from Persia and India, and silks from China all crossed paths here. All of the great works of science and literature could be found within its walls, and the early caliphs began translating them all into Arabic, preserving them for future generations. Baghdad became the world's greatest center of learning during the eighth and ninth centuries. Trade also brought inventions from distant lands, like paper from China.

Trade also allowed for the cultural expansion of Islam. Merchants carried Islam to many new locations, converting members of both the upper classes (who were involved in trade) and the lower classes (who were attracted by the egalitarianism of Islam). The wealth created by trade allowed the caliphs to build new mosques and palaces. Art also found patronage among the government and wealthy merchants.

The Abbasid leadership mixed law and religion. Religious leaders (called *ulama*) not only led prayers at the mosque, they also heard legal disputes and resolved them using sharia. Qualified ulama were selected by the caliphates to serve as chief judges in each city and province. In Islamic countries, the tie between religion and politics was strong.

Socially, the Abbasid leadership defied some Islamic traditions. They instituted the court practices of the Persians, which offended many Muslims, because they seemed to require those entering the presence of the caliph to worship him. They also put themselves and other descendants of Muhammad on a higher social level, in contrast to Islam's egalitarian tradition. However, people in the Abbasid state still enjoyed many freedoms. Villagers could move to cities, non-Muslims could easily convert and join the *umma*, and many slaves, on converting to Islam, eventually found freedom and acceptance in the caliphate.

The Spread of Islam (to 750)

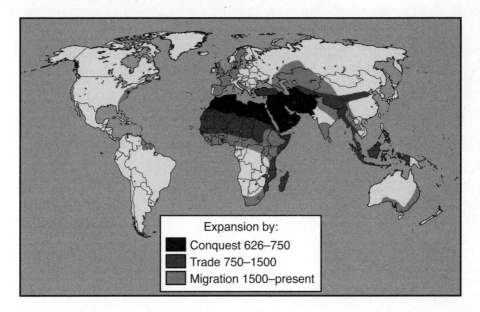

Expansion by:
- Conquest 626–750
- Trade 750–1500
- Migration 1500–present

The Abbasids also introduced the harem, the taking of many wives (polygamy existed in Arab culture prior to Muhammad) and secluding them in the palace, devoid of almost all outside contact. Seclusion was much more severe than that of previous Arab tradition, and even enslaved women enjoyed greater freedom than the wives in a harem. The practice of seclusion and veiling of women spread down to the lower classes of society during the Abbasid rule. By the tenth century, women in the Middle East and North Africa existed solely within their family, with no influence or protected freedoms in the outside world. While polygamy was traditional in Arab society, the number of wives exceeded previous traditions, and without clear rules of succession, conflicts soon arose between potential heirs to the caliphate.

The heirs turned to mercenaries and then to slave soldiers (called *mamluks*) to protect themselves and help win them the title of caliph when their father died. While the armies might win a caliph his position, the caliph often found that his troops refused to disband and instead became a drain on his revenues. Conflicts between these mercenary armies created economic disruption. When their pay didn't arrive, the mercenaries sometimes even turned on the caliph, assassinating him in favor of someone more likely to pay them. Eventually, to pay the mercenaries, the Abbasids turned over whole sections of the empire to the mercenary leaders so they could collect taxes directly from the residents. The captains pillaged the land, creating an agrarian disaster, as villages were destroyed or abandoned. Irrigation works and other infrastructure collapsed entirely. Pieces of the empire broke away into independent states (whose new rulers sometimes took the title of caliph). Eventually, the Abbasids lost all political power, maintaining the position of caliph only as a religious figurehead until the last one was killed by the Mongols in the thirteenth century.

African States
West Africa

Between 600 and 1450 several African societies rose in economic and political importance, creating important states in both West and East Africa. In West Africa, gold and salt provided incentives for traders to establish caravan routes across hundreds of miles of desert. The new technologies (like the camel saddle) allowed large amounts of goods to be transported efficiently across the desert. The newly generated wealth allowed local leaders to build empires, controlling surrounding societies through military force. The first, Ghana, formed in the third century. Originally, the leaders of Ghana depended on the belief that their lineage was sacred, which provided them with religious authority. After converting to Islam, the rulers used it to solidify their power, basing their power on religious authority as the rightful successors to Muhammad.

Weakened by wars along the caravan routes, Ghana eventually faded as the Malinke people rebelled and founded the Mali Empire. The Mali emperors used Islam to build support for their authority as well. By building mosques, converting to Islam, and supporting members of the Islamic community, they won the people's loyalty. Dependent on agriculture, the armies of Mali brought many diverse village populations into the empire in order to expand their agrarian base. Merchants followed, looking for more sources of gold and markets for trade items that arrived in the cities from such faraway places as China. They also brought new technology and continued the spread of Islam into West Africa. Ibn Battuta, a Muslim, was the greatest traveler in the ancient world; he visited sites from Mali to China, traveling close to 75,000 miles. Ibn Battuta spoke highly of the Islamic legal system in Mali, but he was offended by the freedom given to Muslim women, who could even have private conversations with men not of their family.

The hunt for gold proved very successful. In 1324, Emperor Mansa Musa's pilgrimage to Mecca brought so much gold into the Egyptian economy that it caused rampant inflation. His return brought new artists and architects to his lands. Great mosques and libraries were built. Trade made the Mali city of Timbuktu one of the foremost centers of learning in the world. But most of the inhabitants of the large empire continued to live on small farms. No large landowning class developed; instead families produced small surpluses of food that provided for the large trade cities. The villages also failed to integrate into a larger cultural group. For the most part, they continued their own religious and social traditions; even when adopting Islam, they made it conform to local custom. However, the empire allowed for a more peaceful coexistence, as long as it remained strong.

Mali's power faded when the gold ran out. New discoveries moved trade in other directions, leading to the rise of the Songhai Empire in the eleventh century. Songhai formed during the height of the Mali Empire, but it remained a minor power in the region. In the late fifteenth century, Sonni Ali led the Songhai in the conquest of Mali and eventually expanded his empire well beyond Mali's borders. Like Mali, the Songhai depended on agricultural production as much as the gold trade and took care to bring large areas of western and central Africa under their control. They also continued to mix Islamic culture with native beliefs, never fully adopting the strict Islamic beliefs characterized by sharia law, although many in the clergy pushed for this.

Africa's East Coast

As in West Africa, the peoples of East Africa mixed their own culture with that of their Islamic trade partners. In East Africa this mixing created a much stronger, unified culture, although it did not create any great empires. The culture took the name of its common language: Swahili. Swahili mixed the Bantu language with Arabic to create a new tongue. The culture established itself in the coastal trading ports. In the towns, Muslim elites controlled politics and economics, but they depended on Africans from the interior to bring them items for trade: ivory, gold, iron, and slaves. In fact, few people beyond the cities converted to Islam, and as in West Africa, Islam was fused with local traditions like the priority of the maternal line, not the male line, for the inheritance of property. Islam was most prominent among the rulers of the coastal towns, who converted to Islam because they dealt with Arabic merchants. But as the merchants did not penetrate inland and the towns did not establish themselves as larger political units, Islam did not become a major cultural force in East Africa.

Remote Africa: Beyond the Reach of Islam

The other areas of Africa—the forests of Central Africa and grasslands of the South—were far less influenced by outside trade. In modern Nigeria and areas to the east, city-states arose, each with a unique culture and prosperous because of active trade among the states. Many kings ruled based on divine status, but some groups, such as the Yoruba, used representative forms of government to temper the power of the divine king. They depended on the loyalty of traditional tribal rulers who paid homage and taxes to the king (that is, a simple feudal system). Along the lower Congo River, an agrarian-based Bantu-speaking kingdom grew to command a substantial territory. A hereditary king ruled the Kongo and possessed the authority to appoint local chieftains, giving the monarch wide control over the people. In the Kongo, pottery, iron and copper works, wood carving, and weaving produced opportunities for long-distance trade. Women managed agricultural production, giving them an economic importance uncommon in other areas of the world at the time—including Europe, the Islamic states, and China.

The Indian Ocean Connection

The monsoon winds that provided water for the crops around the Indian Ocean also powered an extensive oceangoing trade network. Small sailing ships like the Arab dhow used the innovative lateen (triangular) sail to make short coastal voyages from East Africa to modern Indonesia, using the seasonal monsoon winds. For part of the year the monsoons moved trade north along the coast of East Africa and eventually to the western coast of India. Ports along India's East Coast could send goods to Southeast Asia. The process then reversed itself as the winds changed. This allowed for regular movements of goods and created very stable economic growth all along the shores of the Indian Ocean.

Politically, no single state controlled the trade. Greek merchants, operating out of the Red Sea, traded with Indians, who in turn dealt with Chinese or Thais, who traveled from the Straits of Malacca. The expansion of Islam encouraged Arab merchants to become very active along the routes, but no single state dominated any significant portion. The ships only made short trips, exchanging goods at the nearest port before returning when the monsoon winds shifted. Merchants made a profit at each exchange, with the goods slightly rising in price at each stop.

More important, the Indian Ocean route allowed for a massive diffusion of culture and technology over a large part of the planet. It allowed the innovations of China to impact the libraries of Timbuktu. Chinese, Islamic, Persian, Greek, Roman, and Indian learning moved through and enhanced the cultures all along the route.

Chinese Dynasties
Sui and Tang

In 581, the Sui succeeded in unifying northern China into a new dynasty. They restored the centralized Confucian bureaucracy, established a system of merit-based appointments for government officials (based on exams over Confucian philosophy), and improved the defenses of the country. Emporer Wen of Sui repaired and enlarged the canal system to provide for more agricultural production and rebuilt parts of the Great Wall. He also led the military into the south to expand his empire.

To weaken his rivals, he redistributed land from powerful landlords to the peasants, based on family size (the equal fields system), and lowered their tax burden. Making the peasants happy—as well as working to control floods—was *always* the top job of a successful Chinese government. This conformed to basic Confucian values concerning the importance of peasants, the family, and the emperor's responsibility to provide for each. In fact, culturally, very little changed in China during the Sui; its importance lies in the fact that the Sui reunified the state. The dynasty collapsed in 618, early in the reign of its third emperor, Emporer Yang. General Gau Zu declared that the Mandate of Heaven had passed to him, and he founded the Tang dynasty.

The Tang ranks second only to the Han in laying the foundation for Chinese culture. During the long interval of disunity after the Han, Buddhism entered China. The Tang fully integrated Buddhism into the Chinese imperial system. They also adopted an even more thorough examination system that firmly established government bureaucrats as the source of the economic and social elite.

Once they controlled the north China plain, the armies of the Tang spread out in all directions, extending China's borders to their greatest historical limits. Korea and northern Vietnam both came under Tang control, and a Tang army even fought Arab forces at Samarkand in modern Uzbekistan. The wealth of this vast empire soon became too great an endeavor for the Tang to control, and policies like the equal field system and price controls faded away. What did not go away were taxes.

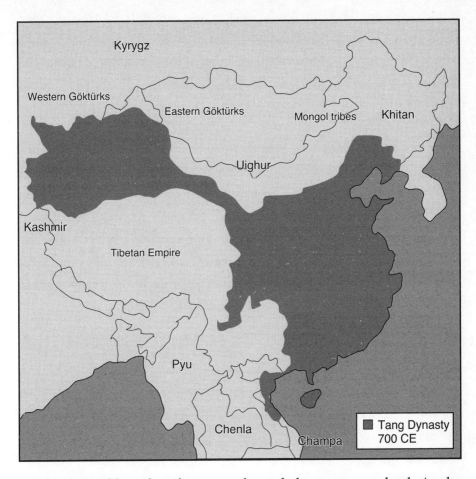

The Tang, like other dynasties, depended on a tax on land. At the start of the dynasty, Buddhist monasteries controlled many acres of land and did not pay taxes on it. This economic power allowed them to influence the emperor. At one point, the Empress Wu, the only woman ever to directly rule China, used Buddhists to circumvent the Confucian bureaucrats who refused to accept a woman ruler because of Confucian teachings. However, the monasteries' continued accumulation of land and the potential of the monks to rival the military finally gave the Confucian bureaucrats enough leverage to convince an emperor to seize much of their lands and establish government controls over who entered and who ran the monasteries. Also, Confucianism itself began to focus on a metaphysical (outside of the physical world) basis for their moral behavior. This previously lacking religious element to Confucian philosophy (labeled Neo-Confucianism) established it as an alternative to the Buddhist and Taoist religions. Each of these traditions influenced the major art and literature of the Tang period.

Weakened Rule

After Wu's rule, the dynasty saw a series of weak or inattentive emperors. Nomadic incursions and rebellions weakened central authority, allowing local landlords greater freedom to establish their own taxes and push peasants off their land. Dependence on Turkish mercenaries to keep out invaders resulted in a military collapse, because the army's loyalty demanded more money than the government could collect. Without threat of military force, the central authority disappeared from many regions. In 907, the last Tang emperor, Emporer Ali, abdicated.

The Song Dynasty

In 960, Emporer Taizu of Song succeeded in unifying northern China, creating the Northern Song dynasty. Although smaller in area, Song economic growth created the largest and wealthiest urban centers on the planet. Kaifeng, the capital, had a population of almost 1.4 million, making it the largest city in the world in the eleventh century. Demand for manufactured goods and imports to the large urban centers fueled a huge increase in manufacturing. Iron and steel tools and weapons gave the Song a high standard of living and stability. To facilitate trade, the Song expanded the use of paper money (called flying money), which had been developed during the Tang dynasty. They also focused more on a trade tax than the land tax. This made them wealthy and kept the peasant populations secure in their land holdings.

Over time, nomadic groups put pressure on the Song, who eventually moved their capital south. This forced them to turn toward ocean trade and move goods into Southeast Asia and the Indian Ocean via Arab and other merchants. A large number of Chinese also migrated to the key port towns along the trade routes, bringing some aspects of

Chinese culture and invention with them. Even with the move, the Song remained the largest and most urbanized (still probably less than 10 percent of the whole population) civilization on the planet. Their new capital, Lin'an, boasted a population near 2.5 million, whereas Venice, the leading city-state of Italy and the hub of European trade at the time, had 50,000.

This great wealth produced a cultural and technological boom in China. Paper matched with block printing produced the world's first book culture. Education, which was important for the Confucian bureaucracy, became affordable for many in the cities, allowing a true meritocracy (rule by those with talent or ability) to develop, although over time corruption entered the system as families tried to maintain their status by getting their sons government positions by cheating on exams, bribing exam graders, and lowering standards on tests.

TANG/SONG INNOVATIONS

Paper	Block Printing	Books	Rudders
Paper Money	Gunpowder	Rockets	Use of Coal
Porcelain	Compartmentalized Ships	Stern	Compasses

At its height, the Song appeared ready to conquer the world, possessing a military and nautical advantage that Europe could not match for centuries to come. But in the end, the Song did not go forth and explore. Men of ambition did not become merchants and adventurers; instead, they studied the classics and sat for exams to earn a place among the scholar-gentry ruling class. Eventually, as the integrity of the government declined, the northern Song fell to nomadic invaders, although the south managed to defend itself and even mounted a recovery of some of the previous prosperity. Eventually, though, Mongol invaders defeated it.

Feudal Japan

Beginning in the seventh century, Japan's imperial system was loosely modeled after the Chinese. Both Confucianism and Buddhism made significant impacts on Japan. Confucian relations established the family structure in Japan as it had in China. Confucian thought also influenced social order, but in Japan a warrior class, the samurai, replaced the idea of the Confucian bureaucracy in the social hierarchy. Chen Buddhism from China became Zen Buddhism in Japan, but many of its adherents valued the martial training it provided. Samurai practiced the meditation arts to become more efficient killers in combat. Also, Shinto, the native religion of Japan, blended with Buddhism. Shinto worshiped nature spirits called *kami*. Many Buddhist temples were founded in natural settings and used Shinto elements in their architecture. Shinto shrines also used elements of Buddhist garden designs.

In the late twelfth century, the military elite took over Japan. The first shogun (military leader) unified all of the various warlords into a single feudal government based at Kamakura. Called the Bakufu, or tent government, it exercised loose control over the kingdom, receiving promises of loyalty from the samurai in return for the Bakufu's protection of the lord's right to his land. (For a comparison of the European and Japanese feudal systems, see the chart on page 175.) After about 150 years, civil war overthrew the shogun's family and another took the title. The new shogunate never fully solidified its control over the whole of Japan. Local lords, given the formal title daimyo, balanced the demands of the shogun with their own desire for autonomy. By the fifteenth century, Japan entered into a cycle of constant civil war.

The Mongols and the World

In 1206, Genghis Khan unleashed on the world a destructive force unlike any before it. Within a generation, well-organized Mongol hordes destroyed the independent political systems in China, Central Asia, Vietnam, Korea, Russia, and the Middle East, bringing down well-established systems like the Abbasid and the Song. Their success rested on a very few key factors. First, as nomads, almost every Mongol knew how to fight and ride. Second, their bows rendered useless the defenses of armored soldiers from the knights of Europe to the cataphracted (armored horse and rider) cavalry of the Song. Third, the Mongol steppe pony provided mobility, maneuverability, and stamina that other mounted troops could not match. The Mongols brought many changes to the areas they encountered.

China

When the Song dynasty fell, a Mongol dynasty replaced it, called the Yuan, founded in 1271 by Kublai Khan, grandson of Genghis Khan. Kublai admired Chinese culture and followed the basic Confucian system of government. He reordered the social structure by placing the Mongols above the Chinese. During his rule, roads and canals were constructed that linked all areas of the nation. Education and science found government support. Public granaries stored food for distribution to peasants during lean years. He also maintained a large military, which was not typical of China. Twice, he launched massive invasions of Japan, but both times his fleets were destroyed by storms at sea (called the "divine wind," or kamikaze, by the Japanese).

Korea

After resisting the Mongols for more than 25 years, the Korean kings finally submitted as vassals to the Mongols in return for cultural independence. They remained vassals for 80 years, until the decline of the Yuan dynasty in China.

Persia

In Central Asia, the Mongols sacked the city of Samarkand, in what is now Uzbekistan. They then moved on to Persia. By using Chinese engineers and brutally punishing those cities that resisted their advance, they quickly annexed the region into their empire. As in China, the

Mongols did little to interfere with local traditions. They allowed the local elites to maintain local autonomy if they paid taxes (tributes) to the Mongols; they allowed Islam and other minority religions to continue (the Mongols themselves had animistic beliefs and did not try to convert others to their beliefs); and they encouraged a continued flow of trade through the region via the Silk Road.

Russia

The Mongols conquered several principalities in Russia, most notably Kiev. The defeated Russians paid tribute to the Mongols until 1480. Because the tribute went through the prince of Muscovy (Moscow), that city became the political and economic center of Russia and, when independence came, the new capital. The collection of taxes for tribute led to the creation of a strong feudal system in Russia in which massive numbers of serfs were dominated by a small nobility, called boyars. The connection with the east shaped centuries of Russian policy, pushing the Russians to expand eastward in order to drive back the nomads, which disconnected the Russians from many of the advances being made in Europe during the sixteenth and seventeenth centuries. As in other areas, the Mongols did not force a new religion on the Russians. In 988, the prince of Kiev officially adopted Eastern Orthodox Christianity, the religion of the Byzantine Empire.

Europe

In early April 1241, two forces of Mongols moved into eastern Europe: one into Poland and a larger force into Hungary. Within a few days, nearly 100,000 of Europe's best warriors lay dead on the field of battle and all of Europe was open to the Mongol horde's conquest. Then the Mongols learned that their khan had died and withdrew to the steppe to select a new leader. They never returned.

Abbasids

In 1258, a Mongol horde under Hulegu, a grandson of Genghis Khan, sacked the city of Baghdad, destroying its mosque, museums, and universities and killing most of its inhabitants. The Abbasid caliph failed to recognize either the power of the Mongols or his own lack of authority; he called for his empire to defend the city, but his real political control amounted to almost nothing. After Baghdad, another Mongol leader died and Hulegu returned to the steppe to select another, taking most of his army with him. A force of Mamluks (Islamic slave soldiers who had won their independence and taken Egypt as a kingdom) drove the Mongols out of the Middle East in 1260; this was the first defeat of the Mongols.

Mongol Impact

The Mongols' rule of the world was short-lived, but it left two very important legacies. First, the Mongols encouraged trade. They protected merchants all along the Silk Road, allowing for more economic activity. This encouraged Europeans who were just entering a new era of development (the Renaissance) to actively seek new routes to China. European explorations moved them toward dominance of the Indian Ocean routes and discovery of the New World. Second, the ease of movement the Mongols allowed linked many remote areas of Asia to the major trade routes connecting the known world. One of these links introduced the bubonic plague to the world.

Europe in the Middle Ages

The end of the Roman Empire plunged western Europe into what is sometimes called the Dark Ages, about 500 CE to 1300 CE. The infrastructure of civilization collapsed, pushing societies back to a farming village–level of existence. People lived in small settlements, usually governed by a lord who offered military protection in return for their labor. Over time the manor system became the standard political and economic institution of western Europe. It included laborers, or serfs, who were attached to the lord's lands and required to work for him; a few free men who specialized in tasks like milling and smithing; and the lord and a handful of men-at-arms, or soldiers. Each manor attached itself to a greater lord, who in turn was attached to another, greater lord. Known as feudalism, this political, economic, and social system governed western European society for nearly 1,000 years.

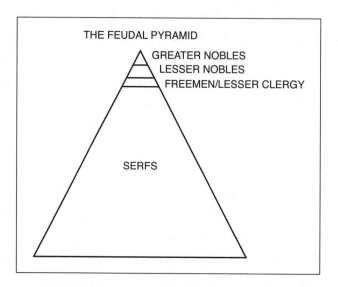

As Germanic tribes gained power in Europe, they established a number of minor kingdoms that subsequently grew into the nucleus of the modern nations of Europe. In theory, a king ran each kingdom, granting lands (called fiefs) to his nobles in return for their loyalty and military service when called upon. The lands provided the income needed to allow the lord and a small body of troops to train for war. Higher nobles received enough land to grant fiefs to their own vassals in exchange for loyalty. In reality, these promises proved difficult to enforce, and very few kings exercised complete control over their kingdoms. Unity came about through religion, not politics.

Christianity survived the fall of the Roman Empire, with the pope maintaining his position in Rome. A wave of missionaries brought Christianity to the Germans, providing some unity to the West. As these priests and monks converted the nobles, the church provided legitimacy to the political leadership. Both ascending to the throne and becoming a knight became, in part, religious ceremonies. (Famously, on Christmas Day in 800, Pope Leo III crowned Charlemagne as the Holy Roman Emperor, an attempt to establish religious authority over the coronation of rulers). The nobles also benefited, obtaining high positions in the church (such as a bishop) for their younger sons. The position gave them more land, and in the feudal Middle Ages, land was power.

In addition to providing a sense of unity in the West, Christianity also provided a haven for literacy. Priests and monks read and wrote Latin as part of their training. Monks hand-copied Bibles and other religious texts. However, they did not encourage new scholarship, just the copying and commenting on previous religious texts. The church also served as one of the few patrons for the arts and architecture through the building of cathedrals and decorative statues, stained glass, and paintings.

EUROPEAN AND JAPANESE FEUDALISM

EUROPE	JAPAN
King held top position but could not control all of the nobles	Emperor remained on the throne but had no political authority
Military service in return for loyalty determined political and economic structure	Shogun held top position but often could not control the daimyo (lords)
The church reinforced feudal obligations	Military power determined the political and economic structure
	Not based on any religious philosophy
The manor system was the basic social arrangement: a lord lived on a manor or in the village while the village serfs provided labor in the fields to produce a small surplus of food, that is, the lord's income	Family honor played an important role in maintaining political loyalties
	Samurai attended to the lord in his castle
	Peasants were taxed, and the proceeds provided for the samurai
Failed as a form of strong centralized government	The early shoguns failed to establish a strong central government for any length of time; however, the Tokugawa shoguns ruled from a strong central position for 268 years

The Byzantine Empire

While Roman civilization survived in the Byzantine or Eastern Roman Empire, it did not exactly thrive:

- Between fighting the Persians, the Muslims (Arabs, Seljuk Turks, Ottoman Turks), and even Norman knights, the empire's territory shrank substantially over time.

- The empire's wealth generated by trade declined. The Byzantines lost control over many of their more productive territories or saw Muslim merchants dominate routes once exclusively sailed by the Greeks.

- The most profitable trade involved the selling of slaves from the Black Sea region to Egyptian Muslims.

- These slaves, many of whom were once warriors from the steppes, became the Mamluks, that is, the slave soldiers of the caliphs.

- These soldiers helped to increase Islamic power and further weaken the Byzantine Empire.

- The bishops of Rome and Constantinople fought over control of the Christian church in Europe. In 1054, this resulted in a schism that permanently split the European church into the Roman Catholic and Eastern Orthodox branches.

- The ecclesiastical split robbed the Byzantines of a potential ally just as the Seljuk Turks moved into Anatolia (modern Turkey), robbing the empire of more territory and putting its capital, Constantinople, on the front lines of future conflicts.

By 600, the Greek remnant of the empire (the Byzantines called themselves Romans but spoke and wrote Greek instead of Latin, the language of the old empire) was already in decline, having reached its peak during the rule of Emperor Justinian (527–565). The culture, though, retained strong remnants of Roman tradition and technology, such as the use of Roman building techniques like concrete, Roman imagery on coins and in art, and the presence of columns and arches in architecture. The Byzantines built architectural masterpieces like the Hagia Sophia

Church and the walls around Constantinople. They continued to discuss the Greek philosophers, although Islamic and Jewish scholars moved rapidly to the forefront of Platonic and Aristotelian philosophy during this period. The Byzantine society was also able to make significant advances in science and medicine by reading the works of Muslim scholars such as Ali ibn Sahl Rabban al-Tabari, who made the first medical encyclopedia. Militarily, the Byzantines even mastered a secret weapon—Greek fire (the exact composition of which is lost to history)—that allowed Byzantine ships to project a burning chemical mixture at enemy vessels. However, these cultural advances were not able to prevent the gradual encroachment of Turkish military forces over Byzantine territory.

THE FALL OF THE BYZANTINES

1095: FIRST CRUSADE	An appeal to the pope from the emperor brought thousands of the faithful to fight the Muslims for the Holy Land. Success in recapturing Jerusalem in 1099 does not help the Byzantines because the western Crusaders kept the conquered lands for themselves
1204: FOURTH CRUSADE	Crusaders sack the city of Constantinople then return to the West with its riches. The city never fully recovers
1300s	Civil war against independent Greek states and dynastic struggles exhausted the strength of the empire
1354	Constantinople comes under direct attack by the Ottoman Turks
1390	The Byzantines lose their last territory in Asia
1402	Turks defeated by Mongols
1453	Constantinople falls to the Ottoman Turks

Challenges to Feudalism

In the late eighth century, Scandinavians, often called Vikings (or Norsemen or Normans), began raiding northern Europe. Their unpredictable attacks on communities, especially the plundering of churches, created terror among the Europeans, who prayed to God to save them. In the end, the Christianization of the Vikings did just that. They adopted feudalism, established trade connections with cities in northern Germany, and became vassals to the European kings. (The province of Normandy in France was given as a fief to the Vikings; later, a duke of Normandy became William I, king of England).

In 1095, Pope Urban II launched the Crusades against the Muslims in the Holy Land. For the commoners of Europe, this opportunity offered salvation from their sins because the pope guaranteed that the souls of those who died on crusade would go straight to heaven. For the nobles, who were short on land, it promised new lands and the power that comes with it. The success of the First Crusade did bring new lands to the feudal lords, but it also challenged the entire feudal system. The crusaders encountered a civilization wealthier and more advanced than their own. Spices, fine textiles, and other luxuries from China and East Africa attracted great interest. Italian sailors ferrying the warriors to the Crusades engaged the Muslim "enemy" in trade. This trade brought wealth to the Italians and attracted interest from other corners of Europe. In northern Europe, a group of free cities known as the Hanseatic League established a complex trading network that linked German cities with Norwegian and English trade centers. Profits came from exchanging wools, salted fish, and manufactured goods. All of these exchanges operated outside of traditional manorial and feudal economies.

By the thirteenth century, Italian traders routinely moved goods from the Middle East into European markets. With the goods, the knowledge of the Greeks and Romans returned along with new discoveries from the Muslim world. The new wealth encouraged Europeans to manufacture goods for trade. This encouraged the development of market towns, some of which grew into cities. The feudal system failed to adapt to these changes. The wealthy merchants and financiers of the cities now had power beyond a fixed area of land. Kings, by taxing the trade of the cities, could raise armies without depending on feudal loyalties. Cities could pay taxes and align themselves with kings and gain a charter to separate them from the control of the nobles. One final blow broke feudalism in western Europe: the Black Plague.

The Black Death

The plague entered the Mongol population in Central Asia and moved into the area around the Black Sea. Italian merchants brought it to Italy. From there it followed the trade routes of Europe, killing millions (possibly as much as a third of the population). Fleas carried the bubonic plague; they lived on rats, and when their hosts died, the infected fleas moved to other hosts, including people. (The pneumonic form of the plague may pass from human to human through inhalation of infected particles.) As the plague ravaged cities, people looked for answers to its cause. Many blamed the wrath of God, fearing they had sinned and failed him. Others blamed Jews for poisoning the water supplies. The deaths and the search for a cause created significant changes in Europe.

In 1347, Europe reached the peak of a population explosion. Good climate conditions early in the century increased the food supply, leading to an increase in population. Even before the plague, crop yields started to decline, leaving a slightly malnourished population in some areas of Europe. The plague eliminated a third of the population, resolving the food problem but creating a labor shortage. Lords and craftsmen in the cities needed workers for their lands and shops. Labor became a valuable commodity, and wages went up as much as five times their previous rates. Prices increased as well, but real wages grew even faster. Feudal duties that tied serfs to specific lands and required they give their labor to one lord no longer fit the economic reality. Serfs could easily relocate and find better work for wages from other landowners or in city shops. In some areas, feudal duties disappeared completely, and in others they took the form of taxes rather than servitude.

The church, too, found its old position destroyed. By connecting the plague to the wrath of God, the people blamed the church for failing them. The population of priests, monks, and nuns—primary caregivers in most communities and thus most exposed to the disease—suffered huge losses. Clergy had to be ordained quickly to fill the ensuing gaps in the church's ranks. Many of these newly ordained clergy attracted criticism for their lack of education and poor ability as leaders. This, too, was read as another sign of God's displeasure with the church. Clergy and laymen (nonreligious persons) began to debate both the policies of the church and its hierarchy.

As the fourteenth century ended, the following changes occurred:

- Politically, Europe saw the development of more centralized states with powerful monarchies (most notably France after defeating the English in the 100 Years' War).

- Economically, greater connection to trade and the development of banking in Italy created a more diverse and complex economy that changed the social order, and a middle class developed in market towns and cities.

- The new forms of credit available from banks and the use of bills of exchange that facilitated long-distance trade provided the new middle class with powerful economic tools to develop wealth to rival that of many noble families.

- Religiously, the church faced stronger political challenges to its power, and those inside the church debated its core beliefs and future.

- Society changed as a middle class developed. Serfs gained greater economic rights and some class mobility as they bought land for their own farms. With few exceptions, women did not see a great change in their fortunes.

- Innovations from the rest of the world, including the reintroduction of some Greek and Roman technology, spurred further technological development. Great improvements were made in shipbuilding and navigation as Europeans (most notably the Portuguese under the sponsorship of Prince Henry the Navigator) looked for their own routes to the riches of India and East Asia.

- Art flourished in Italy as the wealth earned from international trade allowed merchants and bankers to become patrons of the arts. This period of artistic, cultural, and economic rebirth became known as the Renaissance.

In the Americas
Mesoamerica

By 900 the Mayan people dominated the region that now includes southern Mexico, Belize, Guatemala, Honduras, and El Salvador. As many as 12 million people inhabited the region, many living in independent city-states. The Mayans built large buildings, including step pyramid temples that required a high degree of sophistication. They developed an accurate calendar and complex mathematical concepts, including the number zero. The temples and the calendar played important roles in the worship of their pantheon of gods. Like other early civilizations, they adopted a hieroglyphic writing system, the most complete of all found in the Americas, to adorn their temples and palaces with histories of their civilization and instructions for religious rituals.

The greatest challenge presented to the Mayan and other Mesoamerican civilizations concerned agricultural production. The Mayan depended on corn and a few other rain-forest roots as dietary staples. They developed some advanced forms of farming, using terraced fields along mountain slopes and irrigation canals, but due to the nature of the soils of the rain forest, slash-and-burn agriculture provided one of the best short-term solutions for farm output.

At some point in the tenth century the Mayan civilization suffered a sharp decline. In some cities, construction projects stopped and many buildings fell into disrepair. Entire populations abandoned other cities. No Mayan record explains the collapse. Archaeologists note that many city-states warred against each other almost continuously; the Mayans devastated their own civilization in a manner similar to the early Greeks. Also, food production from slash-and-burn agriculture requires new lands every few years; eventually the sources of food are too far removed from the established population centers. Some of the northern Mayan cities survived longer, but by 1100 the most dominant fell to foreign invaders. By the fifteenth century, there was no dominant city, making the area an easy conquest for the approaching Spanish conquistadors.

To the north, the Zapotec culture flourished for a time, creating several large urban centers. In the valley of Oaxaca, just south of modern Mexico City, the most powerful of the Mesoamerican cultures established a new empire. In the mid-fourteenth century, the Mexica, or Aztecs, built the huge city of Tenochtitlan and launched an expansion campaign. By the start of the sixteenth century, the Aztec Empire controlled central and southern Mexico and lands stretching to Guatemala. They, too, built massive pyramids to their gods and, like many Mesoamericans, made human sacrifices part of their religious ceremonies. (Evidence suggests the Aztecs indulged in the practice more than others.)

South America

In the Andes Mountains the Incan civilization began building an empire at the beginning of the thirteenth century, but it did not spread far. Andean culture, isolated geographically from the early Mesoamerican cultures, developed independently. The Incan Empire conquered the cities of the Andes, bringing them under the rule of an imperial court. Laborers then built more than 13,000 miles of road to link the empire. The emperor allowed local chiefs to continue their administrations, but he brought their heirs to live in the royal court at Cuzco; they served as both hostages and indoctrinated administrators. As a final threat, the Incan emperors, like the Egyptian pharaohs and the Japanese emperors, claimed to be descended from the sun god. Like the Aztec emperors further north, the Incans also measured their success in terms of new conquests.

Andean society changed little after the Incan conquest. The Incans established themselves as elites apart from the Andean commoners. Most Andeans grew potatoes, a staple food source, and herded llamas and alpacas, which were used for food, clothing, and transportation. Commoners owed a substantial part of their labor to the community as a whole. A commoner who looked upon the ruler might face death.

Lacking external trade contacts, the Incans depended on agricultural production and the collection of natural resources. An elaborate system of highways, built and maintained by labor from each community, connected the various production centers of the empire. Food, gold and silver, bronze tools, woolen textiles, and other commodities moved along these highways. The Incas, building on the knowledge of previous Andean civilizations, maintained an accurate calendar, forged tools out of bronze (their Mesoamerican neighbors never discovered this technology), and constructed elaborate stone temples for sacrifices to their gods. For nearly 100 years, the Incan emperors ruled and expanded their empire. In 1525, just before the arrival of the Spanish, civil war broke out over succession to the throne and many conquered peoples rose up against the empire. Waves of European diseases destroyed the last remaining Inca survivors in the sixteenth century.

Multiple-Choice Review Questions

1. Early Islamic society blended what two cultures?

    A.   Arab and Byzantine
    B.   Arab and Jewish
    C.   Mamluk and Persian
    D.   Arab and Persian

2. What statement best explains Islam's early success at expanding its political borders?

    A.   Wealthy merchants carried Islam to other parts of the world and attracted converts with both the message of Islam and the merchants' own success.
    B.   The Byzantine and Persian Empires exhausted their military powers against each other, leaving them vulnerable to the Arab armies.
    C.   The Bedouin tribes excelled at warfare and, by using camels, easily outmaneuvered their foes in battle.
    D.   Islam encouraged the conversion of other peoples to their belief system, drawing away the military strength of those who opposed them.

3. Which of the following is a major difference between the political structure of the Islamic caliphate and the Chinese Tang dynasty?

    A. The caliph possessed both political and religious authority.
    B. The caliph was at the top of a feudal hierarchy.
    C. The caliph ruled over an egalitarian society, not a hierarchical society like that found in China.
    D. The caliph was forced to win election to his post by gaining the support of the Bedouin tribal elders.

4. Buddhism moved into China via Indian missionaries on the Silk Road. What other religion spread primarily because of missionary activity?

    A. Hinduism
    B. Christianity
    C. Confucianism
    D. Islam

Alcazares Reales in Sevilla

5. The image above from a palace built for a ruler in fourteenth-century Sevilla, Spain, demonstrates

A. the strong influence of China even at the furthest ends of its trading network.
B. the renewal of Greek architecture in Europe.
C. the influence of the Christian church over Spain.
D. the strong Islamic influence in Spain.

6. How did the Song dynasty differ from previous Chinese dynasties?

A. It allowed women to take the throne if no male heirs were available.
B. It maintained a large military for conquest and internal control.
C. It ruled according to a feudal system and depended on a landed gentry and allied nomadic tribesmen to enforce their laws and provide troops for the military.
D. It encouraged trade, both domestic (along an extended system of roads and canals) and foreign (using some of the most advanced ships of the time).

7. What statement correctly identifies a similarity between the Mali Empire in West Africa and the trade cities of the East African coast?

A. Islam, introduced through trade, became the dominant religion of the elites in each area.
B. Islam failed to establish itself in these areas because the Mali were well beyond the main trade routes dominated by the caliphs.
C. Islam, because of its egalitarianism, became the religion of the lower classes, but the ruling elites did not give up their traditional belief systems and the prestige granted to them.
D. Islamic merchants introduced Islam to each area, but the religion failed to take hold and replace the areas native animistic religions.

8. How did a feudal kingdom differ from the Islamic caliphate?

   A.   Feudal kings ruled through military alliances and did not depend on religious authority to support their rule, while the caliphs, as successors to Muhammad, incorporated religious authority in their rule.

   B.   Feudal kings ruled a highly centralized state, while the caliphate was only a loose alliance of Muslim rulers.

   C.   Feudal kings depended on their lords for their military power, while the caliphs maintained their own military forces.

   D.   Feudal kings lacked any authority over the church, while caliphs were also leaders of the *umma*, the community of all Muslims.

9. What explains the chief economic advantage for the Song in printing paper money instead of issuing new copper coins?

   A.   A shortage of copper could limit the ability to mint new coins, slowing the economy and causing instability in the value of coins already minted.

   B.   Paper currency required all trade goods to remain in China.

   C.   Other nations also valued copper and would drain coins out of the Chinese economy.

   D.   The vast supply of paper allowed the Song to print as much money as they wanted.

10. To what event(s) do the following two quotes refer?

I don't know where to begin. Cries and laments arise on all sides. Day after day one sees the Cross and the Host [the consecrated Eucharist carried by a priest to deliver last rights] being carried about the city [Piacenza, Italy] and countless dead being buried.

   By January 21, [1349,] Cairo had become an abandoned desert, and one did not see anyone walking along the streets...The dead were very numerous, and all the world could think of nothing else...

Everywhere one heard lamentations, and one could not pass by any house without being overwhelmed by the howling.

A.   The Mongol invasions
B.   The Black Death
C.   The First Crusade
D.   Viking raids

Answers to Multiple-Choice Questions

1.   **D**. The Arab conquest quickly overran the old Persian Empire and many converted to Islam, because they were attracted both by the tenets of the religion and the social benefits gained by being Muslim in the caliphate.

2.   **B**. While A and C are both true, the early success rests on the failure of both the Persians and the Byzantines to mount an effective defense against the attacking Arab armies.

3.   **A**. The Tang leaders ruled with absolute political authority based on a Confucian philosophy of government. But Confucianism is not a religion, and the Tang emperor, although identified as the son of heaven to stress his role in maintaining harmony, did not rule over a state religion or have authority over all of Buddhism or Taoism.

4.   **B**. Christianity moved into the Roman Empire through missionaries. Later, during the early Middle Ages, missionaries introduced it to the German kings, the Balkans tribes, Russian princes, and the Vikings.

5.   **D**. Both the use of mosaics in a geometric pattern and the Spanish location indicate Islamic art and influence.

6.   **D**. Confucianism traditionally viewed merchants as a low social class, and Chinese governments rarely encouraged practices that helped merchants. However, innovations such as paper money, also known as "flying money," helped both the government in tax collection and management of their monopoly on salt and iron as well as facilitating trade within China.

7.　**A.** In both areas the ruling elites adopted Islam as their religion. In West Africa, Islam also spread to many areas beyond the ruling palaces. However, along the East Coast, few besides the elites in the trading ports converted, and inland, Islam failed to become a religious force.

8.　**C.** Feudal kings depended on the promise of military service from their vassals in order to exercise power. Often, these promises failed to meet the military demands of the king. However, an Islamic caliph paid mercenaries or purchased and trained slaves for their armies. These tended to be larger forces than those available to a king, but their loyalty was also an issue that might weaken the power of a caliph.

9.　**A.** Paper currency, called "flying money," allowed for greater economic expansion as the production of copper mines failed to keep up with demand and some copper was drained away by other nations due to international trade (this latter part of the answer is found in choice C, but A is a more complete answer).

10.　**B.** Both quotes refer to the Black Death, a worldwide phenomenon during the fourteenth century. The plague struck China, India, the Islamic world, the Byzantine Empire, and western Europe.

Free-Response Examples
Continuity and Change Over Time

Directions: You are to answer the following question. You should spend 5 minutes organizing or outlining your essay. Write an essay that:

- Has a relevant thesis and supports that thesis with appropriate historical evidence.
- Addresses all parts of the question.
- Uses world historical context to show continuities and changes over time.
- Analyzes the process of continuity and change over time.

Explain the continuities and changes along ONE of the following trade routes/regions between 600 and 1450:

- The Silk Road
- The Indian Ocean
- The Mediterranean Sea

Comparative Essay

Directions: You are to answer the following question. You should spend 5 minutes organizing or outlining your essay. Write an essay that:

- Has a relevant thesis and supports that thesis with appropriate historical evidence.
- Addresses all parts of the question.
- Makes direct, relevant comparisons.
- Analyzes relevant reasons for similarities and differences.

Analyze the similarities and differences between the political and social structure of feudal Europe and an Islamic caliphate.

Content Review Part 3:
Conquests and Journeys

1450 to 1750

The fifteenth century included a number of sweeping global changes that laid the foundations for a truly New World.

The Fall of Constantinople

In 1453, the Ottoman Turks conquered Constantinople, bringing to an end the Byzantine Empire in the east. The Ottoman Turks, originally a tribe from the steppes, arose as a powerful force in Islam after the Mongol attacks. The Turks slowly grew in size as they moved into the Middle East, and in the eleventh century, the Turkish Seljuk dynasty replaced the Arabs as the leading power in the region. Already followers of Islam, the Turks adopted Islamic culture and benefited from the trade moving through the region.

In the thirteenth century, the Ottoman dynasty arose in modern Turkey and gained territory by pushing the Byzantines out of Asia. In 1453, the Ottomans constructed several large cannons and placed them against the heretofore-impregnable walls of Constantinople. The city fell in less than two months, and the 1,000-year-old Byzantine Empire collapsed, providing a convenient point to mark an end to the Middle Ages. For the next 300 years, the Islamic Ottoman Empire assaulted Christian Europe. By the time of the Industrial Revolution in the late eighteenth century, the Ottoman Empire was a second-rate power. It was eventually signed out of existence by the Treaty of Versailles at the conclusion of World War I.

The Portuguese Round the Cape

After the Crusades, the Italian city-states (notably Genoa, Florence, and Venice) dominated the trade between Western Europe and Asia. Other nations wanted to find their own routes to Asia in order to better profit from the trade. Portugal took the lead when Prince Henry the Navigator established a school to collect all knowledge on shipbuilding and navigation and then teach it to Portuguese captains. The school taught navigators to use the latest version of the astrolabe, an instrument used to determine position based on the position of celestial bodies. These navigators set sail on newly developed ships—known as caravels—that used lateen sails, allowing greater freedom of navigation. The new ships allowed the Portuguese to build a series of forts and trading stations along Africa's West Coast as they explored their way around the continent toward the Indian Ocean. The slave trade provided profits, but it took almost 50 years for a Portuguese captain to finally pilot his caravel around the Cape of Good Hope. A few years later, in 1497, Vasco da Gama carried out the first trade mission to India.

The Muslim and Indian merchants who Vasco da Gama encountered found little value in what the Portuguese offered for trade, but they could not ignore the Portuguese military force. The Portuguese established dominance over the Indian Ocean trade by bombarding coastal cities and taking hostages linked to important local elites. Since the typical ship involved in the trade was designed to travel short distances and lacked room for many armaments, the Portuguese found that their armed caravels gave them a military advantage over the other powers along the routes. Fifty years had made a big difference.

The Ming Voyages

In 1405, Zheng He, a Muslim eunuch (castrated slave) and favorite of the Ming Yongle emperor, set out on an Indian Ocean expedition. The largest of his ships (about 450 feet long) could easily have carried all of the ships and crew that Christopher Columbus used in his voyage to the New World. Eventually the Ming launched seven expeditions into the Indian Ocean. They established relations with more than 20 kings and traveled as far as the East Coast of Africa, returning to China with giraffes for the imperial zoo. The voyages of hundreds of ships and thousands of men demonstrated a maritime power that no other nation could match. However, the voyages did not fit Chinese tradition. China stood at the center of the world (its name means Middle Kingdom), and the Confucian bureaucrats saw no purpose for the voyages. After the Yongle emperor died, only one more voyage took place. Later, when an eight-year-old ascended to the throne, bureaucrats, with the support of the generals, dismantled the fleet and allowed the official contacts with the Indian and African kingdoms to die. Sixty years after the last voyage, Vasco da Gama's few ships and several hundred men dominated what Zheng He's hundreds of ships and tens of thousands of men gave up.

The New World

In 1492, in an attempt to strengthen the just-unified kingdom of Spain, Christopher Columbus led a small fleet of three ships westward via a new route to reach India or China, which would allow Spanish merchants to trade without depending on the Italians and other middlemen. Columbus, however, reached uncharted lands. For nearly three decades, Spanish and other explorers attempted to find a way around these new lands so they could reach China and India. In 1520, Ferdinand Magellan, a Portuguese captain sailing for Spain, finally made his way into the Pacific. One of his five original ships returned to Spain in 1522, completing the first circumnavigation of the world. Soon after this voyage, the Spanish found treasure worth their attention in the Americas.

The Columbian Exchange is the name given to the transfer of products, ideas, and technology between the New World of the Americas and the Old World continents of Europe, Africa, and Asia. The following chart shows some examples of what was exchanged.

OLD WORLD TO NEW	NEW WORLD TO OLD
DISEASES	
Smallpox	Syphilis
Typhoid	
Plague	
Influenza	
Cholera	
Measles	
Typhoid	
Yellow fever	
PLANTS	
Wheat, oats, millet, rice, rye (all major grains but corn)	Avocado
	Bell and chili peppers
Sugarcane	Cocoa
Watermelon	Peanut
Lettuce	Pineapple
Olive	Potato (responsible for a substantial increase in the global population when it entered cultivation in Europe and Asia)
Onion	
Apple	
Almond	
Black pepper	Rubber
	Squash
	Strawberry
	Sunflower
	Tomato
	Corn
	Tobacco

OLD WORLD TO NEW	NEW WORLD TO OLD
ANIMALS	
All but dogs and the four animals listed from the New World	Alpaca
	Guinea pig
	Llama
	Turkey
RELIGIONS AND PHILOSOPHIES	
All major world religions, with the Roman Catholic Church being the most dominant	
TECHNOLOGY	
Metallurgy (only the Incas produced any important metal tools, using bronze)	
Saddle	
Wheeled cart	
Gunpowder	
Paper	
Printing	
Many others	

The exchange impacted societies on both sides of the Atlantic and the Pacific. In the Americas, the native population with no immunities to the new diseases may have lost 80 percent of their pre-Columbus populations (numbers vary widely, as does the debate about how many people populated the Americas and what caused their deaths). Those who did not die found themselves overwhelmed by European technology and quickly under European domination. Many native cultures completely disappeared or became dependent on foreign influences like the church. For Europe, the new crops opened new fields and led to improved diets and larger populations. Some of the crops became staples of European diets, like potatoes in Ireland or the tomatoes in Italy. These crops also spread into many areas beyond Europe. China benefited greatly from potatoes, as it opened areas for new calorie-intensive cultivation, and peppers became staples in Southeast Asian cooking.

The Aztecs and the Incas

Both the Aztec and Incan Empires ruled over populations of millions and controlled areas comparable to the largest Asian empires. The Aztecs deified their emperor and royal family. They honored warriors in society by rewarding them with nontaxable land. To prove oneself as a great warrior, one needed to take captives in battle and sacrifice them to the gods.

Socially, the native people belonged to clans. These possessed their own lands and worked hard to improve the clan, including maintaining schools for warriors. Just as in European, Asian, and African societies, the vast majority of people were farmers who grew beans, corn, peppers, and other crops. They paid part of their crops as taxes and owed the rulers an amount of labor each year. Also, they were expected to provide victims for sacrifice to the gods.

The Incans likewise deified their rulers. Both Aztecs and Incans claimed ancestry from the sun god. Incans also identified themselves through large clans. As the Incans conquered other societies, they integrated them into the Incan culture, moving them to new locations and assigning them public works projects as partial payment of their taxes. They also took the images of the societies' gods, put them in the Incan capital, and subordinated them to the Incan gods. All males paid a tax in labor as well as crops. The Aztecs did not integrate conquered peoples into their society; they enslaved many and exacted tribute from the rest.

The Conquistadors

Despite the regional superiority of these societies, they were unable to resist European technological dominance. As the Spanish explorers came upon these empires, they brought few troops but benefited from several factors. The Aztecs, who sacrificed thousands of the people they conquered, found no allies among the other native peoples. Many natives were willing to join Spanish leader Hernando Cortes in the fight against Aztec emperor Montezuma II. Also, the capture and death of the emperor shook the Aztecs' faith in their gods. Finally, the Aztecs' wooden swords were ineffective against Spanish steel armor, guns, and

horses. Once defeated, the Aztecs and the other tribes were then deci-
mated by disease, leaving Mexico open to Spanish conquest.

The Incas fared little better. They had bronze tools and weapons
(which were not a match against steel), and they did enjoy greater support from all of their peoples, but they were in the middle of a civil war
over succession. The death of an Incan ruler invited challengers for the
position. At the time of Francisco Pizarro's arrival in Peru, one such civil
war, touched off by the death of the emperor due to smallpox (which
arrived about four years ahead of the Spanish) had only recently produced a new emperor. Pizarro killed the new emperor and installed a
replacement whom he controlled. The Spanish immediately began to
benefit from collections of wealth and labor from the Incas. It took them
20 years to conquer the whole of the Incan Empire.

Encomiendas

As the Spanish brought thousands of square miles of the Americas under
their rule, they needed a system to govern this empire, but they could
not simply transplant the manorial and feudal system of Spain to the
New World. Instead, they relied on the Roman Catholic Church and the
native Americans. The church, especially through monastic orders like
the Franciscans, came to the New World to spread Christianity. Their
settlements (or missions) served to concentrate local populations and
make them more manageable. The Spanish Crown then instituted the
encomienda system to facilitate settlement and claims to the land. The
grant of an encomienda provided a landowner with labor by requiring
the native population to work the land; this could include agricultural
work and mining. While it also called for the native Americans to receive protection and religious and language instruction, in practice, the
natives were slaves. The system lasted into the eighteenth century, but
even from the beginning it failed to produce all of the labor needed. Too
many natives died of disease, and the mines always needed more labor.

The Atlantic Slave Trade

By the fifteenth century the Ottoman Turks used a plantation system to manage agricultural production over large areas of land. To work the land the landowners purchased slaves from East Africa or from traders from the Black Sea. The Portuguese encountered this system as they engaged in the Indian Ocean trade. When they received Brazil as a colony (the Treaty of Tordesillas divided the New World between Portugal and Spain by drawing a line down the center of the Atlantic; Brazil ended up on the Portuguese side), the Portuguese established large plantations to take advantage of the region's favorable climate for growing sugarcane. They then began the large-scale importation of slaves.

The plantation system moved up the coast of South America into the Spanish colonies of the Caribbean. Sugarcane remained the chief crop, but it was joined by tobacco and later cotton in the southern British colonies. An economic system developed around this production, which historians refer to as the Triangular Trade.

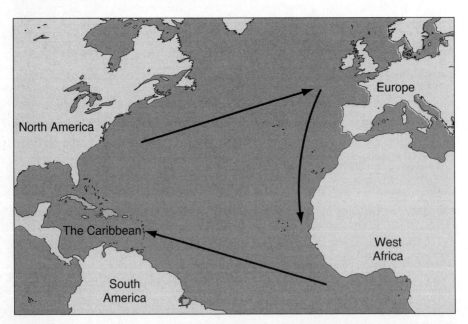

The system took the raw materials from the New World—mostly cash crops, some resources, and rum—and traded them in Europe. In Europe, the goods were used to buy manufactured items. Many of these manu-factured items then went to Africa to barter for slaves; African kings especially liked European guns. The slaves were then shipped across the Atlantic in what was called the Middle Passage. In the Americas, the slaves were sold at auction. In the seventeenth century, more than 1.3 million slaves were transported from Africa to work on these planta-tions, and more than one-third of these went to Brazil alone.

In the European colonies the slaves tried to retain some of the culture they had known in Africa. Many converted to Christianity and learned Western languages. Others mixed their more traditional beliefs (like vodun) with Christianity. However, the adaptation of some Western beliefs did nothing to improve the Africans or their descendants' posi-tion on the social scale. Even if they gained their freedom or had a child with a European, their skin color restricted them to the lowest class. The following chart shows the class hierarchy in Latin America, which depended heavily on skin color.

LATIN AMERICAN SOCIAL ORDER

PENINSULARES	Europeans born in Europe (Spain)
CREOLES	Born to European parents in the Americas; ranked just below Peninsulares, as their loyalty to the Crown could be questioned
MESTIZOS	Mixed European and native parents; laws and custom severely restricted political and economic opportunities
MULATTOS	Mixed race with African ancestry; the most restricted class besides slaves

THE IMPACT ON AFRICA

The initial slave trade followed the previous pattern established by Muslim merchants along the East Coast. Interior kingdoms sold criminals and prisoners of war to traders. As the cultivated areas of the Americas grew, the supply of slaves failed to keep pace. Bands of slavers began taking slaves from villages along the West Coast of Africa. Adolescent males were viewed as the best field workers, so slavers raided villages and kidnapped the most desirable individuals with the highest worker potential. Agricultural production in Africa fell after the key workers were taken away, and the imbalance of males and females resulted in fewer families and fewer children. The natural development of society was interrupted. By the nineteenth century, no society existed that could effectively prevent greater European incursion into Africa.

The Gunpowder Empires

The sixteenth and seventeenth centuries saw the last challenges to European dominance. Three empires—the Ottoman, Safavid, and Mughal—adopted gunpowder and modern weapons and embarked on campaigns of conquest.

The Ottoman Empire

The power of the Ottoman Empire peaked in the sixteenth century during the rule of Suleiman the Magnificent (called the Lawgiver by the Turks). Suleiman expanded the empire into modern Hungary and even threatened Vienna, the capital of the Holy Roman Empire, the largest state in Europe. The Hapsburgs, the ruling family of both the Holy Roman and the Spanish Empires, managed to stop the Ottomans at Vienna, but they did not seriously weaken them. For several centuries, the Ottomans continued to threaten Vienna and central Europe. Like other Islamic states, the Ottomans built a powerful force of slave soldiers, called Janissaries. The Janissaries came into service as children. They were taken from non-Muslim families, educated in Islamic tradition, and converted to Islam. Talented Janissaries earned high-level positions in the government bureaucracy.

Ottoman power went beyond mere military might. Suleiman built an extensive infrastructure of roads and ports to facilitate trade. The Ottomans sought to control trade in the eastern Mediterranean and act as the gateway for European trade. They also continued the learning tradition established by earlier Islamic states by building a strong education system.

Like other Islamic conquerors, they won many converts in their new territories. They introduced a second population of Muslims into Europe (the first was in Spain, although by 1492, it was mostly driven out).

After Suleiman, things went badly for the Ottomans. At Lepanto, off the coast of Greece, they suffered a serious naval defeat that denied them the trade dominance they sought in the Mediterranean. At the start of the seventeenth century, the Turkish nobles tried to disband the Janissaries, but were eventually enslaved by their own troops when the upset Janissaries staged a coup. This also meant that real power was transferred to the Janissaries and stayed there until their overthrow in the nineteenth century. Janissary rule stagnated the empire. The Turks failed to adopt any new military technologies or match Europe's economic gains. As Europe moved toward manufacturing, the Turks fell behind and became dependent on European goods. This was an unfortunate situation for them, because they often found themselves at war with the European powers.

The Safavids (Persians)

In 1502, a new Persian dynasty, the Safavids, rose to power. Like the Ottomans, their power rested in the use of gunpowder and cannons, although they were slower to do so and would eventually require European training in the deployment of guns against their Ottoman rivals. One key difference with the Ottomans and of significant historical consequence was the religion of the founder. The Safavids practiced Shiite Islam and established Shiites as the dominant group in what is now Iran and parts of Iraq.

Safavid rulers continued the traditions of a centralized bureaucracy established by the Persians centuries before. Their capital became a center for Shiite religion and culture, noted for its religious tolerance, architecture, and art. But the capital could not secure the empire. The government bureaucracy failed to attract the loyalty of non-Persian tribes along the edges of the empire, who demanded greater autonomy. It also failed to keep pace with European economic incursion into the region's trade. By the early eighteenth century, the dynasty was beset by enemies and finally fell in 1722 to an Afghan invasion. They would briefly come to power again from 1729 to 1736, but would never be able to regain their former glory.

The Mughal Empire

The last great Mongol conquest took India in 1526. Babar, a descendant of Genghis Khan, led a Mongol and Turk army into northern India. He began the process of defeating each of the independent rulers and establishing a new empire: the Mughal, named after the Mongols. Babar's grandson, Akbar, completed the conquest of almost all of India by using gunpowder to destroy the old fortresses of the rulers and establishing his own bases of operation. Akbar sought to rule India by more than sheer force. The Mughals were Muslim, and many converted to Islam after the conquest. Akbar wanted Hindus to also accept his rule. He brought them into the military and fiscal bureaucracy and married Hindu, Zoroastrian, Jewish, and Christian wives as a sign of his religious tolerance.

A unified India produced great wealth, which Akbar and his successors spent on public art and architecture. His grandson commissioned the Taj Mahal, the architectural symbol of India. A generation later, however, the emperors emphasized Islam and drove many Hindus and others out of the government and enforced the traditional Islamic tax on non-Muslims. The Muslims also destroyed Hindu sites in an effort to expand Islam into all communities. This created internal dissension in the empire and encouraged the independent Hindu kingdoms to revolt.

Economic problems also contributed to the Mughal decline. By the 1600s, European trading ships regularly landed in the ports of India seeking fine cotton textiles. The Dutch and English government chartered companies (the Dutch East India Company and the British East India Company) to establish factories, trade stations, and eventually colonies. While Mughal merchants engaged in trade with the Europeans, they became dependent on the European demands. Mughal economic policy failed to support manufacturing centers or other economic activities.

More and more, the European companies dictated Mughal actions and encouraged a breakup of the central authority. Company policies also rewarded local leaders who could use their plentiful supplies of cheap labor to produce more cotton textiles, then a near-luxury item in Europe.

ASIAN EMPIRES

OTTOMAN	SAFAVID
Ruled by a sultan	Ruled by a shah
Sunni Islam	Shiite Islam
Multiethnic, including Turks, Slavs from the Balkans, and Greeks	Persian
	Built up territory using European tactics
Built by conquest	Failed to integrate other groups
	Conquered by Afghan tribesmen
MUGHAL	**MING DYNASTY**
Ruled by a Muslim emperor	Ruled by an emperor; founded by peasant revolutionary
Originally tolerant of Hindu and other faiths	Rule based on Confucian/Neo-Confucian philosophy
Later rulers favored Islam, leading to dissent among the Hindu elite	Followed traditional policy of isolation after seven major expeditions into the Indian Ocean
Traditional regionalism caused the initial disintegration of the empire	Rebuilt the Great Wall
Finally fell when India was brought into the British Empire	Following the dynastic cycle, corruption weakened the central government; dynasty fell to nomadic invaders, the Manchus

Japan

In the sixteenth century, feudal Japan was consumed by civil war. By 1590, General Toyotomi Hideyoshi had brought all corners of Japan under his rule. To maintain the peace and his dominance, Hideyoshi disarmed the peasants, destroyed the military capability of the Buddhist monasteries (many of whom taught their monks martial arts and often interfered in politics), and sent 150,000 samurai to invade Korea, which prevented the samurai from destabilizing Japan. His death resulted in two years of civil war that ended with Tokugawa Ieyasu's victory at Sekigahara.

To avoid the problems of the previous shoguns, Tokugawa instituted a number of changes in order to centralize power at the capital. First, he required the daimyo (lords) to attend the court every other year, putting them under the shogun's direct observation. Second, families of daimyo remained hostages in the shogun's capital. Third, the Japanese did not practice the same policies toward property. At any time, the shogun could require a daimyo to give up his land and move to another area of Japan. Fourth, the shogun outlawed the manufacture of guns by anyone but him. He then limited the total output to a handful each year, effectively removing guns as a weapon on the battlefield. To further enforce this ban, all outside contact was prohibited, except for minimal trade contacts with China and the Netherlands. Also, to reduce foreign influence, Christianity was outlawed and most Christians were either imprisoned or executed. The result was a highly centralized feudalism that lasted until the mid-nineteenth century when foreigners could no longer be kept out.

Japanese Cultural Borrowing

Like Korean and Vietnamese societies, the Japanese borrowed heavily from the Chinese. Architecture and art copied Chinese traditions. Literature also moved from China to its neighbors. Japan adopted not just literary forms but also the tradition of high literacy rates and even the written characters of the Chinese. Still, the Japanese made their own contributions. A woman of the imperial court wrote what many consider the first novel, *The Tale of Genji*. The Japanese also benefited from ties to China and European contacts by importing new technology, but they restricted usage, much as they had done with firearms. For instance, Tokugawa banned the construction of oceangoing ships and made no use of navigational tools made available by trade.

Creating a Dominant Europe
The Renaissance

Noted more for its artistic expression than for the economic development that fostered it and the philosophy it sparked, the Renaissance fundamentally changed European society. Starting with the economic recovery in Italy, the Renaissance then followed the money, first to France, and then the wealth of the New World brought it to Spain and England. As it moved through Europe, affluence upset the established balance of political power. Wealthy cities provided a different source of revenue for kings. Professional soldiers, paid with tax money, provided kings with the ability to centralize control of their kingdoms. It also gave kings the ability to take on the power of the Roman Catholic Church. By the seventeenth century, feudal politics no longer worked in western European nations.

Economics served as the fundamental source of change during the period. In feudal Europe, land equaled wealth. Very little economic exchange used actual money; barter was the more common method. Renewed trade required a return to currency exchanges. The Italians developed a banking system to facilitate this. They also invented double-entry bookkeeping to better allow businesses to manage their assets and liabilities. New World gold and especially silver allowed for the rapid expansion of European economies. Needing specialists to conduct the trade, manage the banks, and produce new products for exchange, the Europeans developed a middle class, something that did not exist in feudal states. The material demands of the new middle class stimulated further economic development.

The money economy stirred great social change. Already, the serf class was fading because of the impact of the Black Death. Peasants remained poor in general, but some were able to gain ownership of substantial lands. The agricultural revolution in Europe introduced the following techniques:

- Crop rotation allowed for fields to remain productive each year
- Composting improved the fertility of the land without raising costs

- Farmers alternated planting food crops with crops like alfalfa and clover that fed livestock and improved the soil
- Roman techniques of land preparation were reintroduced after more than 1,000 years

With the overwhelming majority of Europeans still involved directly in agricultural production, this provided them with some economic benefits. As a result, their lives became economically more stable.

Wealth also brought great change to the arts. In Italy, paintings, sculpture, and architecture benefited immensely from the new wealth, because city-states and wealthy families fought each other on the cultural front. Artists like Michelangelo found patrons across Italy who were willing to pay large sums for their work. This represented a historical shift in art production because now private citizens, not just the church, could serve as art patrons. Literature began to thrive as more people learned to read, due to their professions. This expanded literacy created markets for works by authors like Dante Alighieri, whose *Divine Comedy* established the basis for Italian literature for centuries to come. Many popular writers, such as Alighieri, wrote in the vernacular language of the people instead of using scholarly languages such as Latin. This practice led to a widespread reading culture among all members of society. Theater, too, expanded with the increased disposable incomes of a growing middle class. In England, William Shakespeare pushed the English language to its greatest extent yet, mixing ancient Greek themes and the tradition of the tragedy with politics, romance, and comedy. The wealth of the Renaissance helped redefine a new European culture.

One area did not change: the lot of women. Economic activity did not include women in any significant way outside of the home. They continued to work primarily within the family, either on farms or as part of workshops. In the developing middle class, women enjoyed more access to wealth, but the laws of the land still favored males in inheritance and social custom made little allowance for women to manage their own economic affairs. In the aristocracy (the nobles), some nations did allow women to inherit land and to even rise to political power (for example, Mary I and Elizabeth I in England and Maria Theresa in the Holy Roman Empire). Women who rose to power and exercised independent control over their own lives were the exception to the rule. In general, not much improved in the political, economic, or social areas for women due to the Renaissance.

Russia: The Other Europe

In 1480, Ivan III threw off Mongol control of Russia. For the next several centuries, the Russians continued to push farther east to prevent a renewed threat to them from the steppes. It also kept Russia from following many of the developments in Europe. Already separated from western Europe by religion, the Russians practiced Eastern Orthodoxy. The attention to the east and the Ottoman Empire in the south kept Russia out of many conflicts in the west. This choice resulted in a Russia that lagged behind Europe in many ways.

Politically, the Russian czars saw themselves as heirs to the Roman Empire. In theory, czars ruled as absolute monarchs in charge of both church and state. However, military units, just as they did in ancient Rome, might depose of a powerful czar in favor of a younger, weaker heir. The boyars (the landed nobles) also presented a challenge to the absolute authority of the czars.

Economically, the mercantile empires of western Europe bypassed the traditional Asian land routes that also connected to Russia. Without a warm-water port, the naval routes bypassed Russian merchants. The goods of the world traveled to other nations, and Russians paid much higher prices for luxuries and spices that were commonplace in European markets. Lacking trade routes, Russia failed to develop a middle class as western European nations did. Also, agriculture remained the key component of the Russian economy. The boyars, not wanting to lose their livelihood, did not offer greater economic opportunities to their serfs, who remained little more than slaves.

At the start of the eighteenth century, Tsar Peter the Great defeated

Sweden after a long war. The victory made the construction of St. Petersburg possible. While not ice-free year round, it did give the Russians greater access to Europe by opening up a seasonal warm water port along a major trade route. Interested in naval and military expansion, Peter spent a great deal of money hiring European experts to build ships and guns for him. His interest went beyond just the military; he wanted Russia to be European. His new capital, St. Petersburg, looked European. He even demanded that his people look European, and he forced the boyars and others to shave their beards, as was the style of the European upper class. He forced all who did not Westernize to pay taxes, such as the Beard Tax, to maintain their own beliefs. His goal was to create a Russian capital that mirrored the major cultural centers of Europe in dress, activity, habits, and architecture. But beyond building up military production, Peter did not move the Russian economy toward capitalism. The Industrial Revolution, which was already building momentum in England, did not include Russia, and no significant middle-class-driven Enlightenment upset the political or social order. Peter's Russia remained a second-rate power until the great upheavals of the twentieth century.

The Reformation

Renaissance philosophy—humanism—recalled the past teachings of Greece and Rome and emphasized the ability of human reason. It did not reject religion, but humanism allowed a discussion of topics other than religion to become part of the intellectual conversation at European universities. As humanism moved into northern Europe, a number of religious leaders began to question the modern Roman Catholic Church, especially the church hierarchy from the pope down. These leaders questioned whether the church was remaining true to the teachings of the Bible. Eventually, the leaders rebelled when Martin Luther posted his 95 Theses.

While the Roman Catholic Church typically dealt severely with heresy and any criticism of church doctrine, Luther found a political situation in northern Germany that favored his cause. The German princes wanted greater independence from the Holy Roman emperor, and thus they sided with Luther as a form of rebellion. The emperor, Charles V, actively fought Luther's followers, but he was faced with rebellion in the Netherlands and a war with the Ottoman Empire (at its height under Suleiman the Magnificent), and so he was forced to allow the princes to determine the religion—Protestant or Catholic—in their own lands.

A century later, the 30 Years' War devastated Germany as the Catholics and Protestants fought for the right to worship. All of the major powers in Europe eventually joined the fight. In the end, the Protestants won and their ally, the Catholic nation of France, emerged as the most powerful state in Europe. France, more worried about the power of the Hapsburg family, rulers of the Holy Roman Empire, supported the Protestant side financially and militarily. The 30 Years' War would demonstrate that nations like France now fought for political reasons and economic gain above all else.

Several strands of Protestantism arose in parts of central and western Europe.

LUTHERANISM

- Founded by Martin Luther, a German monk
- Based on humanist philosophy
- Challenged core beliefs of the Roman Catholic Church
- Believed in salvation by faith alone
- Did not support the Roman Catholic Church hierarchy
- Did not support social change (Luther wrote against the peasant revolt in Germany that turned to him for inspiration)
- Luther translated the New Testament into German

CALVINISM

- Founded by John Calvin, a French theologian
- Also a humanist, he further rejected the teachings of the Roman Catholic Church
- Preached the idea of predestination (those going to heaven were already chosen by God)
- Rejected hierarchy but encouraged a religious state to enforce a strict morality
- Calvin and his followers established a religious state in Geneva, Switzerland

THE ANGLICAN CHURCH

- Founded by Henry VIII of England
- Arose over a dispute with the pope that included the right of Henry VIII to divorce
- Much of the change was placing the king as head of the church in England and seizing church lands (20 percent of all the land in England at the time)
- Over time, it would take on its own theology, differing from both the Roman Catholic Church and the new Protestant faiths

Absolute Monarchy

The 30 Years' War ended a series of political conflicts in Europe that used religious differences as a catalyst to inspire their populations to wage war. It also created the idea of the modern nation-state with definite political boundaries and sovereign governments. French king Louis XIV built a government that took advantage of the new wealth, military technology, and recent French victory. He sought to establish himself as the ultimate authority, the absolute ruler of the state. Absolutism, the type of government he envisioned, attracted many rulers in western Europe. The kings, even after feudalism's decline, continued to face powerful nobles who avoided taxes and possessed the resources to bring rebellion into the kingdom. Louis XIV appointed officials from lesser noble families and new wealth (mostly from the middle class who benefited from economic prosperity) to his bureaucracy. They depended on him for their position; should his power fall, so would theirs. The king, ruling by divine right in theory, controlled all aspects of the state, from foreign policy to religious freedoms.

THE ORIGINS OF THE ABSOLUTE MONARCHY

- Rule by divine right
- Absolute power was the only way of guaranteeing order among the masses
- Restored order after the chaos of the Black Death and religious wars
- Wealth of the New World allowed kings to buy the forces they needed in order to rule
- Growing middle class wanted protection of their property and wealth; some saw this as achievable under a strong leader
- Centralized power made a state stronger when it competed against others; survival of the fittest

Many European rulers sought absolute power, but they faced a new competing interest. While the middle class supported greater restrictions and higher taxes on the nobles, they also wanted more political rights: rights to limit their taxes and protect their property from the nobles, the church, and the king. Restrictions on the absolute monarch inspired parliamentary movements in England and other nations. This desire for a greater say influenced a new philosophy: the Enlightenment.

The Enlightenment and the Scientific Revolution

After the 1688 Glorious Revolution in England, John Locke wrote *The Second Treatise on Government*, which supported rule by parliament and not an absolute monarchy. At the heart of Enlightenment politics was the idea of the role of government as the protector of individual rights. Previous humanist philosophers saw government as the protector of the overall state, sometimes at the expense of individual rights. The Enlightenment included discussions as to what individual rights existed, including freedoms of religion, press, speech, and private property.

Along with the revolution in philosophy, another revolution took place; this one also affected philosophy. In the early seventeenth century, British philosopher Francis Bacon published a series of works explaining the modern scientific method: experimentation, analysis of data, and application in the natural world. He took science out of philosophy. The greatest debate of the day took advantage of his new thoughts. Polish astronomer Nicolaus Copernicus published the theory that the Earth and other planets orbited the sun. Not accepting the theory, Danish astronomer Tycho Brahe made detailed observations to create a model of an Earth-centered system. Brahe managed to create his new model of an Earth-centered system, but at his death, his assistant, Johannes Kepler, created a simpler and more convincing model with elliptical rather than circular orbits of the planets. The emphasis on observation and new data contradicted the classical Greek and Roman view of the universe, which required people to accept scientific principles without question.

Galileo, an Italian mathematician, used an early telescope to make observations further supporting Copernicus's theory, including finding moons orbiting Jupiter. The Earth-centered model argued that all heavenly objects orbited the Earth. In response to his findings, the Roman Catholic Church put Galileo on trial. The successes of the Protestant Reformation encouraged church leaders to go after anyone who questioned church teachings, which included the idea that the Bible placed the Earth at the center of the universe. Already over 60 years old, Galileo spent his final days under house arrest.

NEWTON'S CLOCKWORK UNIVERSE

The true end to the classical view of the universe and the beginning of science's position of esteem in the West came with English physicist and mathematician Sir Isaac Newton. His laws of motion and theory of gravity explained the orbits of the bodies around each other based on mass and gravitational attraction. Newton developed a new form of math (calculus) to work the theories. Science now looked to explain the universe as a series of mathematical equations, a complicated clockwork that was understandable by man. The church and classical philosophers opposed this view, but the already limited power of the church could no longer silence the new knowledge. The economic benefits of science applied to industry only won it more converts, as the scientific revolution merged with the growing Industrial Revolution.

Multiple-Choice Review Questions

1. What group initially replaced the Arabs at the core of Islamic power?

   A. Ottoman Turks
   B. Seljuk Turks
   C. Mamluks
   D. Sunnis

2. What statement best explains Portuguese attempts to sail around Africa into the Indian Ocean?

   A. Portugal's king desired slaves who were available through trade with Africa's East Coast.
   B. Portugal sought to establish its own trade route to the spices and other products of the East and bypass the Italian merchants who controlled the Mediterranean routes.
   C. Portugal, concerned over the growing power of Spain, wanted a route to bring in trade that the Spanish did not control.
   D. Portugal's Prince Henry was able to use government resources to fund his interest in sailing.

3. Which of the following did NOT assist the conquistadors of Spain in their conquest of the Aztec and Incan Empires?

    A. Gunpowder
    B. Metal weapons
    C. Overwhelming numbers
    D. Diseases spread among the native populations

4. Which of the following statements best characterizes the political system of Japan before contact with European explorers?

    A. Japan was ruled by a divine emperor with absolute power.
    B. Japan was ruled by a Confucian bureaucracy similar to that found in China.
    C. Japan was ruled by a strong lord, the shogun, who enforced feudal obligations on the samurai (warrior) class.
    D. Japan was ruled by local lords who owed feudal obligations to a single lord, or shogun, but tended to ignore these because the shogun was weak.

5. What statement best explains the failure of the Gunpowder Empires to match the political and economic development of western European nations from 1500 to 1700?

    A. European nations refused to trade with Islamic states.
    B. The social order of the Gunpowder Empires did not allow for the development of a middle class to champion economic investment or demand political change.
    C. European nations developed guns and cannons earlier than the Gunpowder Empire, who never caught up to the Europeans and thus lost their trade routes and previous economic advantages.
    D. The Gunpowder Empires refused to develop overseas trade routes, preferring to depend upon the older land routes that traveled through their empires.

The Great Buddha, Kamakura, Japan

Buddha Yungang Grottoes, China

White Marble Buddha, Hai Van Pass, Vietnam

6. The images above are an example of

   A. imperialism.

   B. cultural diffusion.

   C. ethnocentrism.

   D. cultural relativism.

TRANSATLANTIC SLAVE IMPORTS BY REGION, 1450–1900

REGION	NUMBER OF SLAVES
Brazil	4,000,000
New Spain	2,500,000
British West Indies	2,000,000
French West Indies	1,600,000
British North America/United States	500,000
Dutch West Indies	500,000

7. Based on the table above, what New World economic activity required the greatest number of slaves?

   A. Cotton production

   B. Mining

   C. Sugar production

   D. Textiles

8. Which statement below best explains the cultural advances made in western Europe during the Renaissance?

    A. The declining power of the Roman Catholic Church allowed artists greater freedom in their works.
    B. The wealth brought into Europe by renewed trade contacts allowed prosperous individuals to become patrons of the arts.
    C. The return of Greek and Roman learning inspired artists.
    D. New contacts with Islam encouraged European artists to match Muslim works of art and architecture.

9. Which of the following statements best explains the success of the Reformation in sixteenth-century Europe?

    A. Charismatic leaders like Martin Luther and John Calvin gained followers among the masses while the Roman Catholic Church failed to counter their arguments.
    B. Renewed interest in the Bible convinced the masses that the hierarchy of the Roman Catholic Church no longer practiced what the Bible taught.
    C. The Roman Catholic Church no longer had political support in Europe, so it could not enforce church doctrine or rules.
    D. Many political leaders gained advantages, both political and economic, by siding against the Roman Catholic Church and its political allies.

10. Which of the following was NOT a long-term impact of the Columbian Exchange?

    A. Massive worldwide population growth
    B. Millions of deaths, mostly in the New World
    C. The breakup of the Roman Catholic Church in Europe
    D. The rise of European nations to global powers

Answers to Multiple-Choice Questions

1. **B**. This is a basic knowledge question. The Ottoman Turks came after the Seljuk rise to power. Mamluks and Sunnis are not ethnic groups. The question asks about Arabs, an ethnic group, so the answer should be an ethnic group.

2. **B**. Portugal's aims were about making money. Portugal's own route would provide them with the greatest income and weaken potential Italian rivals. A and C occurred later, so they do not fit the time in question.

3. **C**. The conquistadors never had superior numbers over the Aztecs or the Incas. They did have native allies, especially against the Aztecs, but the other choices are clearly advantages the conquistadors enjoyed against one or both of their adversaries. The Incas had bronze (metal) weapons, but the Aztecs did not. In both cases, Spanish steel was far superior to the weapon materials of the Aztecs and the Incas.

4. **D**. Like European feudalism, Japanese feudalism before the Tokugawa shoguns tended to be decentralized, because weak shoguns could not consolidate control over the entire country. Note: there was an emperor, as there has been since the seventh century, but he was politically weak.

5. **B**. The economic expansion of Europe was fueled by the early adoption of a capitalist economic system. This system produced a middle class, which drove innovation as it sought its own wealth. The Gunpowder Empires from the Ottoman to the Ming did not allow social change, this allowed their elites to protect their positions, but economics and innovation stagnated.

6. **B**. The similarity of the images and the presence of Buddhism in the three different locations that do not include India (the original home of Buddhism) clearly demonstrate the phenomenon of cultural diffusion. While imperialism also transplanted Christianity to other areas of the world, no single conqueror occupied all of the areas included in the question.

7. **C.** There are two ways to reach this answer. First, if you already know that sugar was the number-one crop in the Americas, you do not need the table at all. Second, the table indicates that Brazil and the Indies received the most slaves, and you should know that sugar production was the dominant economic activity in these regions. Hopefully, even if you knew that sugar was the main cash crop, you referenced the table to back up your knowledge and discovered that the sugar-producing areas received by far the most slaves.

8. **B.** It's the economy. Money from trade allows greater job specialization, including artists, painters, sculptors, and architects. A ignores the fact that the church provided much of the money for art and that religion remained a dominant theme in the art of the Renaissance. C is true, but the trade connections result in a return to Greek and Roman knowledge, and the return of the arts does not pay for the production of new art, which makes A the better answer.

9. **D.** German princes, Henry VIII of England, and many other politicians, even devout Catholics like Louis XIV, all found great advantage in turning against the Roman Catholic Church and some of its political supporters, like the Hapsburgs of Spain and Austria.

10. **C.** The potato led to massive population increases in Europe and Asia. Diseases new to the Americas wiped out native populations with no built-up immunities. The increase in the global supply of silver from the mines of Peru and Mexico, led to D, the growth of European empires—especially Spain, Portugal, France, and Britain.

Free-Response Examples
Continuity and Change-over-Time Essay

Directions: You are to answer the following question. You should spend five minutes organizing or outlining your essay. Write an essay that:

- Has a relevant thesis and supports that thesis with appropriate historical evidence

- Addresses all parts of the question
- Uses the world historical context to show continuities and changes over time
- Analyzes the process of continuity and change over time

Analyze the political and economic impact of European exploration and colonization between 1500 and 1750 on ONE of the following areas:

- China
- Latin America
- West Africa

Comparative Essay

Directions: You are to answer the following question. You should spend 5 minutes organizing or outlining your essay. Write an essay that:

- Has a relevant thesis and supports that thesis with appropriate historical evidence
- Addresses all parts of the question
- Makes direct, relevant comparisons
- Analyzes relevant reasons for similarities and differences

Analyze the similarities and differences between the growth of the Spanish and the Ottoman Empires between 1450 and 1750.

Content Review Part 4:
Industrialization and Integration

1750 to 1914

European Enlightenment and Hegemony

While the AP World History Exam purposely focuses on non-European societies (the test should include at least 70 percent non-European questions), by the start of this time period, Europe's early explorations were now becoming political and economic conquest. By 1914, you cannot discuss any region of the world without including the external influences exercised by European powers (along with the United States and Japan). The influence covered all areas of culture: politics, economics, religion, social order, innovations, and the arts.

The Enlightenment philosophy in Europe acts as a key starting point for this period of world history. Like Confucius, Socrates, and Plato at the start of the classical period or Islam in the seventh century, the Enlightenment ushered in a new system of thought that dominated a large area of the globe. At its core, Enlightenment philosophy focused on the rights of individuals. John Locke, an English Enlightenment philosopher, spelled it out with the simple notion that the state's greatest responsibility was to protect an individual's life, liberty, and property. Frenchmen Voltaire and Jean-Jacques Rousseau both continued to push the importance of individual liberty and the role of the state in protecting individuals. Their ideas produced tangible results:

the American Declaration of Independence and Constitution and the French Declaration of the Rights of Man and of the Citizen and the Napoleonic Code.

The First Global Conflict

In 1756, Prussia and the Hapsburg Austria dragged most of the rest of Europe into a conflict that grew into the first truly global war. The Seven Years' War, as it became known, soon involved combat in the Americas, Africa, and India. Navies patrolled the world's trade routes, from the Caribbean to the Indian Ocean, seeking to destroy or capture the economic lifeblood of their enemies. In Europe, massive armies engaged each other on battlefields in Germany and Austria. In other areas, due to a lack of available European manpower, native soldiers joined Europeans to fight other natives to help establish the dominance of a European power over their lands.

Just prior to the start of the European conflict, French and British colonists in the North America, supported by troops from their mother countries, engaged each other in a fight over the territory just west of the Appalachian Mountains. Known as the French and Indian War in American history, this conflict set a very common pattern that lasted well into World War I: regular army troops would join with colonist and native forces to fight other European powers and their native forces in order to establish control over a territory.

In this case, many native tribes fought for the French, because the British colonists clearly acted as invaders of the native lands. The colonists wanted to move large populations into new territories, intent on clearing the lands for new farms. The limited number of French settlers seemed less of a threat, especially when many acted as trappers and traders of furs who came to trade and then left. Some did help the British, who promised to respect the tribe's lands; this would cause future conflict between the colonists and the king.

On the other side of the globe, Britain and France sought to pick up the pieces of a once fabulously wealthy state. The Mughal rulers of India started to fade from power in the eighteenth century. Prosperity, driven by the planting of commercial crops like sugarcane, indigo, tobacco, and cotton, benefited both rural peasants and local leaders. Textile manufacturing also made many entrepreneurs very wealthy. This money allowed local leaders to build up military forces to defy the Mughals. By the time of the Seven Years' War, central power was almost nonexistent, and India seemed back on the path toward regional fragmentation. However, the Dutch, French, and English all saw great economic potential in India, and each resented the flow of silver out of their nations in exchange for Indian goods. Mercantilist policies emphasized a positive flow of silver and gold into the nation. The war would allow the English to ally with local Indian leaders in order to beat the rival French and their allies. By war's end, the British restricted the French to just two territories and limited their military manpower. Soon India saw another period of political unity, but this time the core of that unity originated in London, not New Delhi or any other Indian state.

The Atlantic Revolutions

In Europe, the Enlightenment produced a constitutional monarchy in Great Britain. By 1750, British middle-class merchants and businessmen shared some political power with large landowners and the old nobles. The Enlightenment's promise of protecting individual rights and sharing political authority was not yet a complete reality, but as wealth increased, more and more found themselves with greater access to political power or, if limited, a greater need of access to power to protect what they had. In several cases, this need for greater access produced a political revolution.

The American Revolution

Greater political freedoms in Britain and the economic protections they provided produced the first serious challenge to the colonial order. British colonists in the Americas began to resent mercantilist policies that limited the profits they might make. As Parliament faced the huge debt generated by the Seven Years' War (the French and Indian War being part of that conflict), the members looked to the colonists to pay for the war. Many in the colonies benefited from the conflict, winning new lands across the Appalachian Mountains, so the members of Parliament voted new taxes on the colonies, beginning with the Stamp Act in 1765. Resentment and defiance of the tax eventually forced its repeal, but the British would not give up nor allow their subjects to defy the government. By 1775, Parliament enacted several additional taxes along with restrictions on trade between the colonies and other ports. Violence broke out on occasion.

Open rebellion began as the colonists attempted to protect guns and ammunition stored at the towns of Lexington and Concord. The colonial leaders met in Congress and eventually declared independence from Great Britain. Several years of conflict produced no clear victor in the northern colonies; Great Britain took many major cities but could not capture the leaders or destroy the Continental army. Eventually the combat shifted south and, with critical help from the French (both financially and militarily), the colonists trapped the main British army at Yorktown and forced its surrender.

The new government eventually established under the American Constitution reflected the ideas of the Enlightenment and the interest of the middle class behind the initial revolution.

- It guaranteed political and economic rights
- It *did not* create a new nobility or privileged class
- It created a republic that granted middle- and upper-class men political power
- It *did not* grant equal political representation to all; it excluded slaves and women, requiring property or other qualifications for participation in state government and voting
- It instituted a system of checks and balances over political offices so no single individual or group (oligarch) could monopolize power

The French Revolution

The French government of Louis XVI supported the American Revolution as a tactic to weaken the British, because the French had recently lost much to the British in the Seven Years' War. Initially, French assistance included guns, funds, uniforms, and training. Later, thousands of French troops and the French navy actively joined the war against the British. Some of the ideas of the revolution seem to have travelled with troops when they returned home.

By 1788, Louis XVI faced a series of challenges to his rule that encouraged these revolutionary ideas.

- Many Enlightenment authors were French, and their works were already in wide circulation; these works all called for greater limits on the power of the king, the church, and the nobles
- The American Revolution left the French deep in debt; they could not make payments on the loan or get additional credit
- Industrialization in France was in depression, leaving many unemployed in the cities
- Successive bad harvests, especially in 1788, drove up bread prices; many in the cities could not feed themselves
- Peasants wanted relief from feudal duties (high taxes and labor obligations) owed to the nobles
- Those in the Third Estate (First Estate was the clergy, Second Estate was the aristocracy, Third Estate was everyone else), though many were wealthy merchants and businessmen, did not have any political clout

In 1789, Louis XVI called representatives of all of the estates together in an attempt to deal with the financial crisis. The initiative quickly turned into a broader movement to reform the entire system. Louis failed to act against the Third Estate as it pushed for political representation. Violence broke out and the revolution began.

Like the American Revolution, the middle class and Enlightenment ideas were instrumental in the initial move toward revolution in France. However, the working poor of the cities and the peasants in the countryside also played a major role. Unlike the American Revolution, those leading the political changes did not reach a quick consensus on what they wished to achieve. As the revolution developed, divisions formed between the leadership. Some wanted a constitutional monarchy like that in Britain. Others wanted to found a republic, removing the king and the aristocracy. The various parties mobilized the masses of urban workers to win support for their positions. However, the situation turned violent. The early Enlightenment ideas faded as the more radical revolutionaries established a dictatorship, executed the king and queen, and then found themselves victims of the guillotine.

Ultimately, in a coup d'etat, or blow to the state, Napoleon Bonaparte, a military leader, took over the government and, with popular support, made himself the emperor of France. Years of internal fighting and the threat of invasion had the French looking for a savior, and Napoleon offered stability and the military talent to defeat France's enemies. He also instituted some of the ideas of the Enlightenment in the French legal system through the Napoleonic Code.

COMPARING REVOLUTIONS

AMERICAN	Inspired by Enlightenment ideas
	Middle-class revolution
	Taxation and economic opportunities were limited by British government
	Support from the French helped achieve a military victory
	Resulted in the establishment of a republic based on Enlightenment philosophy
	Revolution was not social; neither class nor gender roles changed

FRENCH	Inspired by Enlightenment ideas
	The Third Estate (middle class, urban poor, and peasantry) all wanted change
	Economic crises, bad harvests, and feudal duties all contributed to the initial revolution
	Violence in Paris, other major cities, and in the countryside all contributed to fear and radical political change
	The Revolution executed the king and queen
	This caused the nations of Europe to declare war on France
	Napoleon, a military hero, first saved the government then overthrew it
	In the end, the French Revolution did not succeed as an Enlightenment revolution
	The revolution involved efforts to affect social change but failed in the long term to address issues of the working classes; it did remove the final feudal duties owed by peasants
	Women failed to achieve any of their early revolutionary goals even though many worked to spread the Enlightenment sentiments that inspired the early legal changes
HAITIAN	Inspired in part by the revolution in France
	Freed blacks and mulattos led the slaves in revolt
	Abolished slavery
	Won independence from France
	The revolution did remove the white elite, but ultimately replaced them with a similar social hierarchy
	Women fought for freedom but did not gain any more political rights or economic freedoms than women had in other Caribbean societies
LATIN AMERICAN	Revolution of elites
	Peninsulares (Spaniards born in Europe) occupied the top positions in colonial government; they made their fortunes then many returned to Spain
	Creoles (born in the Americas to European parents) were heavily invested in the colonies but could not work in the colonial administrations

LATIN AMERICAN (CONT.)	Creoles revolted to replace the Peninsulares as the political rulers
	Spain, engaged in the Napoleonic Wars in Europe and weak, could do little to hold on to its New World colonies
	The new governments did not make changes reflecting Enlightenment ideas
	The revolutions simply replaced one elite with another
	Women in the Creole class gained little political recognition under the revolutionary governments; they would take on a role similar to elite women in Europe, promoting charity and social discussion, such as occurred in the salons of Paris
MEXICAN	Creoles were joined by mestizos and natives in revolting against Spanish rule
	Mixed set of objectives
	Creoles wanted to replace the Peninsulares in power (like in other Latin American states)
	Mestizos, mulattos, and natives wanted relief from taxes and other obligations
	Some sought a society based on Enlightenment ideas
	Creoles led the initial revolution; especially prominent was a priest, Father Miguel Hidalgo
	The egalitarian concerns of Father Hidalgo did not match with the goals of many of the Creoles in Mexico
	An eventual Creole victory resulted in a military dictatorship, not an Enlightenment government

The Haitian Revolution

The Haitian Revolution stands out among the other anticolonial revolts during the late eighteenth and early nineteenth centuries because, at its core, it was a slave revolt. The French Revolution inspired freed mulattos and African slaves in the colony to revolt in order to abolish slavery as well as win independence from France.

Initially, the slaves revolted because the revolution in France seemed to promise them freedom but did not move in that direction. To control the half million slaves, the 30,000 French colonists needed the help of free blacks. So they extended full citizenship to them in return for service in the colonial militia. The French government, appealing to the larger masses, abolished slavery in 1793, leaving the wealthy planters in Haiti with little support. As the revolution in France evolved into the military dictatorship of Napoleon, Haitian revolutionary leader François-Dominique Toussaint Louveture pushed for more autonomy. Betrayed by a French invasion in 1802, Toussaint Louveture was imprisoned in France as Napoleon reestablished French control of the colony. However, when it became apparent that Napoleon would reintroduce slavery, a massive revolt broke out and expelled the French. Haiti took on its modern name and declared itself a free nation in 1804.

The Haitians would not follow the path of the Enlightenment where all men were equal, as Toussaint Louveture had sought. Instead, Jean-Jacques Dessalines, who led the final fight for independence, became the new monarch. Like the other Latin American revolutions, the majority of the people would not gain any political or economic freedoms from their new government. A small elite, in this case former slaves, established a new government, although it too would face revolt as mulattos, who were denied government positions, rose up. In 1806, mulattos ambushed the emperor, killing him and putting Haiti on the path of greater political instability.

The uniqueness of the Haitian revolt—a successful slave uprising—inspired many in Latin America and the United States, although in different ways. It inspired slaves to revolt in many nations, although never at a national level. It inspired fear in many plantation owners, especially considering that slave populations were greater in number than the rural plantation owners.

The 1810 Mexican Revolution

Like much of the rest of Latin America, Mexico also revolted against Spanish rule during the Napoleonic Wars. However, in Mexico, it was not just Creole elites replacing the Peninsulares. The initial revolt, led by an inspirational Creole priest, Father Miguel Hidalgo, sought to include the masses of peasant mestizos and natives in a new political order. The death of Father Hidalgo and other leaders sharing his interest in a broader social revolution allowed the Creoles in Mexico to turn the revolution back to their desires for independence from Spain. An elite would be maintained, but they would be the ones in power, not the Spanish. When Creole officers in the army rebelled, the Spanish lost. One former officer established himself as a dictator over Mexico and all of Central America. The non-Mexican regions rejected this, and eventually another military mutiny resulted in the new emperor's death.

Military dictatorships, foreign interference, and lack of political power for those outside of the Creole class characterized the rest of the nineteenth century in Mexico. They lost lands to the United States after the Texas Revolution and the Mexican-American War. When the government failed to pay its debts to European nations, the Europeans invaded. With conservative backing in Mexico, France supported the establishment of a new empire under the Hapsburg prince Maximilian. Later, when Maximilian tried to follow a moderate political agenda, conservatives withdrew their support, and he was forced to rely on French troops to remain in power against a growing guerrilla war. The end of the American Civil War allowed the United States to demand that the French leave the continent. Without French support, Maximilian was defeated, captured, and executed by a firing squad.

A liberal government followed Maximilian's empire, but a poor economy and the president's attempts to gain greater power caused another brief civil war. General Porfirio Diaz established a new liberal government based on the ideas of positivism (faith that the pursuit of science would guarantee the progress of humanity). Improving global economic conditions allowed him to ally with the wealthy elite in Mexico, improve the economy, and attract foreign investment to support further economic growth. At the same time, he pushed peasants off their lands because he viewed them as backward and allowed many of the wealthy to expand their landholdings. The former peasants were to supply labor for industrial growth, thus becoming an urban working class. While some of the liberal elite agreed with the necessity of the sacrifice of some for the betterment of others, many did not and supported calls for a return of the land to the peasants and more social programs to help the poor. When Diaz, at age 80, announced he would not run for president in 1910, the opposition fielded several candidates. Then Diaz changed his mind and rigged the election, touching off another bloody revolution in 1911.

The Slavery Issue

The Industrial Revolution and Enlightenment philosophy both contributed to the abolition of slavery. The Industrial Revolution ushered in a period of mechanical innovation that reduced the need for some of the agricultural labor involved in the production of both food and cash crops. This changing economic model reduced the need for forced labor. In Europe, the surplus farm labor and overall increase in population provided an abundance of labor for new factories. In the colonies, mercantilist policies did not allow for industrialization on a large scale, so a reduction in the need of labor affected the previous economic model that relied on slave labor.

A sugar glut at the end of the eighteenth century and rising slave prices also changed the economics of the Atlantic trade. This mixed with the growing moral objections to slavery and made change inevitable. Britain and France both abolished slavery in the early nineteenth century. In Britain, the formerly wealthy sugar lobby lost ground to manufacturing interests that saw no profit in the slave trade, but rather saw Africa as a potential treasure trove of mineral resources for their factories. In France, the revolution banned slavery as contrary to the new constitution and individual rights. Even after the revolution failed, slavery never regained its place in colonial France.

Initially, African slavers continued to ship slaves by Spanish or Portuguese ships, but the British navy began an active program of ending the shipment of slaves from Africa, intercepting any ships suspected of carrying slaves. This interruption of the slave trade combined with fears of successful revolts like that in Haiti forced planters to look for other sources of labor. As the European empires expanded and connected all corners of the globe, planters found tens of thousands who were willing to work as indentured servants in return for transportation to new lands and hopefully a greater chance of economic progress. Massive numbers of Indians, Chinese, and Japanese moved into Latin America to do the work formerly done by slave labor. These indentured servants and freed slaves formed the basis of the peasant–poor classes across Latin America. Brazil, where the Portuguese first introduced the plantation system to sugar production, became the last American state to outlaw slavery in 1888.

The Industrial Revolution and Western Dominance

THE KEY TECHNOLOGIES

TEXTILES
The first mechanized area of production
Flying shuttle for weaving
Mechanical carder for combing wool fibers for processing
Cotton gin for separation of fibers from seeds
Spinning jenny for spinning thread (multiplied single-user production by a factor of eight and then doubled that)
Water frame to mechanize spinning jennies (also encouraged factory system)
Power loom for weaving allowed production of cloth to keep up with thread production

MILITARY WEAPONS
Breech-loading rifles and cannon (loading a gun or rifle by a breech in the barrel significantly increased the rate of fire)
Ironclad and steel warships
Repeating rifles
Machine guns
Wireless communication (used first by military ships during the Russo-Japanese War in 1904–5)

OTHER FIELDS
Steam engine allowed for the location of factories anywhere (flowing water was no longer needed to power machines)
Steamships to provide reliable transportation of raw materials and manufactured goods
Railroads for rapid overland transportation (opened new markets and allowed for the concentration of factories, thus reducing costs)
Bessemer process for the production of less-expensive steel (lighter and much longer lasting than iron)

The Economics

The Industrial Revolution altered the culture of Western Europe. The capitalist economies of Western Europe, first mercantile then free market, produced a tremendous amount of wealth. They turned this wealth into global power.

Under the rules of mercantilism, the Western powers competed for resources and markets by establishing colonies. Early colonizing states like Spain and Portugal failed to industrialize, depending on older colonial models that rewarded the nobles and established near-feudal conditions. Once these colonies failed or rebelled, the home countries became dependent on the manufacturing sectors in newer powers like Britain, France, and Prussia (the future core of a united German state). Starting with Britain, these economic changes forced political realignment. The older aristocracy/gentry (the term *gentry* refers to large landowners, most of whom had titles of nobility) class of Britain lost ground to the new industrialists and merchants. This rising urban upper and middle class soon came to dominate politics in Parliament. Old laws favoring the nobles were repealed. National policy favoring industrialization and foreign policy took on a clear economic focus, avoiding binding military alliances in favor of profits.

Other nations also followed this path, although with less conviction. The French Revolution favored middle-class economic interest, but a return of the monarchy and more revolutions in 1830 and 1848 slowed France's economic growth. The newly united nations of Italy and Germany also pushed rapid industrialization as the only means of achieving great power status and remaining independent. Rapid industrialization demanded strong governments, and both Italy and Germany produced republics that favored industrial and middle-class interests, but they encountered problems when dealing with the working-class poor of the cities. A few Enlightenment philosophers, especially in Germany, began to develop new socioeconomic models that fell broadly under the term socialism. In Germany, Karl Marx and Friedrich Engels published their works on communism. The communist call for the violent overthrow of the existing class structure caused governments and those with political power to favor politically conservative parties. They feared that liberal parties would only invite more rapid change and cause those currently in power to lose their economic and political advantages.

The economic realities drove Europe to expand and innovate at a rate never encountered before in history. Few in the wider world managed to resist the armies and navies of an industrialized Europe.

Imperialism

Since the time of Columbus, the European powers sought overseas colonial possessions. The Seven Years' War (1756–1763) demonstrated that a European conflict could ensnare any part of the globe. After the war, the powers continued to expand their control over large populations. The British, using existing allies in India, slowly brought each of the independent states under the British Raj (rule). The French and the Dutch, both driven from their Indian territories, each expanded into Southeast Asia; the French into Vietnam and the Dutch across Indonesia.

Colonial administrators faced growing demands from home for raw materials, cash crops, and new markets for manufactured goods. In the colonies, they lacked many of the bureaucratic resources to get the job done. By the mid-nineteenth century, many powers introduced Western education into their colonies to raise a generation of bureaucrats to manage the more complex imperial institutions in the colonies. Like the previous recruitment of soldiers from native populations, the new educated elite allowed for the expansion of European control and greater diffusion of European cultural values around the globe. On the surface, this meant the adoption of European dress by a new set of elites in nations like India and Japan. The European calendar that kept the schedules of steamship lines at all ports of call now supplanted local calendars; the seven-day week became the international norm.

European culture also included political and social ideas that challenged traditional systems and the newly imposed European order itself. In many areas, the institution of slavery fell early in the nineteenth century due to Europeans protesting the actions of their governments (Brazil became the last nation to abolish the practice, in 1888). Teaching the same philosophical values to the conquered colonials produced the potential for political and social upheaval.

- Western-educated elites used European legal systems to challenge colonial practices that denied them rights.
- Failure of the Europeans to grant their colonial subjects the same rights they enjoyed created a social backlash.
- Nationalist leaders used the anger created by the denial of rights against their colonial rulers.
  - Some pushed for further adoption of European culture and the use of public opinion in Europe to gain freedom (Indian National Congress).
  - Others pushed for establishment of their own institutions in place of European controls (Imperial Japan).
  - Finally, some nationalists sought a return to fundamentalist or basic social traditions, rejecting European influence (the al-Mahdi revolt in the Sudan).

COLONIAL SNAPSHOTS

EGYPT

1869: completion of the Suez Canal makes Egypt a valuable territory for the British and other colonial powers

1875: Britain buys a large interest in the Suez Canal Company from the ruling *khedive* who was facing financial difficulties

1882: British troops intervene to support a Turkish minority government and protect their interest in the canal

While nominally independent, Britain would maintain a military force in Egypt until 1954

Summary:

- Small local elite become dependent on European forces to stay in power
- Colony becomes dependent on an export-driven economy based on cotton; without British factories, the economy would collapse
- Locals turn to traditional ideas and attack the Egyptian elite and European troops
- British troops prevail, but the ruling elite loses legitimacy in the eyes of many Egyptians

JAPAN

1853: Commodore Matthew C. Perry initiates negotiations between the United States and Japan; the Tokugawa shogun wished to avoid any external contacts, but American military strength forced negotiations and an eventual treaty

1868: A samurai revolt forces the resignation of the shogun and the establishment of an oligarchy, including the emperor

To remain independent, Japan adopts many political and economic institutions from Europe and Japan

1894–95: Sino-Japanese War; Japan defeats China, becoming an Asian empire, but losing some gains as Russia forces the return of lands in Manchuria

1894: Britain becomes the first to agree to remove the unequal treaty obligations in effect against Japan

1902: Japan and Britain sign a formal alliance recognizing each other's interest in Asia and agreeing to come to each other's military aid

JAPAN (CONT.)

Summary:
- Elite realize the need to adopt European political and economic systems
- Nationalism, championed by the government, produces strong support at all levels of society for modernization along Western lines
- Traditional customs dropped to demonstrate desire for acceptance by the Europeans (empress stopped blackening her teeth in order to get Japanese women to drop the custom)
- Nation industrializes but finds itself in conflict with other European nations competing for markets and resources in China

SOUTH AFRICA

1652: Dutch farmers settle southern Africa

1835: Great Trek; Boers move north out of British territory

1879: Britain subdues (although suffering an embarrassing defeat) the Zulus, the largest tribe in Southern Africa who had opposed Boer incursion into their land

1890: British South Africa Company (BSAC) formed by Cecil Rhodes to take advantage of gold and other mineral deposits found in the region

1893: BSAC starts a series of small wars with local tribes that are resisting its control

1895: BSAC begins encroaching on Boer territory (Rhodes himself orchestrates a raid to encourage anti-Boer sentiment)

1899–1902: Boer War; British force the Boers to accept British rule, although providing them some degree of autonomy

Summary:
- Early European colonial populations displace native groups
- As colonial populations increased, more native areas come under pressure
- Mineral wealth encourages the home country to take an active role in administering the colony, even overriding the interests of the colonists

Spheres of Influence
The Scramble for Africa

As the competition for colonies increased, the vast unexplored regions of Africa became the target of European expansion. Many regions of Africa provided a challenge for Europeans to occupy due to difficulties with transportation, disease, and native populations. However, the demands of industry for raw materials like rubber and improved methods of transportation and communication eventually made African colonization both profitable and possible. Earlier efforts of Christian missionaries opened up the initial routes of exploration. Portugal and Belgium both sponsored large expeditions that resulted in annexation of territory. The British occupation of Egypt in 1882 pushed the other great powers to action.

To avoid potential conflict, German prime minister Otto von Bismarck hosted the Berlin conference in 1884 to set guidelines for the colonization of Africa. The conference, attended by 14 powers and no African states, produced a new map of the continent, dividing it into colonial possessions based on existing claims and the desires of a few European monarchs. Only two states—Ethiopia and Liberia—remained independent. After the conference, European businesses and militaries descended on the continent to secure and exploit the new territory. Natives that resisted quickly fell to modern European weapons.

Mines and agricultural production required large amounts of labor. In the Congo Free State and other areas, colonial officials forced Africans to work as a means of paying a tax to their colonial masters. Failure to meet quotas could result in brutal consequences. In the Congo, the Belgian King Leopold I's officials maimed thousands in order to force more villagers to collect rubber from wild trees, kill elephants for ivory, and to work in the copper, diamond, and gold mines. The brutality eventually resulted in Britain and the United States pressuring Leopold to renounce his personal rule over the territory and turn it over to the Belgian government. While conditions improved in the Belgian Congo and other areas due to increased international scrutiny, Africans remained impoverished and under the control of Europeans.

Qing China

In 1644, the Manchus, a seminomadic people from the northeastern portion of modern China, conquered the failing Ming dynasty. Establishing themselves in Beijing, the Manchus declared their possession of the

Mandate of Heaven and named a new dynasty: the Qing. At its height in the mid-eighteenth century, Qing agricultural refinements—the introduction of corn and sweet potatoes and the double cropping of rice—touched off a massive population boom. In 50 years the population nearly doubled. At the same time, the increased population provided for more agricultural laborers to cultivate more acreage, increasing food production to a point. Soon, agricultural demands exceeded the available lands. Government flood control and irrigation systems failed to meet the growing agricultural requirements.

The larger population provided labor for the increased production of trade goods. Merchants were able to trade the increased production to European merchants, thus supplying a growing consumer society. Everything from silks to teas drove increasingly large numbers of Europeans and Americans to establish merchant ties to China. However, the Qing took little advantage from the increasing economic demand. Most production remained preindustrial, as peasant families produced products at home as a side business. Laws that dealt very little with property rights and a government and social system that considered merchants a lower class of society made it impossible for Chinese entrepreneurs to follow the pattern of industrialization established in Europe.

In Europe, the large influx of silver from the New World during the sixteenth and seventeenth centuries created conditions for the adoption of capitalism and the Industrial Revolution. In China, this failed. No large middle class developed. Qing policy and Confucian beliefs prevented merchants from advancing their interests and instituting changes that might increase the economic power and national strength of China. The failure of the government and merchants to work together invited more European influence.

Wanting to halt the drain of silver from their economies to China, the British, French, and other mercantile powers actively sought products to trade in the Chinese market. In the early nineteenth century, after the financial drain and political distraction of the French Revolution and then the Napoleonic Wars, Britain needed to increase exports to China to balance its trade and then discovered a market in China for opium. With the most productive poppy-growing regions in the world found in northern India (modern Pakistan) and Afghanistan, Britain soon moved from a trade deficit with China to a surplus. Like the drug trade today, the illegal (according to Chinese law) trade fueled a criminal class in the cities and created thousands of drug addicts.

The opium trade only added to Qing troubles. By the start of the nineteenth century, the Qing faced growing challenges to their rule. The Chinese themselves resisted foreign control. The traditional Confucian bureaucratic elite already suffered from corruption. The emperors failed to take an active role in managing the country, and the palace elite, wives, and slaves drained valuable resources from the treasury for their own luxury. It seemed that the Qing were following the classic dynastic cycle and would soon face losing the Mandate of Heaven. But in 1839, bureaucrat Lin Zexu was given the task of ending the opium trade, and he confronted the British in a very traditional Chinese manner: he wrote a letter to the queen.

LETTER FROM COMMISSIONER LIN ZEXU TO QUEEN VICTORIA, 1839

A communication: magnificently our great Emperor soothes and pacifies China and the foreign countries, regarding all with the same kindness. If there is profit, then he shares it with the peoples of the world; if there is harm, then he removes it on behalf of the world. This is because he takes the mind of heaven and earth as his mind....

But after a long period of commercial intercourse, there appear among the crowd of barbarians both good persons and bad, unevenly. Consequently there are those who smuggle opium to seduce the Chinese people and so cause the spread of the poison to all provinces. Such persons who only care to profit themselves, and disregard their harm to others, are not tolerated by the laws of heaven and are unanimoly hated by human beings....

Suppose there were people from another country who carried

opium for sale to England and seduced your people into buying and smoking it; certainly your honorable ruler would deeply hate it and be bitterly aroused. We have heard heretofore that your honorable ruler is kind and benevolent. **Naturally you would not wish to give unto others what you yourself do not want....** Now after this communication has been dispatched and you have clearly understood the strictness of the prohibitory laws of the Celestial Court, certainly you will not let your subjects dare again to violate the law.

Note: The tone is clearly Confucian. Victoria, as a good ruler, must follow the example set by the Chinese emperor, who acts as a model of virtue and does not allow opium because it causes harm to his people. Lin expects Victoria to accept this lesson and police her people now that she understands the responsibility of a proper ruler (he even uses the Confucian version of the Golden Rule to chide the queen into proper behavior). Historically, Victoria likely never saw the letter.

When the letter failed, Lin seized and destroyed the yearly shipment of opium in Canton. British merchants took the matter to Parliament and argued the necessity of protecting private property. This pushed the British Parliament into sending military forces against China. The resulting Opium Wars (from 1839–1842 and again from 1856–1860) shattered the myth of Chinese power in the East. China failed to stop the small British force from advancing up the coast and taking cities at will. The Qing surrendered at Nanjing in 1842. The treaty established the pattern of unequal treaties that would dominate imperial diplomacy for the next 60 years.

THE TREATY OF NANJING: MAJOR CLAUSES

- Indemnity as payment for seized or destroyed opium and the cost of the war

- Annexation of the island of Hong Kong (British returned it voluntarily in 1997)

- Embassy in the Qing capital of Beijing (Europeans had been excluded from the city)
- Opening of five treaty ports to trade
- Control over China's ability to set tariff rates
- Extraterritoriality for British subjects in China (exempted British citizens from criminal prosecution and punishment in Chinese courts; this did not end until after the Second World War)
- Most-favored-nation status guaranteeing Britain treaty advantages granted by China to any other nation

As if on cue, the defeat at the hands of a foreign invader triggered a number of internal revolts. The most serious, the Taiping Rebellion, ranked as one of the bloodiest events in human history and almost destroyed the dynasty. Started by Hong Xiuquan (a minor official who came to believe himself to be Jesus's younger brother), the rebellion quickly captured large sections of central China along the Yangtze River. Nanjing, the southern capital, fell in 1853, and the Taiping army commanded by peasant generals seemed unstoppable. In the areas of their control, the Taiping sought to end the opium trade, fought hard against gangs and bandits, and redistributed lands to the peasants. They also pushed gender equality, outlawed prostitution, and discouraged foot binding.

Hong failed to continue his leadership over the movement. As he focused on religious doctrine, his generals fought each other, and the large landowners put together a modern military force, trained and led by Europeans and equipped with modern weapons. The Qing also sent an army against the Taiping. By 1860, much of the Taiping territory was lost. Nanjing, the final stronghold, fell in 1864 to the Qing. As a sign of the complexities of Chinese politics, while fighting the Taiping, the Qing also fought the French and British in the Second Opium War. This war resulted in the capture of the Chinese capital and the sacking of the emperor's Summer Palace. One of the British officers responsible for the plundering would later lead the final assaults against the Taiping fortresses along the Yangtze River, winning a victory for the Qing emperor he had just helped to defeat.

The Boxer Rebellion

By this point most in China felt that the dynastic cycle had run its course and the Qing were destined to fall. But European, American, and Japan's governments wished to keep the Qing in power to protect their interests in China. Many Chinese sought a way to modernize their system and join the great powers as an equal. In 1895, after suffering defeat at the hands of Japan, many at the highest levels were willing to work with a new generation of Chinese intellectuals. Reformers, with the backing of the emperor, were able to institute a wide range of reforms in 1898.

These included removing much of the old bureaucracy, establishing modern academic institutions, adopting Western industrial practices, medicine, science, rules of commerce, and a patent system. Reformers also revised the legal code to protect individuals and attack official corruption. Since most of the reforms threatened the traditional privileges of the Chinese elite, the reformers faced stiff opposition. Within four months of the changes, the Empress Dowager Cixi imprisoned the Guangxu emperor and arrested or executed most of the reformers.

To add to China's troubles, Cixi then encouraged an anti-foreign Taoist cult, the Society of Righteous Harmonious Fist (called the Boxers by Europeans), to attack Europeans in China. After attacks on several missionaries and the murder of a number of Chinese Christians, the dowager declared war on the foreigners in China and sent her armies to join the Boxers. A multinational force of American, British, French, German, Japanese, and Russian troops invaded northern China. The imperialist powers, despite their own differences, would not tolerate resistance to their authority. The force captured Beijing and forced the court to flee. The eventual peace treaty forced the Chinese to execute many government officials who were involved in the war, to destroy the defenses of Beijing, to stop the importation of firearms, and to finance a war indemnity that took four decades to pay off.

The empress did an about-face and allowed the bureaucracy to institute many of the previously banned reforms, but it was too little, too late. The emperor died, and Cixi's death followed the next day. The last emperor, Puyi, came to power before his third birthday and abdicated in 1912, just after he turned six. A Qing general promised a newly formed national assembly he would create a republican China, but he declared himself emperor in 1916. The provinces rebelled and the government turned against him. His death that same year marked the beginning of a long period of warlordism and civil war in China.

The Old Man of Europe

By the eighteenth century the Ottoman Empire already appeared as a failing power. The leadership had failed to keep up in several areas. First, the empire remained primarily agrarian, dependent on large plantations for substantial portions of their tax income. Britain and France were already in the early stages of industrialization. Germany, Russia, and the Austrian-Hungarians also were moving in that direction. The Ottoman Empire was left out of this international movement. Second, since the sixteenth century, trade routes to China and India opened by the Portuguese and Spanish replaced the overland routes to the Mediterranean. This once lucrative network had supplied the Ottomans with wealth and innovations. It also made them a major force in the Mediterranean and therefore European politics. As the British, Dutch, and French took over the global trade routes, the Ottomans faded further.

This failure to keep up with Europe carried over into other areas. Early during the Ottoman rule, the sultan instituted the millet system that allowed various religious groups a degree of self-rule within the empire. The non-Muslim groups did not enjoy equal status with Muslims, but as long as taxes were paid and national loyalty maintained, the religious leaders could govern their communities. This system failed when nationalist movements began to sweep the Baltic in the eighteenth century. The Ottomans had done nothing to unite the people of the empire into a single, cohesive group. Ethnic revolts tore at the empire from the inside, and so did its military.

For centuries, the Ottomans utilized a special corps of slave soldiers called Janissaries. At one time, the troops—taken from Christian families within the empire—were the most feared warriors on the Continent. However, in the seventeenth century, they had become more interested in politics and were involved in several rebellions and even overthrew a sultan in favor of his eventual replacement. To maintain their position of power, they resisted the military innovations originating in Europe and put the Ottomans farther behind the other armies on the Continent. They also resisted attempts by the sultan to create a larger military by recruiting from other sources. In 1826, the sultan sought further reforms and pushed the Janissaries into revolt, and then he surprised them with a secretly trained, modern military force. The Janissaries were completely defeated.

The reform-minded sultan continued to push for changes, but he faced too many challenges. The Tanzimat reforms he and his sons instituted beginning in 1839 focused on education and law. The decree announcing them sounded like a constitution that stripped special privileges from Muslims and made the tax and conscription systems more equitable. Many bureaucrats were educated along Western lines to improve the functions of government. Some believed the Tanzimat reforms did not go far enough and pushed for a Western-style parliamentary government. When a new sultan instituted authoritarian rule and removed the reforms, this group—known as the Young Turks—attempted to oppose him. This along with military pressure from Russia and ethic revolts throughout the Balkans seemed to mark the end for the Ottomans.

In 1908, a revolt forced the sultan to restore the reforms, and the next year the Young Turks formed a new constitutional government. However, Austria-Hungary's annexation of Balkan territory, new independence movements, the threat of Russian invasion, and the desire to restore Ottoman rule in Egypt (then controlled by Britain) all served to distract the government from making any real progress. Two Balkan wars just before World War I cost the Ottomans money, manpower, and territory. The Young Turks allied with Germany in World War I, believing in the power of the German army and looking to force the British out of Egypt. This proved disastrous. At the end of the war, the Ottoman leadership disbanded the empire, and the state of Turkey arose in its place.

Russia and Japan: Two Roads to Modernization

In the early eighteenth century Peter the Great sought to bring Russia up to the economic and technical standards of a great European power. His defeat of Sweden gave him the potential trade connections to complete part of his goal. However, instead of using the new Baltic ports to promote an increased trade and then adjust government policies to promote economic growth and freedoms, Peter's new revenues brought European military and armament experts into Russia to build weapons and train armies. His successors continued this policy with mixed results. By 1800, Russia was a major player in European politics and an important ally in the Great Power's efforts against Napoleon, although the young Czar Alexander I admired the French emperor.

The defeat of Napoleon after the devastating invasion in 1812 made Alexander a hero to many in Europe and confirmed Russia as a great power. However, the initially reform-minded Alexander turned against Enlightenment ideas and greater political freedoms after the Napoleonic Wars. Russia again failed to follow Western Europe as it modernized its economic and political systems. Alexander and his brother, Nicholas I, embraced autocratic rule and reinforced the power of the nobles over the peasants and fledgling industrial class. Only armaments advanced, but without greater manufacturing, the government saw little increase in revenues, which pushed it to increase the tax burdens on the peasant and working classes. The defeat in the Crimean War at the hands of the British and French who aided the Ottoman Empire demonstrated

Russia's weakness. The next czar, Alexander II, attempted reform, even emancipating Russia's 52 million serfs. However, Russians still lacked many of the freedoms and economic opportunities available in Europe. As he attempted to push new reforms past the Russian nobility, Alexander was assassinated.

Alexander III sought a return to a more autocratic Russia and championed the power of the nobles over the peasants and working class. He distanced himself from European courts and parliaments. His nationalism and strong support for the Russian Orthodox Church lent support for the anti-Semitic pogroms of his government; a million Jews fled Russia for Europe or the United States. Rail lines across Asia encouraged him to expand Russia's influence in central Asia, risking conflict with Great Britain. The rails also pushed Russia to become more interested in the Far East, especially a warm-water port in China capable of supporting a Russian Pacific fleet.

Alexander's son, Nicholas II, would see Russia's desire for a warm-water port in China fulfilled with the annexation of Port Arthur. Originally, the Japanese defeated China, gaining this Yellow Sea port, but they were forced by French and Russian threats to return it, only to have the Russians then seize the site. It would be Nicholas II's handling of Japan that would lead to Russia's greatest international crisis before World War I and the ultimate revolution that would bring down the czar.

Japan: From Feudalism to Imperial Capitalism

In 1600, the Tokugawa family took over the military rule of Japan. The new shoguns then officially isolated the country, baring all Europeans except for a limited number of Dutch traders from the islands. Along with banishing foreigners, the shogun's government also sought to eliminate the community of Japanese Christians, banning the religion and executing many who would not renounce the faith. Behind this wall of cultural isolation, Japan developed a unique system of centralized feudalism.

By the late eighteenth century, Japanese culture possessed some surprising attributes. First, the economy boasted a robust internal trade system. The shogun's government, called the *bakufu*, or tent government, in an effort to monitor the daimyo, built five major highways out of Edo (modern Tokyo) and required each of the daimyo to build connecting roads. This network provided rapid and safe transportation to all corners of Japan. Merchants prospered using this network to transport their own goods. In the many castle towns, markets formed as farmers brought in their produce and looked to buy items. The presence of large numbers of samurai serving the daimyo encouraged the merchants to maintain permanent locations in the towns. These grew into some of the first department stores anywhere. The requirement that daimyo travel to and from Edo to serve the shogun also created a demand for inns, teahouses, theaters, and other conveniences for the daimyo and their samurai. Merchants, too, wanted these accommodations and distractions.

Support for the theater led to an expansion of popular arts, including books illustrated with wood block prints. As merchants and others were forbidden to buy many of the permanent luxuries (finer clothing, bigger homes) reserved for the samurai class, they instead bought fine foods, attended the theater, watched sports (sumo being very popular), took vacations, and read. The trade-travel network helped standardize the language as well. This cultural boom is similar in some ways to the Renaissance in that it helped to establish a strong national identity.

But not all was ideal. Merchants and others with wealth lacked any legal protections when their rights might conflict with the samurai. Several times the shogun's government forced moneylenders to forgive loans granted to samurai. Samurai themselves found that merchants and others of a lower status had much better lives, and some chose to leave their rank and pursue other careers. Many of the daimyo, forced to meet their obligations to the court, could barely maintain any samurai in their service, creating a class of unemployed warriors, known as *ronin*, who might create some upheaval in the countryside. All of these were challenges for even the best shoguns and bureaucrats of the *bakufu*. Then, in 1853, an additional issue arose.

At the request of President Millard Fillmore, American naval commander Matthew C. Perry sailed a group of American warships, including two steam-powered vessels, into Edo (Tokyo) Bay and demanded to meet with officials of the shogun's government. This violated Japanese law, but lacking a means of dealing with the American ships, the shogun sent his representatives. Perry delivered a letter from the president, requesting normalized relations between the two countries. Perry promised to return in a few months for the shogun's answer. The next year, the United States and Japan signed the Treaty of Kanagawa. The treaty opened two Japanese ports to American shipping, allowed for the rescue of shipwrecked sailors or the harboring of damaged ships, and established formal diplomatic relations. Soon other nations followed.

The Meiji Restoration

By 1868, the *bakufu* clearly lacked the ability to deal with the foreign influences in the country. Raising the banner of the new Meiji emperor, a number of daimyo rebelled against the shogun, who officially resigned to the emperor and his new government. Because of the relatively peaceful nature of the revolution—there was some violence, but very little, considering a government was overthrown—the new government was immediately able to move Japan forward. The boldest step the Japanese took was to send representatives to the United States and Europe to see how the Japanese might modernize. Within a decade, Western-style government, education, and military technology were well integrated into Japanese society.

The emperor ruled in name, but a strong cabinet dominated national policy. Military leaders and industrial groups (called *zaibatsu*) created the climate for rapid industrialization. Purchasing European equipment allowed the Japanese to create a textile industry almost overnight. The zaibatsu worked with government policies that allowed them to take over the national banking system, free up land for investment, and herd tens of thousands of displaced peasants into the cities to work in the new factories. Many of these workers were women and children who left families in villages to earn cash while the rest of the family continued to tend the fields. Government support of their investments also brought in heavier industries over time, including steel, railroads, and shipping.

The emperor also modernized his military along the Prussian and British models. When the last of the samurai class revolted over issues of pensions and economic opportunities, this new army defeated them soundly. Taking a cue from the Europeans, the Japanese looked toward building an empire in East Asia to support their manufacturing exports and increase their access to resources. The first step involved Korea.

In 1894, Chinese and Japanese troops helped the Korean government put down a revolt. However, after the revolt, neither power withdrew their armies. Japan acted first, attacking the Korean government directly. War broke out on August 1. China, expecting an easy victory over what it and most of the world still considered a backward country, found itself in full retreat. The Japanese army occupied all of Korea and defeated China's forces in Manchuria, capturing Port Arthur, a major base on the Yellow Sea. The Japanese navy all but eliminated its Chinese opposition at the battle of the Yalu River. In April 1895, the Japanese became an imperialist power, taking control of Formosa Island (modern Taiwan) and several other Chinese territories as part of the peace treaty ending the war.

Russia wanted Port Arthur for itself and worked with France and Germany to get the Japanese to return the port to China, who then was forced to allow it to fall under Russian control. Japan turned to their naval partner, the British, for assistance. Early in the Meiji period, the Japanese began buying British ships and hiring British naval officers to train their navy. They consciously modeled their military after the rank structures used in England and France. As a result, the samurai class lost social authority under the new military system that required that all classes bear arms. In 1894, the British had already signed a treaty with Japan that did away with extraterritoriality and established relations with Japan as an equal nation. Other nations soon followed. Japan's assistance in the West's efforts to put down the Boxer Rebellion created a very positive opinion of the nation in England. In 1902, the British signed the Anglo-Japanese alliance, promising to come to Japan's aid if it were attacked by more than one power. This was a first in modern history: the acceptance of an Asian nation as a military ally. It also opened the door for Japan to attack Russia.

In 1904, the Japanese launched a sneak attack on the Russian Pacific Fleet at Port Arthur. Japanese army units occupied Korea and marched into Manchuria to engage the Russians. They also landed near Port Arthur and put the city under siege. Eventually, after 30,000 Russian and 60,000 Japanese casualties, the city fell. At sea, with its smaller Pacific fleet trapped in port, the Russians sent their main fleet from the Baltic around Africa and into the Indian Ocean. After months at sea, it entered the Pacific and moved up the Chinese coast. To resupply the fleet of 27 warships, the Russian admiral planned to head first to Vladivostok, the Russia port at the end of the trans-Siberian Railroad. To do so, he entered the Sea of Japan through the Tsushima Strait. Here, the Japanese waited for him. The battle cost the Russians almost 4,400 dead and 6,000 captured, along with the loss of 21 ships. The Japanese had 117 dead and lost three small craft.

Defeats in Manchuria forced the Russians to ask for peace. The victorious Japanese were out of men due to horrendous casualties in the Manchurian fighting and agreed to let American president Theodore Roosevelt host a peace conference in Maine. The resulting treaty recognized the Japanese victory but did not give Japan the territory won in the war. The United States believed in the territorial integrity of China, and so both sides were required to leave Manchuria. Victorious, but not satisfied, the Japanese military began looking at long-term plans to establish a greater empire in Asia. The Russians, humiliated by a non-Western power, faced internal discord. Military units revolted and riots occurred in major cities. Strikes and peasant uprisings against landlords also added to the unrest. However, the czar's police and military eventually put down the revolts and executed many of the leaders. Later, Vladimir Lenin and other communist leaders credited the 1905 revolts as the beginning of the socialist revolution in Russia.

The defeat of Russia by Japan offers a chance for a quick comparison on how nations outside of Western Europe adopted to the new industrial–imperial reality of the nineteenth century.

RUSSIA	JAPAN
Autocratic rule	Oligarchy of the imperial office, military commanders, and industrialist
Politics influenced by landed aristocracy	
No middle class	Zaibatsu (a collection of powerful industrialists) worked with the government to manage the economy
Built a land empire across Asia but did not gain access to greater trade routes or markets	
	Substantial middle class invested in industrialization
Revolutions rising from the poor peasant class led by an intellectual elite	Sought to establish an empire for markets and resources
Failure of the economy to modernize	
Militarization of the economy (government spent a great deal of money on military production but ignored other areas)	Modern economy based on European models
	Slogan, "Rich country, Strong army"

The Road to War

The Russo-Japanese War demonstrated that Japan was indeed a world power. It also revealed a larger global trend. At the start of the twentieth century, the world no longer stood open to new conquest by the imperialist powers. Everything was occupied.

- Latin America, although mostly independent and protected by the threat of American force should anyone try to establish a new colony, belonged to the great industrialists nations of Europe, especially Great Britain, who bought its resources and enabled its elites to stay in power.

- The Pacific islands were now way stations for American, British, French, and German navies.

- Africa fell to the "Scramble" in the late nineteenth century, with only Liberia and Ethiopia remaining independent.

- India belonged to Britain.
- Russia and Britain spent much of the nineteenth century in unofficial conflict over Afghanistan, Iran, and other regions of central Asia.
- Southeast Asia supplied tin, rubber, pepper, and oil to British, Dutch, and French colonial masters (Thailand remained independent).
- China belonged to whoever could exploit it; the "Open Door Policy" rejected spheres of influence but allowed all nations to trade and invest without Chinese approval.
- Korea (after 1910) and Taiwan belonged to Japan.
- The Middle East was either British (Egypt–Suez Canal) or remained part of the Ottoman Empire.

The war suggested several courses of action, many of which were already underway. First, nations needed allies to assure their military success. Great Britain was long opposed to alliances, but it would join France and Russia when Germany's aggressive policies in Africa worried British governments. Navies needed more and larger warships. A general arms buildup started in 1905 and carried on into the First World War. Finally, nations needed huge numbers to meet the needs of their armies, considering the high casualties the Russians and Japanese experienced. Nationalism prodded young men when the time came to take up arms and fight.

As 1914 began, 100 years of empire building and industrialization in Europe was about to unleash all that it had created against the world.

Multiple-Choice Review Questions

1. The Seven Years' War established what nation as the colonial ruler of India?

    A. France
    B. Prussia
    C. Portugal
    D. Great Britain

2. Which of the following statements best characterizes the relation-ship between the American Revolution and the Enlightenment?

    A. The American Revolution rejected British attempts to apply Enlightenment economic ideas to trade relations between Britain and the colonies.
    B. The American Revolution sought to establish Enlightenment ideas about political rights and economics currently denied the colonists by the British government.
    C. The American Revolution failed to adopt Enlightenment prin-ciples as the revolutionaries were predominantly middle class and feared a working class uprising.
    D. The American Revolution sought only the rights granted British citizens under the king and Parliament.

3. Which of the following actions would NOT fit with a mercantilist economic policy?

    A. Restrictions on manufacturing in a colony, even though labor may be cheaper than in the home country
    B. Routing of goods through the home country before they were shipped to a colonial port
    C. Limiting the amount of gold and silver available for export from the home country
    D. Restricting the amount of manufactured goods available for export to other colonial powers

4. Which of the following did NOT contribute to the French Revolution?

    A. Failure of the government to enfranchise (give political rights to) the French middle class
    B. Failure of the French government to address famine due to poor grain harvests and severe winter weather

C. A revolt of the French military over pay and modernization

D. A meeting of the Estates General to discuss political and financial difficulties

CHINESE–BRITISH TRADE IN CANTON, 1835–1836

BRITISH EXPORTS TO CANTON, CHINA (VALUE IN SPANISH SILVER DOLLARS)		BRITISH IMPORTS FROM CANTON, CHINA (VALUE IN SPANISH SILVER DOLLARS)	
Opium	17,904,248	Tea	13,412,243
Cotton	8,357,394	Raw Silk	3,764,115
All other goods	6,164,981	Vermilion	705,000
		All other goods	5,971,541
Total	32,426,623	Total	23,852,899

Source: *Commissioner Lin and the Opium War* (New York: Norton)

5. Based on the table above, what economic policy supports the exporting of opium to China?

A. Laissez-faire economics

B. Mercantilism

C. Free-market capitalism

D. Imperialism

6. Based on the table, which of the following statements is most accurate about the economic prospects for China in the decade from 1836 to 1846?

A. Tea and other exports will rise as the British now have the wealth to buy more of the Chinese production.

B. China should experience a period of economic growth as the growing import market creates a demand for more manufacturing.

C. China will face a shortage of capital as silver is used to buy imported goods.

D. China should expect increasing revenues from its exports as British demand increases.

7. Which of the following statements best explains the end of the slave trade from Africa to the Americas?

A. Moral objections in Britain encouraged the government to abolish the trade and actively patrol against it.
B. Cheap colonial labor did away with the need to move large numbers of people to new areas as laborers.
C. Aggressive slave revolts forced plantation owners to alter their economic models from slavery to tenant farming.
D. A decline in the global demand for cash crops due to rising industrial output cut the demand for labor in agrarian colonies.

8. Which of the following areas most successfully adopted a Western model of industrial development by 1914?

A. China
B. India
C. Russia
D. Japan

9. In which of the following regions did women make the most economic gains due to the Industrial Revolution?

A. In the Caribbean, as demand for sugar increased the income of small farming families
B. In Western Europe, as factories used women as paid workers
C. In China, where European spheres of influence forced the Chinese to abandon many Confucian ideas about the servitude of women
D. In India, now under British rule, as the caste system was outlawed

10. Which of the following statements best describes Ottoman reaction to political and economic developments in nineteenth-century Europe?

    A.   Recognizing the growing military and economic importance of Western Europe, the Ottomans engaged in a rapid program of borrowing, including adapting republican political institutions and capitalist economic policies.

    B.   The Ottomans failed to develop a unified social and political response to Western European growth, resulting in failed attempts at political reform and a decline in the size and wealth of the empire.

    C.   The Ottomans sought to use Western European legal practices to protest the power of the sultan and force his abdication.

    D.   Recognizing the failure of their own political and economic system, the Ottomans returned to the religious autocracy of the caliphate and attempted to bring all Muslim areas in the Middle East and North Africa back into their empire.

Answers to Multiple-Choice Questions

1. **D**. Britain would become the leading imperialist power as a result of the Seven Years' War and its initial expansion into India. The French and the Netherlands both lost their holds on India due to the war, while the Portuguese were already in economic decline and the Prussians did not expand overseas until German unification in 1871.

2. **B**. America is the child of the Enlightenment. Mercantilist policies of England could not allow the colonists to pursue their own economic interests in manufacturing and other trades. Only political independence and the protection of individual rights would allow for the economic prosperity that many in the American Revolution envisioned.

3. **D**. The exporting of manufactured goods could potentially bring more hard currency (generally gold and silver) into a nation's economy.

The point of mercantilism is to increase the hard currency available to your nation, because economic power is the measure of the power of the whole nation. All of the other choices promote the flow of hard currency to the home country.

4. **C.** The French military did not revolt en masse during the revolution. Some units did join the revolution later or fight as loyalists for their officers.

5. **B.** Opium provided the positive balance of trade in China that Britain and the other imperialist powers sought. Britain, with access to the largest supply of opium in the world growing in northern India and Afghanistan benefited the most from the trade.

6. **C.** The table indicates that China would be paying out large amounts of silver unless it is able to increase its production of other goods or find new products. Unfortunately, a nation beset by drug addiction and the criminal activity that goes with it is unlikely to undertake new and productive economic reforms.

7. **A.** The growing moral argument against slavery allowed the British Parliament to take military action to stop the export of slaves from Africa. Also, the industrial economic model in Britain did not require slavery, so there were no economic reasons not to actively pursue its end.

8. **D.** Japan. China failed and Russia did not make the social adjustments to promote an industrial middle class. India was not free to act on its own; it was under British rule.

9. **B.** The availability of work outside of the home offered some limited economic freedom for working-class women, although reality saw them get half the pay as men, and society still favored married women to be at home, not working.

10. **B.** The Ottomans attempted several reforms, but internal opposition consistently resulted in little real or permanent change to the system until it was too late (World War I).

Free-Response Examples
Continuity and Change Over Time

Directions: You are to answer the following question. You should spend 5 minutes organizing or outlining your essay. Write an essay that:

- Has a relevant thesis and supports that thesis with appropriate historical evidence.
- Addresses all parts of the question.
- Uses world historical context to show continuities and changes over time.
- Analyzes the process of continuity and change over time.

Explain the economic and social changes in one of the following areas between 1750 and 1914.

- Western Europe
- Latin America
- Africa

Comparative Essay

Directions: You are to answer the following question. You should spend 5 minutes organizing or outlining your essay. Write an essay that:

- Has a relevant thesis and supports that thesis with appropriate historical evidence.
- Addresses all parts of the question.
- Makes direct, relevant comparisons.
- Analyzes relevant reasons for similarities and differences.

Compare the Japanese and Chinese response to European imperialism in the nineteenth century.

Content Review Part 5: Accelerating

1914 to the Present

The First World War

The June 28, 1914, assassination of Archduke Franz Ferdinand, heir to the Austrian-Hungarian throne, by a Serbian nationalist released a torrent of forces in Europe and around the world. Since the mid-nineteenth century, the growing pace of imperialism pushed the major powers of Europe closer to war by fostering the creation of military alliances between nations. By 1914, the demand for control of more markets and resources, shifting political alliances, growing nationalist sentiments, and an unsustainable arms buildup all signaled a great powers showdown. The assassination provided a ready excuse to "let slip the dogs of war" (*Julius Caesar*, by William Shakespeare).

CAUSES OF THE FIRST WORLD WAR

IMPERIALISM	Nations were seeking greater control over resources for industrialization and manufacturing as well as markets for manufactured goods
	The scramble for Africa in the late nineteenth century completed the colonization of most of the world

IMPERIALISM (CONT.)	Germany's aggressive stance toward expanding its influence in North Africa led to two crises in the decade before 1914 and pushed the French and British governments toward greater cooperation
	The decline of the Ottoman Empire had both Austria-Hungary and Russia interested in acquiring its territory as the Ottoman borders shrank
	Japan, as a new imperialist power in East Asia, had already defeated Russia in 1905 and sought a greater sphere of influence in China and in the Pacific
	Britain and France, the two largest colonial powers, were forced to spend more of their national budgets to secure their far-flung lands
ALLIANCES	Military alliances, once designed to maintain a balance of power in Europe, became more a tool of potential intimidation and actually encouraged potential conflict
	The British, French, and Russians established the Triple Entente as a counter to the Triple Alliance of Germany, Austria-Hungary, and Italy, which had formed to protect each from the potential threat of either Great Britain, France, or Russia
	The Triple Alliance treaty called for secrecy, voiding the deterrent that a defensive alliance should produce
	Both alliances discussed potential gains should a war break out in Europe
NATIONALISM	The people of the Great Powers and those ethnic groups in Europe who found themselves part of an empire belonging to another people all experienced a growing sense of nationalism
	Public opinion in the Great Powers, fed by newspaper stories designed to generate greater readership, pushed for more aggressive measures against other powers in Europe
	Ethnic groups, especially those in the Ottoman Empire and the Austrian-Hungarian Empire, all called for greater autonomy or outright independence

NATIONALISM (CONT.)	The Great Powers used ethnic nationalism for their own advantage, especially Russia and Austria-Hungary in the Balkans
	The minority ethnic groups knew they could manipulate the larger powers by offering alliances
ARMS RACE	National budgets in each European power strained to keep pace with new military technology and the military buildup of other European nations
	The naval buildup of Germany forced the British navy to launch new construction programs as well
	New weapons like the machine gun required new expenditures for equipment and new training programs
	The threat of war forced greater mobilizations of men, costing more in equipment and training
	All of the nations were struggling to keep pace with the rising costs, each fearing it would be defeated if it could not

Ultimately, the assassination of the Austrian-Hungarian heir provided the excuse everyone needed for war. Austria blamed the Serbian government for the attack and issued a series of demands called the July Ultimatum. These demands were very harsh, and Serbia only agreed to eight out of ten. Austria used the Serbian failure as an excuse to declare war. This caused the Russians to declare war on Austria, in order to aid Serbia, and the Germans to join their ally Austria. France joined Russia, and Germany responded by invading Belgium as an easier way into France. Great Britain, claiming that it could not tolerate the violation of Belgium's neutrality and fearing a powerful Germany, came to the aid of France. The Ottomans joined Germany, and Italy chose to side with France and Great Britain in order to gain Austrian territory. All parties initially expected a quick war, and young men flocked to enlist as not to miss the excitement.

In the Trenches

The German invasion of France was designed to strike a quick and fatal blow to the Allies. With all of the resources of the German army advancing on Paris, the city could not hope to stand. A quick defeat would convince the Allies (Britain, France, and Russia; later Italy would join as well) to agree to peace terms, and it would win Germany and Austria-Hungary (the Central Powers, along with Bulgaria and the Ottoman Empire) concessions in Europe and abroad. The Germans, however, failed to throw the full weight of their army at Paris, because they were fighting a two-front war with France and Russia, and the French army was able to resist the German advance. British, French, and German troops now dug in along what was to be called the western front. Tens of thousands died as the stalemate solidified along hundreds of miles of trenches. Over the next four years, millions of soldiers joined the ranks of casualties as neither side could force the other to give ground. New weapons like machine guns, tanks, and mass-produced artillery and mortars rendered old tactics obsolete and killed men faster than in any war before.

All of the Great Powers in Europe mobilized for total war; they were prepared to throw the full resources of the economies and manpower into defeating their opponents. Membership in the armed forces reached numbers never seen before. To replace the lost workers in factories, women, especially married women, joined assembly lines to produce weapons and ammunition. This patriotism would earn them the vote in many nations. Families accepted rationing of strategic materials, and governments took over greater control of the economies.

The war took on a global scale from the start. Great Britain, France, and Germany all possessed overseas empires. Fighting broke out in Africa, especially in the east between Belgian, British, and German colonial troops. Members of the Commonwealth—South Africa, Canada, New Zealand, and Australia—all sent men to Europe. Colonial troops from Africa and India also traveled to Europe to fight. In Asia, Japan joined its ally Great Britain and attacked German interests in China and seized German islands in the Pacific. It also conducted naval operations against German ships in the Pacific and South China Sea. Arabs fought for the British, who promised them independence, against the Turks in the Middle East to protect the Suez Canal.

In an effort to cut the Allies off from their colonial resources and manpower, the Central Powers, behind the naval might of Germany, attempted to block the sea lanes to Great Britain and France. The German surface navy hesitated to engage the larger British navy, but German submarines scored many successes against merchant shipping headed for Britain. Submarine attacks, however, created collateral damage for the Germans. Many of these ships were coming from the United States, which had declared its neutrality in 1914. As a neutral country, the United States could trade with both sides, but the British blockade of Germany cut U.S. shipments there by 99 percent. The sinking of the passenger ship *Lusitania* by a submarine turned American public opinion strongly against Germany. The turn of public opinion was further facilitated by the Zimmerman Telegraph, which revealed German attempts to bring Mexico into a war with the United States and resulted in a declaration of war on Germany in April 1917.

Tons of material and more than a million American soldiers joined the fighting on the western front. A last German offensive—fueled by troops taken off of the eastern front, where Russia had signed a separate peace after a revolution in early 1917—failed as American soldiers reinforced the lines. The failed attack left the German army weak, and the Allies finally broke through. As they advanced towards Germany, the Central Powers signed an armistice to end the fighting. After four years and almost 40 million casualties (nine million dead), the fighting ended.

The staggering losses of the war allowed many in the colonies to question Western civilization and the benefits it could bring. Never in memory had so many died. India and the African colonies that provided many troops for the war started to think in terms of rewards for their service. They were losing hundreds of men in a fight that only served to make their masters stronger. Some began campaigns to obstruct recruitment, but the colonial governments took this very seriously and cracked down on the leaders. Other leaders in India and Africa cooperated, but they talked of rewards once the war was over.

Versailles: The Spoils of War

The Allies held the negotiations for the final treaty to end the war near Paris at the Palace of Versailles. President Woodrow Wilson, armed with a fourteen-point peace plan, wanted to change the face of war, making the Great War (as it was then called) the last war between the European powers. However, the other allies had different ideas. The British and the French dismantled the Austrian-Hungarian and Ottoman Empires as punishment for waging war against the Allied Powers. They also took large areas of Germany, recreating the nation of Poland and returning lands to France. Germany's overseas empire was distributed among the victors, with Japan gaining islands in the Pacific and areas of German influence in China. Britain and France took the German colonies in Africa. President Wilson's Fourteen Points were only implemented through the creation of a League of Nations to resolve international disputes. However, the failure of the U.S. to join this organization severely limited its ability to bring any dispute to a resolution.

In addition, Germany was forced to pay massive reparations for the war (finally paid in full on October 3, 2010). These reparations devastated the German economy, preventing the new democratic government from formulating any workable recovery plan for the nation. While the United States ultimately refused to ratify the treaty, Great Britain and France readily did so and planned for a new Europe without a strong Germany. Their victory, however, did not immediately fix their own economic problems.

- Both Britain and France had lost a generation of young men (Britain almost a million, France well over that)
- Large numbers of soldiers returning home were unemployed
- America's industry took a leading role in international trade

- Anticolonial parties used the war as a new means of attacking colonial rule

  ○ Specifically, the negotiators at Versailles refused to include a clause in the League of Nations covenant that recognized all races as equal

  ○ The Japanese had pushed for this, but it was opposed by Australia, and President Wilson (who opposed it due to Southern congressional opposition) refused to include it without a unanimous vote (that vote failed)

  ○ Japanese nationalists would use this to argue against future cooperation with the West

History shows that the treaty ultimately created several causes of the Second World War: destabilization of Germany, the Italians' anger at the perceived failure of their government to "win" the war by gaining more from the Treaty of Versailles, and America's rejection of the treaty and refusal to join the League of Nations.

The Russian Revolution

Well in advance of the First World War, Russia's political, economic, and social systems were all subject to increasing internal pressures to change. In 1861, the czar officially emancipated the serfs of Russia, symbolizing the attempt of the government to move Russia into the modern world. However, little actually improved for the peasant in the countryside who both owed their former landlords for the lands they now farmed and lacked the earning power to purchase enough land to make them economically independent.

In the cities, the rush toward industrialization recreated the social upheavals seen earlier in other European states, like prerevolutionary France. Rapid industrialization created a working poor subject to rising prices and economic cycles that created booms that attracted more workers and then recessions, leaving many unemployed and starving. In 1905, after the humiliating defeat of Russia at the hands of the Japanese, riots turned to revolution. Although the czar survived this first revolt, he was forced to make some changes, including consenting to allow a limited parliament, the Duma. However, the changes failed to give any real power to those outside the royal family or nobility.

When World War I began, Russia saw an opportunity to use the war to quell internal dissent because patriotism and a quick victory would silence opposition to the government and improve the economic situation. But a quick victory did not come. Wishing to lead the massive Russian army himself, Nicholas II moved to the front with the forces and left his wife to run the government. The large number of troops lacked adequate equipment, and Russian industry failed to keep pace with wartime demands. Also, conscription and the need for labor in the factories led to a reduction in agricultural output. By 1917, the Russian people could no longer stand the war or the government.

THE RUSSIAN REVOLUTION

CAUSES	Failure of the working class to achieve economic stability
	Limited rights of the people to participate in government
	Consistent agricultural failures
	Denying peasants the ability to purchase enough land for their own economic survival
	Defeat during the Russo-Japanese War
	Failure of the czar to maintain the political gains promised after the 1905 Revolution, especially the promises made to the middle class and landowners, giving them some legislative powers
	Tremendous losses on the eastern front against Germany in World War I
EFFECTS	Withdrawal of Russia from the war
	Loss of larger amounts of territory in eastern Europe to Germany as part of the peace treaty between the two powers
	Rise of the Bolsheviks as the more moderate revolutionaries fail
	Elimination of the royal family and removal of the nobles
	Collectivized agriculture; although this proved unworkable
	Civil war (Reds vs. Whites) and foreign intervention from 1917 to 1922

EFFECTS (CONT.)	Bolshevik Revolution creates a totalitarian state based on communist-socialist principles

The First Postwar World

Gender

World War I saw a mobilization of global manpower unequaled in history. On the home fronts in Britain, France, Germany, Russia, and the United States, women took on the jobs vacated by men who were called to serve. Many of these were in war-related industries like munitions that had not previously employed women. Other jobs included expanded clerical positions in government. Some even faced the horrors of war by nursing the troops near the front lines. Prior to the war, women tended to leave the workforce when they married.

Not only did the war interrupt women at home, it also interrupted the suffrage movements in various Western nations. As a whole, most of the suffragettes lent their support to the war efforts. Some even campaigned for government war bonds and recruitment. However, a few protested the war effort as part of a larger peace movement. With the end of the war, the suffragettes returned to their political cause and won the vote in most Western countries by 1920. There was not an immediate rush of women into politics (actually, the first American women in Congress entered in 1916, four years before the Nineteenth Amendment enfranchised women across the nation), but political parties in the West were forced to quickly find potential women candidates and take stances on women's issues, including prohibition, better public education, and health care.

A New Scientific Revolution

In the early twentieth century several major scientific breakthroughs fundamentally changed the understanding of the universe. Albert Einstein introduced the general and special theories of relativity. These theories improved the understanding of gravity well beyond that originally explained by Sir Isaac Newton. Additional work by Einstein and others also paved the way for the harnessing of atomic energy both for power and destruction. Other physicists developed models of the universe based on the new understanding of gravity. Galaxies were proven to exist, and the idea of an expanding universe was first postulated, eventually becoming the big bang theory.

Medicine built on the important discoveries of the nineteenth century as researchers looked for efficient ways to kill bacteria that were now known to cause many illnesses. Scottish scientist Alexander Fleming made the most important discovery when he produced the first antibiotic: penicillin. Other researchers pushed for more work on vaccines, especially against smallpox and polio (an effective vaccination program would eliminate smallpox in nature by 1979, and polio may disappear by 2015). By the late twentieth century, many of the biggest bacterial killers in history were being managed by concerted efforts of government, international organizations, and medical researchers. This contributed to reduced infant mortality, increased life expectancy, and global population increase. However, even with this advanced medical knowledge, new challenges arose.

The integration of global markets continues to present challenges to the medical profession. Like the spread of the plague, the movement of people after the First World War created a pandemic as it spread an influenza virus around the world. The so-called Spanish flu is estimated to have killed more than the previous four years of war. Several other flu pandemics occurred, although none was as devastating as the 1919 pandemic. Greater integration also contributed to the spread of a new viral disease, HIV/AIDS, out of Africa into the global population in the 1970s. Early in the twenty-first century, SARS moved out of a remote region of China onto several other continents, forcing quarantines in places as diverse as Ulan Bator, Mongolia, and Toronto, Canada. Transportation technology and economic integration provides, as always, a continued challenge to medical professionals and settled societies.

The Colonies

During the war, tens of thousands of colonial troops fought along the western front. Workers in the colonies provided raw materials for the war effort, and in India there was a push to increase local manufacturing capacity so Great Britain could focus on wartime production. As the soldiers returned home and the home countries adjusted their economies to peacetime production, little money was left for the needs of the colonies. Many conquered people saw this weakness as on opportunity to seek greater independence.

Prior to the war, a number of Indians, under the banner of the Indian National Congress Party, sought a greater degree of economic and political freedoms within the British Empire. In 1920, Mohandas Gandhi, a British-trained lawyer, joined the Indian National Congress and reorganized it, expanding membership from a small, elite group of Western-educated Indians to a mass movement desiring complete Indian independence. Gandhi had previously fought the colonial administration in South Africa to protect Indian rights. While in jail, he read Henry David Thoreau's *Civil Disobedience*. Gandhi incorporated these ideas of nonviolent protest into the Indian National Congress's strategy for opposing British colonial administration and his own later movement to teach Indians to lead a simple life and reject manufactured goods and other Western influences. The rejection of manufactured and other Western goods particularly hurt the British administration in India and gave Gandhi's nonviolent movement a powerful weapon for change.

In many of the other colonies, similar opposition to European rule was on the rise. A small core of Western-educated colonials often protested for independence based on Western ideas about democracy and freedom. Others pushed more radical Western ideas about socialism and revolution. For the most part, these movements met with little immediate success. The majority of colonial subjects trusted more traditional ideas and leaders. They, too, failed to expel their European colonial masters.

The Neo-Colonialist

Starting in the late nineteenth century, the United States found itself outproducing its market demands. Factories were turning out goods in excess of the demands of domestic and foreign markets. Without an extensive empire, the United States began to actively look for available markets where their products might find a new demand or replace European goods. Latin America, close and independent, proved the most attractive region.

By the end of World War I, the United States had replaced the British as the primary foreign investor in the region. Latin America provided a host of valuable mineral resources like copper and harvested materials like rubber needed for industry. In return, the nations imported many manufactured goods that their economies did not produce. The United States became financially and militarily linked to the region. By 1929, 40 percent of all international investment from the United States went to Latin America. Also, American troops intervened in no less than seven Latin American countries, some multiple times, during the first three decades of the twentieth century. These interventions were part of Theodore Roosevelt's Big Stick Doctrine, which argued that the U.S. had the right to use the military to enforce foreign policy.

Great Britain and the other European nations continued to invest in the region, and many Europeans immigrated to South America, especially Argentina, joining previous generations of Germans and others already there. The income from this investment continued to favor a small elite in most of the Latin American states, although liberal groups did gain some ground. Movements like positivism promoted scientific and technological learning and attacked the power of the Roman Catholic Church. However, the same movements also allowed small elites to restrict democratic reforms in the name of economic and social progress.

An American Decade

At the peace negotiations at Versailles, American president Woodrow Wilson brought his 14 Points to the negotiation table and promoted the idea of collective security through the League of Nations and greater international integration. However, the U.S. Senate rejected the entanglements that collective security seemed to require. But American businesses did not miss the opportunity offered by the opened markets. This greater economic involvement of the United States included American banks who financed recovery efforts in Europe and helped the German economy recover from the hyperinflation of the early 1920s that made its currency worthless.

Along with American money came music and arts. The motion picture industry in the United States became a global leader. American jazz and early big band music flourished in Europe's capitals and, with the help of radio (public radio stations began appearing globally in 1919), across the globe. Even with public sentiment in the United States following traditional isolationist tendencies, America became a key player in the international community.

By the late 1920s, America's manufacturing economy—driven by new products like the affordable automobile and home appliances and global demand—produced large profits for investors. These profits attracted more people and institutional investors like small banks into the stock market. By 1929, America's prosperity bolstered the international economy. America also successfully negotiated the Kellogg-Briand Pact with the other great powers of the world. This Pact argued against aggressive war as a mechanism of foreign policy, seemingly ushering in an era of international cooperation and peace. By outlawing war as an "instrument of national policy," except as self-defense, the Kellogg-Briand Pact allowed America to avoid entangling alliances while promoting peace (since the pact did not require nations to take any actions either through political or economic sanctions or force against those nations who broke the agreement).

The League of Nations would officially register the treaty on September 4, 1929, just as stock market prices began a decline that would lead to the stock market crash and the beginning of the Great Depression. Within a year, the global economy looked devastated beyond repair, and political events moved the great nations of the world toward another global conflict, although many chose not to look toward where their actions pointed.

The Great Depression

The stock market collapse in the United States had immediate repercussions in Europe. The American capital invested in Great Britain, France, and Germany vanished. Without this source of financing, economies in Europe went into recession. In response to the collapse, the United States instituted protectionist policies, including substantially raising tariff rates. This, combined with a drought in the Great Plains, drove America into an economic depression as people lost jobs and stopped spending. The response from overseas only increased the economic woes. Other nations joined America by passing protectionist tariffs. Politically, these were popular, but they only decreased demand for products, leading to increased unemployment and reduced spending. There were real political consequences as well due to the economic and social changes.

A GLOBAL DEPRESSION: THE 1930S

NATION	POLITICAL AND SOCIAL CONSEQUENCES
Great Britain	Labour Party wins elections
	Protectionist tariffs
	Democracy, although attacked by some groups, remains relatively strong, but leadership is considered weak
	Previous recessions had already reduced military spending; this is further cut
	Government efforts for the working poor fall far short of needs, especially in housing
France	Democracy remains the governing principle, but successive weak governments fail to respond well to the crisis
	The loss of American capital means that Germany cannot make reparation payments needed by the French to fuel their economy

NATION	POLITICAL AND SOCIAL CONSEQUENCES
France (cont.)	Industrialization and agriculture remained small scale and less efficient than France's neighbors
	Workers were pushed to accept lower wages in order to remain employed, but this cuts demand for goods and idles production lines
	Domestic issues override military and foreign concerns
Germany	American loans in the 1920s had stabilized the German mark, but the withdrawal of this capital damaged the German recovery
	Tariffs reduced the demand for German industry and rapidly increased the unemployment rate
	The democratic government, already blamed for the poor results at Versailles and the economic disasters of the early 1920s, lost legitimacy with the people
	The National Socialist Party (Nazi Party) gained electoral victory by convincing the middle class of the danger of communist revolts from the workers
	The leader of the Nazis, Adolf Hitler, concentrated all political power in himself and became dictator, which was supported by many Germans who had no long-standing belief or trust in democratic government
Union of Soviet Socialist Republics	Ostracized after making peace with the Germans in 1917, the Soviet Union did not feel as many negative effects from the Depression as Western capitalist economies
	Joseph Stalin, the leader of the USSR, used the Depression as an opportunity to expand his influence in eastern Europe
	Stalin also purged all people in the Soviet system he felt might betray him
	The large number of executions and murders went largely unnoticed in the West, because it was occupied with the Great Depression
	Nazi Germany partnered with the USSR in redeveloping their military, which had been heavily restricted under the Treaty of Versailles

NATION	POLITICAL AND SOCIAL CONSEQUENCES
Italy	Having failed to recover from the war economy in the 1920s, Italy was already under a fascist dictatorship when the Great Depression broke out
	Benito Mussolini used the fear of a worker or communist revolt to gain support from the middle class to win some seats in government; from there he monopolized power and ruled as a dictator
	Fascist government controlled the economy and replaced all unions, civic organizations, and youth groups with government-run institutions, making active opposition against Mussolini very difficult
	Mussolini took advantage of the situation to expand Italian power in North Africa
	He invaded Ethiopia in 1935 and offered military support to General Francisco Franco in Spain
	By the late 1930s, Italy had allied itself with the more industrialized Germany
Japan	Production fell by 50 percent and a bad harvest caused widespread hunger
	Artificial fabrics hurt the silk industry
	Radical elements in the military pushed for expansion to control markets and vital raw materials
	Government leaders, including a prime minister, were assassinated by low-ranking, nationalistic military officers
	The government slowly became dominated by the military and began a policy of expansion
	The army took Manchuria in 1931 and invaded China in 1937
India	Reduction in the demand for cash crops hurt India's rural communities
	British officials forced the continued production of cash crops in order to secure tax revenues
	The poor could find no markets for their crops and could not pay the taxes

NATION	POLITICAL AND SOCIAL CONSEQUENCES
India (cont.)	Colonial restrictions on local industries also meant that tools for farming and other businesses were made in Europe but could not be purchased by the cash-poor Indians
	As prosperity rapidly declined, the movement for independence led by Gandhi and the Indian National Congress gained strength
	Both Gandhi and the congress came under increased pressure by the British officials to stop their campaigning
African Colonies	As in India, local cash crop production produced no revenues, but continued cultivation was demanded by colonial officials
	Harvests of coffee, tea, and rubber could not feed the population or produce the needed income to pay colonial taxes and buy foreign-produced necessities, like metal agricultural tools
	Local independence leaders like Kenya's Jomo Kenyatta pushed for independence but won few concessions
Latin American Nations	The export sector of the Latin American economies drove almost all other economic and political activity
	A small group of elites made their wealth through mining and cash-crop plantations
	Industrial decline reduced demand for raw materials, the main business of South America
	Demand for cash crops like coffee fell along with the economies in Brazil and Colombia
	Elites in some nations, facing high unemployment rates among the masses of poor, used military force to maintain order
	Elsewhere, the elites and small middle class embraced some of the ideas of fascism to remain in power
	In Central America, the United States continued to dominate politics and carried out several military interventions in Haiti and Nicaragua, although these were now fewer as military budgets were shrinking

NATION	POLITICAL AND SOCIAL CONSEQUENCES
United States	Its economic collapse brought down much of the rest of the global economic system
	Initially, protectionist policies made the economic situation worse
	Drought in the Midwest greatly expanded the economic hardships across the country
	Franklin D. Roosevelt won the 1932 presidential election and promised significant changes in the government's economic policy; these changes are grouped under the heading of the New Deal
	The withdrawal of significant U.S. funds from overseas investment hurt the cause of democracy in Germany and Latin America

By the mid-1930s, the world envisioned by Woodrow Wilson and others at Versailles in 1919 and by Aristide Briand a decade later seemed lost. Almost all of the newly created democracies in Europe failed, with Czechoslovakia being the lone exception. Global economic integration and the tenets of collective security were forgotten as each nation looked toward its own interest. The lessons of destruction of the Great War were already forgotten by many who had fought and now seemed determined to fight it again.

The Road to War
China

The last Chinese dynasty, the Qing, collapsed in 1912. Attempts to replace it with a republic led by Sun Yat-sen or another dynasty both failed. Large areas of China remained under the spheres of influence of the European powers even after the imperial collapse. During the First World War, the recognized governments of China joined the Allies, and Japan invaded and took possession of the German sphere in China. After the war, many Chinese, especially those with a Western education, were looking for the negotiations for peace to bring about an independent

Chinese nation that was free of European spheres of influence. They were disappointed.

The treaty not only continued the spheres of interest, but it also awarded the Japanese the former German area. The treaty also failed to provide the international support the Republic of China needed to secure the whole nation. On May 4, 1919, Chinese intellectuals and students led a protest march against the terms of the treaty. The movement failed to make an immediate political impact on the situation in China but started a nationalistic movement and an active populist political base.

WARLORD CHINA: POLITICAL CENTERS IN CHINA IN THE 1920S

WARLORDS	Numerous local "generals" used military force to dominate regions of China
	Weapons came from numerous sources, as tons of military equipment was available for sale after the war
	Foreign powers and investors made arrangements with the warlords to secure markets and sources of luxury products
	Although some warlords attempted to unify larger regions into a recognized state, they could not compete with the military organization and urban and international support given to the Kuomintang
KUOMINTANG (KMT)	Formed by Sun Yat-sen in 1912 as the Qing dynasty came to an end
	Goal was to establish a Western-style republic, with Sun Yat-sen as president
	Initially failed as Qing General Yuan Shikai took over China and outlawed the party
	After World War I and the death of General Yuan Shikai, the KMT rose to prominence due to external support
	The Soviet Union allied itself with the KMT as the most likely successor to power in China
	When Sun died, his brother-in-law, Chiang Kai-shek, the military leader of the KMT, took over

KUOMINTANG (KMT) (CONT.)	Although it was once allied with the Chinese Communist Party (in 1927), the KMT tricked the communist leadership and executed most of them, beginning a civil war that would last until the eventual communist victory on the mainland in 1949
	In 1949, Chiang Kai-shek moved the KMT to Taiwan and maintained the name Republic of China
CHINESE COMMUNIST PARTY (CCP)	Founded by leaders of the May Fourth (1919) protest movement
	Initially tried to organize among the small number of urban industrial workers
	The Soviet Union encouraged the leadership to join the KMT, because the Soviets did not believe China was ready for a true communist revolution
	Broke with the KMT and was almost eliminated in 1927 when in negotiation to realign with the government
	New leadership, especially Mao Tse-tung, recruited the rural peasantry into the party
	During the civil war it slowly built up a loyal following in the northern countryside
	A truce with the KMT allowed both to resist the Japanese invasion in 1937
	At the end of World War II, the civil war resumed, and the CCP quickly gained control of the countryside
	The KMT left in 1949 with American assistance

The chaos in China encouraged the Japanese to view it as an area for expansion. In 1931, the Japanese invaded Manchuria and created the puppet state of Manchukuo. The Japanese launched a full-scale invasion of China from Manchukuo in 1937. Eventually the United States threatened Japan's supply of oil and scrap metal if they did not withdraw from China. This was Japan's pretext for the attack on Pearl Harbor.

Italy and Spain

As the world's powers were ignoring the opening moves of Japan in Asia and the rearmament of Germany by the Nazis, Mussolini's Italians sought to expand their small empire and restore some of the old glory of Rome by invading Ethiopia. While meeting strong initial resistance, the modern Italian military conquered the poorly equipped Ethiopians. More significant than the military victory was the complete failure of the League of Nations to respond to the Ethiopian request for help. The idea of collective security had clearly failed.

In 1936, the republican government of Spain faced a revolt by military forces concerned over recent liberal success in national elections. With the help of German and Italian support, the military moved against the government but met greater resistance than expected. This success encouraged more radical liberal elements—socialists and communists—to try to expand their power in government. They gained the support of the Soviet Union. In many ways, the Spanish Civil War (1936–1939) served as a rehearsal for the Second World War as it pitted fascism against republican and communist forces and tested out the new weapons available to Germany. It also connected art with political expression as Picasso, already one of the foremost artists of his time and a Spaniard, used the fascist bombing of the town of Guernica as the theme of one of his most important paintings. The painting went on display at the 1937 World's Fair in Paris.

Nazi Germany

The Great Depression offered the Nazi Party an opportunity to rise to power in Germany. Growing unemployment and the lack of any influx of capital increased the popularity of more leftist parties: the socialist and communist. Middle-class Germans feared the potential of a communist revolution and had no faith in the ability of the democratic government to manage the situation. Hitler's fascist party provided a nationalist focus, a scapegoat for the economic problems of Germany (the Jews), and a force to intimidate the workers' movements. In 1932, the Nazi Party won the most seats in the German parliament (but not a majority) by running against left-wing socialist and communist groups. Hitler was appointed chancellor in 1933. From here, he quickly seized complete control of the government.

Initially, Hitler focused on consolidating power by funding public works like the autobahn (a national highway) and encouraging violence against opposition groups and Jews. He also made a number of moves that violated the terms of the Treaty of Versailles. He reoccupied territory that was to remain neutral, built up the armed forces beyond the treaty limits, contracted with the Soviet Union to test new weapons and strategies, and united Germany with Austria. When the international community failed to act against any of these moves, Hitler continued with his expansion of German territory by annexing Czechoslovakian territory, which he argued was a natural extension of Germany because it had a large German population. Great Britain threatened intervention, but in meeting with Hitler and Mussolini in Germany, British prime minister Neville Chamberlain gave in to Hitler's demands in a political move called appeasement. Within a year, the rest of Czechoslovakia was annexed by Germany.

By the summer of 1939, Europe appeared on the brink of war. Hitler entered negotiations with Stalin to assure himself that the Soviet Union would not interfere with his plans, which was ironic, considering that part of the Nazi appeal was their tough stand against communism in Germany. With a nonaggression pact between Germany and the USSR signed in August, Hitler moved against Poland on September 1. Great Britain and France, both having guaranteed Poland's independence, responded by declaring war on Germany on September 3, 1939.

World War II

Initially, Germany won a string of victories, capturing most of Poland (the eastern section being given to the Soviet Union as part of the nonaggression pact), Denmark, and Norway through a rapid military advance called blitzkrieg (lightning war). In 1940, Belgium, the Netherlands, and France fell surprisingly quickly, and the British army barely escaped annihilation in northern France. German U-boats (submarines) began unrestricted attacks against all shipping into Great Britain. Germany also began airstrikes against military and civilian targets in Britain. Britain struck back with its own raids against German cities.

Outside of Europe, Italian and German forces fought their way into Egypt, attempting to close Britain's oil supply and supply lines to India. Australia, New Zealand, and Canada sent troops and equipment to aid in Britain's defense. In the United States, sentiment and President Franklin D. Roosevelt favored the British, but not enough to get the United States to declare war. By 1941, the United States negotiated a lend-lease policy that allowed Britain to use American equipment in return for future payments or leases of military bases. However, Britain could not long sustain the war on its own.

Hitler picked this time to turn against Stalin and invade the Soviet Union. This would prove, as it had for Napoleon, his downfall. Initially, the Soviet armies collapsed in front of the advancing Germans. Tens of thousands of Soviet troops were encircled and killed or taken prisoner. But as the Germans neared Moscow, the Soviet winter slowed their advance. Additionally, the vast distances, lack of rail transportation (Soviet rails were a different gauge than the rest of Europe), and scorched-earth policy of the Soviets (they removed or destroyed almost everything of military value) proved too much for the Germans to master in a few short months.

The Soviet invasion took some pressure off of the English, but the submarine attacks were eliminating more ships than the British could replace. Another year could cripple the British homeland. Still, the United States chose not to go to war. American interests were mostly at home or in markets in Latin America. The American possession of the Philippines and close business ties to China made Japan a potential threat. With Europe occupied, Roosevelt took it as America's responsibility to resist Japanese aggression in China, although not with actual combat forces. His ban on further shipments of oil and scrap metal to Japan did, however, get Japan's attention. In response, the Japanese launched a surprise attack on the U.S. naval base at Pearl Harbor, part of a full-scale attack on the United States and the Allies across the Pacific and Southeast Asia. Very quickly, the Allies' ability to strike back was eliminated, as their bases in the Philippines, Malaysia, the Dutch East

Indies (modern Indonesia), Hong Kong, Singapore, and the central Pacific fell to the Japanese.

By May 1942, the Axis powers, as Germany, Italy, and Japan were called, seemed in control of the war.

- The entry of the United States did not immediately change anything on the front lines in Europe.

- The Japanese attacks in the Pacific appeared on the verge of striking directly at Australia and pushing the United States all the way back to the West Coast.

- The Soviet Union appeared like it might collapse, giving Germany access to massive oil reserves in the Caucasus Mountains.

- British supply lines to India were in danger in Egypt, the mid-Atlantic, and from Burma, now under attack by a swift-moving Japanese army.

- Submarine attacks were up during the first months of America's entry into the war.

However, the Axis encountered a series of setbacks.

TURNING POINTS OF WORLD WAR II

THE BATTLE OF MIDWAY	Code breakers identify the location and target—Midway Island—of Japan's next major attack
	The greatly outnumbered American fleet surprise the Japanese fleet and win a stunning victory, sinking four of Japan's aircraft carriers and killing over 400 of the best pilots in Japan
	No longer can the Japanese launch an attack against the United States with a superior number of aircraft carriers
THE BATTLE OF EL ALAMEIN	British forces stop the German Afrika Korps from reaching the Suez Canal in Egypt
	The defeat leaves the Germans with few resources in Africa and they retreat
	Pursued into Libya, the Germans are again defeated and retreat to the small territory of Tunisia; much of the Italian army is captured because they lack transportation to retreat

THE BATTLE OF EL ALAMEIN (CONT.)	Britain may now focus on other theaters of the war as the Middle East oilfields and the link with India is safe
THE BATTLE OF STALINGRAD	Both Hitler and Stalin choose to make this the key battle of the eastern front
	Although Soviet losses are staggering (about 1.1 million killed or wounded), the Soviets encircle the German army
	Over 800,000 Germans are killed or captured as a result of the battle, losses they cannot replace
	The rest of the war in the east will be a slow German retreat to Berlin
INDUSTRIAL PRODUCTION	The key to Allied successes is the productivity of U.S. industry
	The GDP (gross domestic product) of the United States exceeds that of all of the Axis powers combined each year of the war
	From 1942 on, the GDP of the Allies is *at least* twice that of the Axis powers
	The Allies produce over 600,000 military aircraft, more than three times the amount of the Axis
	In 1942, the United States begins to produce merchant vessels at a rate faster than the Germans can sink them (by the end of 1943, German submarines are defeated by improved convoy protection procedures)

Victory

In 1944, the American, British, and Canadian armies staged a massive invasion of France at Normandy. Within a few months, Paris was liberated, and by winter, Allied armies in the west were poised to enter Germany. On the eastern front, massive Soviet formations in excess of a million men pushed the German out of Russia and into the Balkans and Poland.

By April 1945, the Soviets surrounded Berlin, and the American and British armies moved into western Germany. Hitler killed himself to avoid capture, and the remnants of the German government surrendered on May 8, 1945.

In the Pacific, Japan watched as American forces moved closer and closer to Japan. In 1943, bombers from China began attacking Japanese cities. In 1944, the Americans captured Pacific island bases through an island-hopping campaign of military advancement, thus allowing U.S. bombers to fly shorter distances and carry more bombs to drop on Japanese industrial and population centers. The Americans used incendiary bombs that ignited the wooden structures of most Japanese cities and killed thousands of civilian workers, crippling Japanese war production. American submarines also cut off almost all supplies of fuel and metals to the Japanese home islands.

By the spring of 1945, Japan could no longer hope to maintain any of her possessions outside of the main islands, but the government refused to discuss an end to the war. During the war, the Allies had made it clear that they would accept nothing less than an unconditional surrender from the Germans and the Japanese. The Japanese knew this would likely mean the forced abdication of Emperor Hirohito. In July, as preparations began for the invasion of Japan itself, the Allies again demanded the unconditional surrender of the Japanese government. Refusal led to two atomic bombings on the Japanese home islands, one on the city of Hiroshima, the other two days later on Nagasaki. The devastation convinced the emperor to publicly announce Japan's surrender on August 14, 1945.

A New Peace and a New Conflict

After the victory, the Allied powers again sought to design a peace to prevent future conflict. This time, the United States and the Soviet Union held the most influence. The atomic bomb gave the United States the upper hand militarily, but politically, the United States could not put itself into direct conflict with the Soviets; people were tired of war. This resulted in a settlement that restored France and other Western governments, but left much of Eastern Europe under the dominion of the Soviets, whose armies occupied these nations (Albania, Bulgaria, Czechoslovakia, Hungary, Poland, Romania, and Yugoslavia). Germany itself was divided into four occupation zones. The areas under French, British, and American control would become West Germany, the Soviet area would become East Germany. Berlin, in the Soviet sector, was divided into four occupation zones.

This temporary arrangement in Europe lasted until 1991. Winston Churchill labeled the dividing line between Western and Eastern Europe an "iron curtain" separating the free states in the west from the states under Soviet domination and totalitarian governments. As the divide widened, the United States decided to intervene directly when the British government announced it could no longer aid Greece in its fight against a communist insurgency. The United States pledged itself to rebuilding Greece in order to stabilize the government. In 1947, Secretary of State George Marshall offered America's financial assistance to any state needing to rebuild in order to resist communist or other takeovers. Dubbed the Marshall Plan, this effort spent billions of American dollars to rebuild Western Europe, including West Germany.

Similar divisions occurred in Asia, as Korea and Vietnam were both hastily divided between the United States and the Soviet Union. Japan, occupied by the United States, would not see any Soviet occupation zone, but several territories would transfer from Japan to the Soviet Union. Japan also benefited from its own Marshall Plan during the American occupation (this lasted until 1951).

These newly recovered economies joined the United States in resisting Soviet expansion. When the Soviet Union tested its own atomic bomb, the two sides settled into an uneasy peace, labeled by George Orwell a "cold war." Used increasingly by others, the term stuck as a label for the geopolitical reality from 1945 until the end of the Soviet Union in 1991. During this period, very little understanding of politics, economics, and technology may be achieved without addressing the relationship between the world's two superpowers.

The United Nations: The Hope of Peace

At the end of the Second World War, the Allies joined themselves into a new multinational organization designed, like the League of Nations, to provide for global collective security. The United Nations began in much better shape than the previous League of Nations. First, the United States, the world's greatest power, joined the organization; isolationists no longer commanded a dominant political position in the country. Second, the other potential economic and/or military powers, including the Soviet Union, both Germanys, and Japan, joined as well. The charter of the United Nations also created a Security Council with the power to use economic punishment and military force to back up the decisions of the membership.

In addition to the charter, the members of the United Nations adopted the Universal Declaration of Human Rights. The document reflects many of the ideas of the Enlightenment and liberal democratic governments like those in the United States and the United Kingdom. In theory, all of the signatories respect basic principles like life, liberty, equality of race, ethnicity, religion, and freedom of thought. However, many nations violate these basic rights with little recourse available for the United Nations to enforce compliance.

Several areas came under the United Nation's immediate responsibilities. The first was to oversee the trials of war criminals and the implementation of the peace settlements. Second came the necessity of returning territories to their former empires or establishing them as newly independent nations. As the war was a contest of democracy against totalitarian regimes, the return of colonies to their former empires was not in the interest of all of the UN members.

COLONIAL ISSUES

FRENCH INDOCHINA	Modern Vietnam, Laos, and Cambodia
	France demanded the return of the colony; Ho Chi Minh declared Vietnam independent
	A guerrilla war forced the French out

FRENCH INDOCHINA (CONT.)	Divided at the Nineteenth Parallel by UN agreement
	The United States intervened in the region when the communist North supported an insurgency in the South
PALESTINE	Other Middle East mandates became Arab states
	Issue of Palestine involved conflicting Arab and Jewish claims
	The UN created an oddly shaped Israeli nation bordered by a two-part Palestine
	At independence, war broke out between the two
	Israel defeated and occupied parts of Palestine while the rest of the nation remained under Arab control (Egypt, Jordan, Syria)
	As of 2011, the UN continues to monitor the situation without a viable solution
KOREA	Freed from Japan in 1945
	Divided at the 38th Parallel between the United States and the Soviet Union
	The UN ordered elections in 1948, but the Soviets refused
	Both the North and the South formed independent governments
	The North under Kim Il Song invaded the South in 1950
	First UN "war" as the Security Council approved the use of military force against the North (the Soviets boycotted the meeting)
	War eventually involved China as an ally to the North
	Fighting ended near the 38th Parallel in 1953
	War and unification remain unresolved as of 2011
THE PHILIPPINES	U.S. territory conquered by Japan in 1942
	Returned to U.S. control during the war
	Granted full independence in 1947 by the United States
	Democratic but was ruled by a dictatorship during the 1960s and 1970s
	Many in the Philippines migrated to the United States to escape the political unrest and economic conditions

INDIA	Crown jewel of the British Empire
	Had long fought for independence (mostly nonviolent)
	Indian troops fought on many fronts during the war, and Indians supported the British war effort
	Britain wished to maintain control but could not afford the cost and criticism both at home and from its allies
	Granted independence in 1947 but divided into Hindu and Muslim (Pakistan, including East Pakistan—future Bangladesh) nations
	Violence greeted independence
	Gandhi was assassinated by a Hindu in Pakistan
	India remained democratic
	Pakistan has had both democratic governments and military dictatorships
	Several wars have broken out between the two nations
	Both now have nuclear weapons
	Both also saw many of their most educated people move to Britain in search of greater economic opportunity

Western Society

The United States emerged from World War II as a political and military superpower. The Soviet Union joined the United States as a superpower within a few years. However, the Soviets never achieved the economic and social influence of the United States. By 1950, the United States was in an economic boom. Many soldiers returning from the war chose college instead of work as part of the GI Bill. The government funded these degrees, creating a massive surge in the middle class as the soldiers finished their educations and used large savings accounts to purchase homes, cars, and appliances. Manufacturing grew, creating more high-paying jobs and prosperity.

Women, who again had made huge contributions in factories and public works during the war, also pushed for higher education and more independence. While movies and television continued to show them in domestic roles, the introduction of contraceptives allowed them to pursue greater business opportunities and full careers. Slowly, attitudes in the United States and Europe changed to allow and politically protect greater equality for women. By the 1970s, women held many roles in national politics, culminating with the election of Margaret Thatcher as prime minister of the United Kingdom in 1979. Even in other areas of the world where Western cultural influence was not absolute, women were elected to national posts. India and Israel both elected female prime ministers in the 1960s.

Part of this spread of Western ideas was due to technology and popular culture. Television arrived in the United States and Europe just after the war. It allowed an almost immediate transfer of both news and culture across a nation. Imagined by science fiction writer Arthur C. Clarke in the 1940s, communication satellites allowed for the near-instantaneous transmission of voice, images, and data by the late 1960s. Now, news and culture could reach dozens of countries and hundreds of millions of people at a time. The further diffusion of radio, records, and film further contributed to the spread of Western culture. Music by the Beatles and clothing like blue jeans became the height of culture in places as diverse as Tokyo and Moscow.

Along with culture came business. Multinational corporations, although not new, seemed to become the norm. Brand names like Coke and Ford entered every language, even on the other side of the iron curtain. The great wealth of the United States allowed it to invest in almost every area of the globe. Cultures changed habits as American products entered new markets. Europe's multinationals also found markets beyond their old colonial boarders. By the 1970s, Japanese brands—Sony, Toyota, Honda—joined the race to dominate global markets. Koreans joined in the 1990s, and Chinese brands seemed poised to do the same in the early decades of the twenty-first century.

Today, fast-food chains like McDonald's, foods like sushi, and drinks like green tea are global trends. Television shows like *Pop Idol* originated in the United Kingdom, became *American Idol* in the United States, and then found new names and audiences like *Afghan Star* in Afghanistan. Communication and trade have always transferred culture. The advent of radio, television, satellite communication, and the Internet accelerated the process over the last century. With the fall of the Berlin Wall and the Soviet Union behind it, the process now extends into practically all areas of the globe, even into areas like China that attempt to stop or control the flow of information.

The Third World

The Cold War created two camps: the free nations of the West and their allies and the Soviet Union and their communist puppet states. Those nations not brought into the conflict or who fought to remain outside of it found themselves lumped together in a poorly defined third camp: the Third World. Initially, this was a relatively small group of nations. In the 1950s, many Latin American nations found themselves mostly ignored or, due to heavy American investment, part of the United States' camp. Much of Africa remained colonized, as did Southeast Asia and the Pacific. But slowly, political and economic realities changed.

DEFINING THE THIRD WORLD

The original term came from a French economist and used the term *third* in reference to the Third Estate prior to the French Revolution. Like the Third Estate, the Third World lacked political power. The following generally characterizes the nations of the Third World during the Cold War:

- Undeveloped
- Agrarian/rural
- Overpopulated
- Poor
- Technologically backward

For many Third World nations, the description fit. But there were important efforts made by these nations from the 1950s on to influence the superpowers and establish some greater degree of economic development and political independence.

Initially, India and China (communist, but not a great ally of the Soviet Union) called for members of this group to work as a nonaligned voting bloc in the United Nations. They would push their own issues of development, transfer of technology, protection of their resources, and an end to intervention in their affairs. Leaders within the bloc pushed for pan-Arab or pan-African movements to unite those regions under a common political and economic purpose, although this did not produce lasting political change.

By the early 1960s, the nonaligned movement found many more nations willing to work together to balance the influence of the superpowers. For one, there were now more independent nations. In 1945, 51 nations, almost all independent states, started the UN. In 1960, there were 99 member states, and by 1970, 127 (the 192nd member, Montenegro, joined the UN in 2006). The nonaligned bloc could now force the UN General Assembly to criticize the actions of the superpowers, although the Security Council would not take action, because the superpowers could veto any stance against them or their allies. The UN also took on many causes important to developing nations that did not just reflect efforts by the wealthier nations to gain influence. They pushed for greater transfers of technology and aid in return for political acceptance of American or Soviet actions.

KEY ISSUES HINDERING DEVELOPMENT

- Access to capital
- Access to water
- Political stability (especially in nations involved with the superpowers, as they have greater access to military equipment and often find themselves subject to military coups)
- Agricultural technologies; some earlier Western agricultural practices or cash crop production actually caused more harm than good

- Poverty
- Educational access
- Brain drain (educated people could find better work and pay in the United States and Europe)
- Malnutrition
- Disease and access to medical facilities
- Internal conflict; civil wars, especially wars based on ethnicity and religion

Other developing nations took on a more active role, by choice or force, in the relations between the two superpowers.

The Cold War Occasionally Gets Hot

Several times during the Cold War period the expansionist policies of the communist bloc ran head-on into the containment policy (started by President Harry S. Truman) of the United States. The containment policy stated that Communism needed to be stopped from expanding because, if allowed to spread out of its existing territory, it would slowly take over all the surrounding areas. First, in 1949, the Chinese Communist Party finally drove the Nationalist Party (KMT) out of mainland China. The United States connected this takeover of China to the Soviet Union, although Mao Tse-tung had little direct help from Stalin, and China and the Soviets disagreed on many aspects of communism and global political policy.

Mao's victory came because the communists mobilized the peasants, offered them greater opportunities for education, provided them with land, and distributed government resources to their benefit. Within a few years, China's agricultural output was again feeding the population, something not seen since the mid-nineteenth century. However, Mao sought to industrialize China along the lines of the Soviet Union in order to make it a great power. The attempt, called the Great Leap Forward, would depend upon peasant production of the basic items, especially steel, needed for industry. But Mao's faith could not make steel producers of the peasants.

Agricultural production in China collapsed in the late 1950s and millions died. Mao fell from power as more moderate elements of the Chinese leadership took power and tried to renew agriculture and restrict industrialization to modest growth in cities. Mao, not willing to accept his loss of power, turned the peasants and students against the new leadership in what was called the Great Proletarian Cultural Revolution.

The Cultural Revolution destroyed a generation of educated Chinese as it pushed anyone with the taint of intellectualism (basically anyone with an education who questioned any of Mao's decisions or did not seem to support him wholeheartedly) into the countryside and out of official government circles. From 1966 until Mao's death in 1976, China remained closed to most of the outside world and absorbed in this reeducation of its population (although, in 1972, American president Richard M. Nixon reestablished U.S. relations with China in an attempt to end the Vietnam War, which he believed, incorrectly, the Chinese were capable of ordering the Vietnamese to do).

After Mao's death, Deng Xiaoping came to lead China and encouraged greater economic freedoms and contacts with the world. This process began slowly in the 1980s, mostly encouraging peasant farmers to increase food production by allowing them to establish markets in towns and cities. However, with the end of the Cold War, foreign investment, especially from Taiwan, China's long-term enemy, fueled a rapid industrialization throughout the 1990s and into the first decade of the new millennium. The Chinese economy is now second only to the United States, and China still champions itself as a member of the nonaligned bloc, pushing for greater independence of resources and markets, although now it finds itself looking to dominate both resource production and global markets.

In Korea, a more direct Soviet intervention created a hot flash in the Cold War. Kim Il Sung, the Soviet-appointed dictator of the Democratic Republic of Korea (North Korea), launched an invasion of the Republic of Korea (South Korea) that he believed would quickly give him control over the entire Korean Peninsula. However, the United States challenged the invasion with the full backing of the UN. Because the Soviet Union protested the blocking of the People's Republic of China's effort to take Taiwan's seat at the Security Council, it was boycotting the meeting of the Security Council during which a vote was taken on the Korean invasion.) The North Korean army found itself surrounded, and UN forces occupied almost all of North Korea within a few months. At this point, China, fearing a U.S. attack on its soil, intervened, and its army pushed the UN back to the 38th Parallel. For two years, UN forces maintained this stalemate until the North agreed to an armistice; the armistice still remains in place as neither side is willing to negotiate an end to the conflict that started more than 60 years ago.

Cold War tensions moved to Cuba in 1959. A revolution led by Fidel Castro overthrew dictator Fulgencio Batista. Initially, the revolution was seen as potentially democratic and a positive change, as even the United States had stopped supporting its former ally Batista. However, when Castro adopted communism and established a brutal authoritarian government, the United States found itself forced to deal with communism and a potential hot war on its doorstep.

The revolution itself reflected the harsh realities in Cuba. A small elite, like those in many other Latin American nations, dominated an impoverished peasantry. Foreign investment, especially from American banks and corporations, only served to maintain the wealth of the elite and continue the production of cash crops or mineral resources in mines that paid low wages and few taxes. Earlier, in Guatemala, the United States had actively sought the ousting of a democratically elected leader because he threatened to nationalize property belonging to an American corporation: the United Fruit Company (whose board included the director of the CIA, Allen Dulles, and whose legal counsel once included the Secretary of State, John Foster Dulles, Allen's brother). As the Cubans carried out such policies, it became evident that conflict might come.

The United States never invaded Cuba, although it did support a failed invasion by Cuban exiles on the island (termed the Bay of Pigs invasion). The real tension occurred in 1962, when the United States learned that the Soviet Union intended to base nuclear missiles on the island. The resulting Cuban missile crisis pushed the superpowers and the world closer to nuclear war than any other event. As a result, the superpowers initiated a number of discussions, resulting in treaties that reduced the threat of nuclear confrontation.

TWO COLD WAR REVOLUTIONS

CUBA	IRAN (ISLAMIC REVOLUTION)
Dictatorship that favored a small elite and international interest (chiefly American interests)	Dictatorship that favored a small elite and international interest (U.S. and European oil companies)
Core of middle- and working-class rebels	Organized by Shiite religious leaders
Peasant revolution based on some socialist ideology	Religious students formed the basis of the early protest
Charismatic leadership: Fidel Castro and Che Guevara	Lead by the Ayatollah Ruhollah Khomeini, an exiled religious scholar
Guerrilla tactics slowly defeated a well-supplied but ineffectively lead military	Riots, strikes, and rallies by religious and other university students forced the Shah (king) to resign
Instituted socialist policies but not democratic reform	Military abandoned the government due to the public protest
Established an authoritarian dictatorship	New government instituted democratic structures but the power lay in the hands of religious leaders
Depended on the Soviet Union for economic assistance; U.S. embargo of sugar and other products hurt any economic development	Khomeini passed laws to remove all traces of Western culture and development
	Depends on oil revenues to maintain power as the economy has collapsed, generating high unemployment

By far the largest conflict during the Cold War was the U.S. involvement in Vietnam. Like Korea, Vietnam was divided by UN instructions as the two superpowers negotiated a future for the nation. The communist North supported revolution in the South and supplied insurgents with weapons and other equipment. The United States, following the policy of containment, supported the South militarily without attempting to destroy or conquer the North, fearing a more direct confrontation with the Soviet Union. The resulting stalemate cost the United States billions of dollars and created active opposition among the American public against the war. Much of the opposition came as people watched the war on television each night on national news broadcasts. The unpopularity of the conflict pushed the American government to negotiate a peace with North Vietnam that resulted in an American pullout from the region and the eventual conquest of the South by the North in 1975.

Although militarily the United States remained powerful and devoted to the concept of containing communism, politically, Americans showed themselves to be unwilling to accept the status quo when it came to the Cold War. The Soviets were still seen as a threat, but the use of American troops in combat anywhere around the globe for the sake of containing communism now generated debate and laws that limited the freedom of the American president to take action on his own.

One final chapter in the Cold War was the Soviet invasion of Afghanistan. In 1979, the Soviet military moved into Afghanistan to prop up a communist government in the poor Central Asian nation. The decade-long occupation drained the treasury of an already suffering Soviet economy. Unable to afford to occupy the entire country, and without the training needed to successfully combat an insurgency, the Soviet army suffered greatly at the hands of Afghan freedom fighters (*mujahideen*). Supplied secretly by the United States with weapons, the mujahideen kept the Soviets from declaring victory in Afghanistan and forced them into an embarrassing retreat in 1986.

The End of the Cold War and a New Era

The 1980s were not good to the Soviet Union. World oil prices—high because of an Arab-sponsored OPEC (Organization of Petroleum Exporting

Countries) embargo in the 1970s—were starting to come down. Oil was one of the few resources the Soviets produced in quantities sufficient for export. The annual wheat harvest in the Soviet Union fell dramatically as mechanization and modern agricultural techniques were not adopted to keep pace with a growing population and soil degradation. This forced the Soviets to purchase wheat from the United States and other Western sources, spending the little hard currency they had available. Technologically, the space race, once the pride of the Soviet scientific establishment, no longer generated headlines. Computers and other advanced electronics now dominated innovation, and the Soviets were not only behind the Americans, they were behind the Japanese and Western Europe as well. The election of Margaret Thatcher in the United Kingdom and Ronald Reagan in the United States also put new pressures on the Soviets while reenergizing the free-market system both nations helped found.

Not willing to live with the status quo, Reagan and Thatcher began a military buildup and global political campaign against the Soviets. Economically, the people of the Soviet Union were demanding more consumer products, better quality and variety, and more of the benefits due to them as citizens of a worker's paradise as the communists had promised. The drain of the Afghan War and the great expense of the military buildup needed to keep pace with the United States made this impossible. When Mikhail Gorbachev came to power in the Soviet Union in 1985, he attempted to reform the system so it could meet the demands of its citizens and maintain its power against the United States. But the Soviet Union was too far gone.

In 1986, a nuclear disaster at the Chernobyl nuclear power plant in Ukraine caused the release of radiation 100 times greater than the Hiroshima and Nagasaki bombs combined. The disaster showed not only the technological decay of the Soviets, but it also demonstrated the political ineptitude of the bureaucracy. Initial deaths were compounded as the government concerned itself more with covering up the incident than restricting the effects of the release. As many as 15,000 people died prematurely due to the initial explosion and radiation release.

Gorbachev pushed two policy initiatives—glasnost (openness) and perestroika (restructuring)—to change the Soviet system. However, the attempts at change only further demonstrated the economic, social, and political problems of the Soviet system. Economically, the changes angered both conservatives who wanted to maintain state control and more liberal economists who wanted to completely change the system to promote rapid growth. The workers found themselves fearing for their employment. Glasnost opened the door for more outside influences (Western culture), which only seemed to confirm the lack of development in the Soviet Union. The middle class and even the poor in America and Western Europe enjoyed greater access to homes, education, transportation, consumer goods, travel, information, entertainment, and even food. (McDonald's came to Moscow in 1990; 27,000 people applied for the 605 jobs, and 30,000 lined up on the opening day to spend a half day's wages on a Big Mac, fries, and a Coke).

More important, the open political debate of glasnost led to the weakening of the central government in favor of the many Soviet republics. As the central government started to lose control of its republics, disruption in Eastern Europe proved too much for Gorbachev. The Soviets spent substantial amounts of money to prop up the economies of most Eastern European nations, along with other communist allies like Cuba and North Korea. Dwindling aid created internal conflicts in states like East Germany. As East Germany failed to uphold economic arrangements with its communist neighbors, those countries stopped enforcing closed borders. In 1989, East Germans began fleeing to West Germany via Hungary and Czechoslovakia. Those with educations were especially prone to make the attempt, as they were more likely to find work in the West and also better understood the decline in the East.

On November 9, 1989, guards along the Berlin Wall stopped guarding their posts. A few East Germans tentatively moved into the West and found their way open. Soon people were tearing down the wall. When the East German government fell, other communist states in Europe watched for a Soviet reaction and saw none. Peacefully, many people in the communist states of Eastern Europe demanded political and economic reforms, beginning with democratic elections. Aside from a violent and brief civil war in Romania, these changes took place rapidly over the next year. In the Soviet Union, the republics began a push for independence. The Baltic states, annexed in the early days of World War II, demanded complete independence. After a failed attempt to overthrow Gorbachev in August 1991, Latvia, Lithuania, and Estonia declared themselves independent. The other republics, including Russia, followed, and the Soviet Union officially disbanded in December 1991.

Beyond the Cold War
The Arab-Israeli Question

One key political issue that did not always involve itself directly with the Cold War was the question of Israel and Palestine. The Zionist movement began in the late nineteenth century, but Israel did not become a reality until after the Second World War. At the end of the First World War, both Arab Palestinians and European Jews expected the former Ottoman territory of Palestine to become their independent homeland, which the British had promised. Instead, the British ruled the region under a League of Nations mandate and allowed both Arabs and Jews to live in the territory, but they tried to limit immigration and the mixing of the two groups because that often led to violence.

After the Jewish Holocaust of the Second World War, world opinion favored the creation of a Jewish state, and large numbers of Jewish emigrants demanded it of the British and the United Nations. Attacks against the British authority in Palestine led to the United Kingdom's decision to abandon the region to UN control, and the UN negotiated two state settlements.

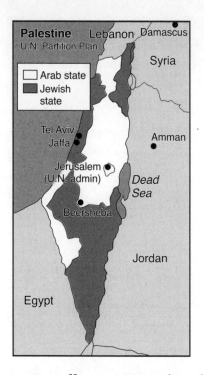

The settlement went into effect in 1948 and produced an immediate war between the Arab states of the region and Israel. Israel survived and took large parts of the Palestinian area into their nation. The UN and many nations around the world refused to accept this annexation of territory, but no outside military force intervened. Israel built itself into a strong and stable democratic state and received international support from nations like Britain and France. Egyptian leader Gamal Abdel Nasser used the plight of the Palestinian refugees to unite the world's Arabs behind the goal of a united Arab state and the nonaligned movement, because the Western powers favored Israel. When Nasser nationalized the Suez Canal in 1956, he was able to force the British, French, and Israelis who all intervened in Egypt to withdraw. He won the revenues of the canal for his government as well as the respect of the Arab peoples for forcing the West and Israel to back down (the United States and the Soviet Union both put pressure on the Israelis to withdraw from Egypt and for the British and the French to withdraw from the canal zone).

Building on this success, Nasser was able to temporarily join Syria with Egypt as part of the move toward a unified Arab state. However, economic and social interests in Syria did not fit those in Egypt, and the United Arab Republic broke apart. Also, in 1967, Egypt, Jordan, and Syria launched their combined military forces against Israel. In six days (the conflict is called the Six-Day War), Israel destroyed the military forces of each of the nations and took territory from all three. These humiliations ended talk of a unified Arab state and also convinced the Palestinians that the Arab states were only looking out for their own interests and would not or could not help Palestine achieve independence.

A number of movements grew out of the defeat, the most significant being the Palestine Liberation Organization (PLO). This group and others began launching high-profile terrorist attacks against Israeli and Western targets in order to gain support for Palestinian independence. The most significant came in 1972, when members of the Black September group murdered 11 members of the Israeli Olympic team during the Olympic Games at Munich. The international television coverage brought great publicity to the Israeli-Palestinian conflict. Numerous other attacks followed over the next two decades, as the PLO pushed to keep its plight in the news.

Into the twenty-first century, the question of Palestine remains undecided. The Israelis, as a democratic government in the Middle East, are recognized and respected by the United States and many Western nations. However, in the 1970s, the Arab states in OPEC learned that they could hurt the global economy by manipulating the supply of oil. An oil embargo after the 1973 Yom Kippur War caused gas prices in the United States to rise by 70 percent and to remain high for almost a decade, even though the embargo only lasted about a year. Although unlikely to stop exporting to the United States again, Arab oil producers and Palestinian terrorist organizations and their allies know that they can disrupt the global economy with attacks on oil production. Because of this, the political settlement of the Palestinian issue remains important to the United States and the United Nations.

Globalization: Independence through Interdependence

Since the fall of the Berlin Wall, the international system sees itself in a period of great economic integration, often referred to as globalization. While not the first time the world experienced a rapid linking of international markets, the globalization of the last 20 years is by far the most rapid and extensive. The creation of this new global system during the decade after the Berlin Wall fell produced a number of positive social changes.

- Greater trade allowed for investment capital to move from developed nations into projects in some of the world's least developed areas.

- The economic integration has pushed governments to make greater efforts to protect basic human rights and adopt democratic reforms while investors demand protection of their investments (property rights) and do not like negative publicity if a government is perceived as oppressing its people.

- The transfer of technology has accelerated as new factories and call centers require modern infrastructure to link to global supply networks (not just roads, but telecommunications, Internet, wireless, cell phones, etc.).

- New factories in developing nations offer women greater economic opportunities and a chance to break free of traditional restrictions, as they did in Europe and America during the Industrial Revolution.

- Greater integration has also produced a more peaceful world (the news does not seem to indicate this, but globally, major conflicts have been on the decline over the last two decades, as have internal conflicts and separatist movements).
  - This was clearly shown in 2002 during the escalation of hostilities between the two nuclear powers of India and Pakistan:
    - International diplomatic pressure pushed both sides to back down;
    - In democratic and globally integrated India, business leaders also applied pressure on the democratically elected government

to back down, because their business interests were threatened by the perception that India may soon enter a war and not be capable of doing business as usual.

- The long-held belief that stability promotes greater trade and wealth holds more truth today than ever before; global corporations and investors look for stability when making decisions to move into a new nation.

- Beyond the United Nations, the International Monetary Fund, established to promote financial stability and responsibility in national budgets, and the World Bank, used to fund development projects, are international organizations that both promote greater dependency on free-market systems of trade and financial stability.

But this integration also produced negative consequences.

- Sustainability is now a serious issue.

  ○ Growing middle classes in China and India especially have increased the consumption of fossil fuels and added to the production of carbon dioxide and other pollutants.

  ○ Raw materials cost of metals and minerals have significantly increased due to the growing demand.

  ○ Efforts to get at more of these resources endanger the environment due to poor mining practices, drilling accidents as oil becomes more difficult to reach (for example, oil spills in the Gulf of Mexico), and excessive logging.

  ○ Resistance to external cultural influences has created and could create even more cases of violent attacks against foreigners and their institutions.

    · The September 11, 2001, attacks are the most obvious of these, as 19 Islamic fundamentalists attacked the United States because of its increased involvement in Saudi Arabia, site of Mecca, the holiest city to Muslims.

- The need for greater global travel and freer movement of individuals has allowed for nontraditional or terrorist attacks against targets in Europe and the United States.

- The transfer of information via the Internet and other digital media has allowed for the spread of weapons information, including information on how to build nuclear devices.

- The increase of global cargo makes the monitoring of imports and exports more difficult, allowing for weapons, drugs, and people to be trafficked with greater ease.

- Multinational corporations like the petroleum giants British Petroleum and Exxon operate in many nations with budgets that far exceed the local national budgets.

    ◦ The enormous wealth generated often maintains local elites in power at the expense of more democratic reforms.

    ◦ Even corporations like Walmart and Coca-Cola have great political influence based on where they choose to build factories and distribution networks.

As the first decade of the twenty-first century ends, the following trends require mention. Politically, the world's people demand greater representation in their governments. Democracies, not yet universal, still produce some of the most stable nations. In the developing world, some democratic institutions still suffer from a lack of legitimacy as tribal and ethnic influences outweigh a larger sense of national identity. Elections in developing nations often produce more of a loot-and-pillage result as the winning ethnic group attempts to divert government and economic resources to only their people or the personal wealth of the leadership. But notable achievements in South Korea, South Africa, and Brazil indicate that democratic governments can produce real change and development.

Economically, the world is richer than ever before, and that wealth is spread into more countries than previously. The stated goal of the United Nations at the start of the century, the Millennium Goals, specifically addressed issues of greater economic development to pull people out of poverty, and the numbers indicate some successes. Trade and technology especially have contributed to greater global wealth, but the interconnectedness of markets also produces fluctuations in national economies that the governments find very difficult to address. A volcano in Iceland can cause farmers to lose their homes in Kenya, because the ash prevents planes from flying to Europe with fresh Kenyan produce, causing farmers to default on short-term loans. An earthquake in Kyoto, Japan, forces layoffs in Taiwan, as the factory that makes memory chips for laptops is damaged, and so the laptop production facilities in Taiwan must reduce production. For wealthy nations, these setbacks don't affect the entire economy, but for many in the developing world with little other economic opportunities, they can devastate an entire economy based on the production of only a few items.

Economics must also face a pushback from the environment. Medical breakthroughs and the Green Revolution produced real benefits for impoverished nations. Cholera, malaria, polio, and many other endemic killers now touch far fewer lives. The Green Revolution increased food production across the developing world, leading to better nutrition, longer life expectancy, and population growth. However, many developing nations now find themselves dependent on food imports as their populations exceed their ability to produce crops. Without major changes in food production and distribution, malnutrition and starvation could return on unprecedented scales.

Disease, too, poses some new problems, even with all of the tremendous medical advances of the twentieth century. As mentioned before, greater economic integration allows for once-isolated strains of disease to spread quickly around the world. Additionally, the widespread use of antibiotics in the late twentieth century led to the development of some strains of disease resistant to current treatments. These new versions of old killers (like tuberculosis) continue to challenge medical researchers and require new investment in the development of treatments that often cost too much for those in the developing world. However, failure to fight diseases in the developing world only opens up the more developed nations to greater threats. People continue to migrate from poorer to wealthier regions. Developed nations cannot halt this migration because they need the inexpensive labor and also must respond to humanitarian crises that can produce massive numbers of refugees that some, either legally or illegally, will find their way into the developed nations. This opens the developed world to diseases left unchecked in the developing nations.

Economic integration also facilitates greater cultural or artistic sharing. Movies from Hollywood in the United States or Bollywood (the word itself is an example of cultural diffusion) dominate the international entertainment market. Sports and television combine to make events like the World Cup for soccer and the Olympics global occasions followed by not hundreds of millions but billions of people. Many cultures feel overwhelmed by these new influences.

Traditional religious ideas and social customs find it very difficult to counteract the influence of global marketing and movies and television. In some nations, governments try to ban outside influences, limiting the screening of foreign films (France) and television shows or banning items like Pokémon cards (Saudi Arabia) as a bad influence on the traditional culture and religious values. Others find a blend of foreign with local: the McVeggie and Chicken Maharaja Mac in India's McDonald's replacing beef hamburgers and Big Macs. But often urban and rural populations adapt to these changes differently, with urban populations moving much faster into global culture and rural areas fighting back. In India and Pakistan, a number of terrorist attacks have come from rural communities and targeted urban centers and government officials who are seen as betraying the values of the nation.

The 2001 attacks on the World Trade Center and Pentagon grew out of a fundamentalist movement that first took hold in some isolated areas in Afghanistan and the Sudan. Extremists in the most remote areas of the globe possess the ability to reach a worldwide audience and promote their ideas with little hindrance. Groups like al-Qaeda, who were responsible for the attacks, present a completely new challenge to the international order. Others, like members of the Uyghur minority in China who want independence, adopt these same tactics to defeat their national governments. World powers like the United States and China, which can mobilize substantial military forces for deployment overseas or at home, find it very difficult to address these new terror threats.

The cultural assault includes gender roles. Western influences and greater economic opportunities both offer women another view of what their roles should be in society. In Japan, a Confucian nation, the legal system since the occupation by the United States after the Second World War has protected the rights of women in society and marriage. However, few women work in high positions within the corporate world. Most follow long-standing expectations of quitting work after they marry and raising children. Those who attempt otherwise often find family and social pressures against them. Even companies generally will not promote women, as they expect them to leave once they are married. Middle Eastern nations face harsh criticism of their legal treatment of women. While the West needs their oil, they can continue these practices. However, little other investment comes into the region, as the treatment of women discourages corporate relocations and even tourism. In Dubai, one of the more liberal nations in the region, a British couple received a fine and was deported for kissing in a restaurant.

Multiple-Choice Review Questions

1. Which of the following does NOT explain a reason for the breakout of a global confrontation in 1914?

   A. Military arms race
   B. Complex military alliances
   C. Economic collapse
   D. Nationalism

2. Which of the following statements best explains the global nature of the First World War?

    A. Colonial troops fought in Europe and in Africa because the European powers needed to mobilize all available manpower.
    B. Much of the fighting was in the colonial territories in India, Africa, and China.
    C. Japan and Russia committed large numbers of troops to the fighting in China.
    D. Countries from all continents fought in the war.

3. Which of the following best explains the poster's argument that the United States was fighting for freedom?

A.   The war was over territorial expansion, but this did not inspire the American public.

B.   The war aims of the Allies were different from the United States, who sought to maintain freedom of the seas and democratic governments.

C.   The war sought to defeat the monarchies of Europe.

D.   The war aims of the Allies were to defeat fascist governments around the globe.

4.   The Treaty of Versailles failed to

A.   punish Germany for the war.

B.   recognize the contributions of the British to the defeat of Germany.

C.   recognize all races as equals.

D.   return Belgium's independence from Germany.

5.   What statement best describes the integration of Latin America into the global economy during the first half of the twentieth century?

A.   Independent Latin American nations started to use the wealth generated by the sale of raw materials and cash crops to industrialize.

B.   Latin America further declined in economic importance as its mineral wealth was exhausted and its cash crops found few markets.

C.   Colonial governments in Latin America failed to provide sufficient profits for continued European involvement in the region.

D.   Latin American elites depended on investment, especially from the United States, in mining and cash crops in order to remain in power without political change.

6. Nations that turned to fascism

    A. lacked industry.
    B. lacked a working poor to promote social reform.
    C. often arose from new democracies with failed economies.
    D. feared the growing influence of the middle class in politics.

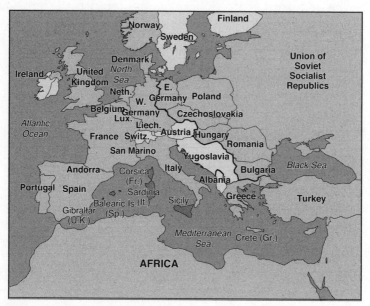

7. What would be the best caption for the map shown above?

    A. Europe after the Treaty of Versailles
    B. Europe after the Nazi invasions
    C. Post–World War II Europe
    D. Europe in 2000

8. Which of the following statements best describes China's role in the Second World War?

    A. The Nationalist (KMT) and the Chinese Communist Party (CCP) were in the midst of a civil war and did not actively involve themselves in the war effort for either side.
    B. The KMT supported the United States, but the CCP supported

the Soviet Union early in the war, preventing any unified action by China for either side.

C. The Japanese invasion in 1937 forced both the KMT and CCP to fight against Japan, joining the Allied effort in 1941 when the United States declared war on Japan.

D. As the European powers became involved in the Second World War, the Chinese KMT took the opportunity to push them out of their specific spheres of influence, winning greater control of China as a whole than any government since the Qing dynasty.

9. Globally, what contributed more to gender equality in the twentieth century than any other influence?

A. Greater economic opportunities for women during periods of industrial development and war.

B. Government regulations granting equality to women.

C. The need for more industrial workers as Western consumer society demanded more manufactured goods.

D. Greater educational opportunities for women as public schools were required to teach both girls and boys.

10. How were the Cuban Revolution of 1959 and the Iranian Revolution of 1979 similar?

A. Both toppled dictatorships dependent on American investment.

B. Both established Soviet-backed communist dictatorships.

C. Both were driven by outside efforts to topple the existing governments.

D. Both used religion (Roman Catholicism and Islam) to inspire the rural peasants to rise up against the governments.

Answers to Multiple-Choice Questions

1. **C.** No severe economic collapse directly preceded the First World War. The cost of continued military expenditures, growing complexities of alliances as each power sought greater support, and internal calls for national self-determination (especially in Austria-Hungary) all created the grounds for conflict. Also, newer powers like Germany and Japan sought greater empires.

2. **A.** The extensive colonial possessions provided key resources, especially manpower, for the war effort in the West. There was fighting in Africa, and Japan did seize German territory in China and the Pacific, but the greater effort was the movement of troops from the African colonies, Australia, Canada, India, and New Zealand to the western front.

3. **B.** The United States adopted a policy of isolationism and only entered the war as a result of attacks on merchant shipping by German submarines. To get the American public behind the war effort, President Woodrow Wilson made the conflict more about the protection of democratic governments and international law, such as freedom of the seas. His allies were more interested in territorial acquisition.

4. **C.** The treaty's language initially had a clause, pushed by the Japanese, that would have declared all races equal, recognizing the contributions of colonial soldiers from India and Africa, the Arab rebellion in the Ottoman Empire, and Japan's attack upon German possessions in China and the Pacific. However, Wilson feared the loss of support from Southern senators and had the clause removed.

5. **D.** Latin American governments sought to appease the masses, surviving due to investments from the United States in raw materials that allowed small groups of elites, fearful of populist rebellions, to appease the masses without real political or economic reform. It also allowed the governments to train militaries that would back the elites if faced with liberal reforms.

6. **C.** Fascism depended on a middle class fearful of a workers' revolt

(communism) and not trusting of democratic institutions that seemed to have failed to stabilize the government. The failed democratic institutions in Argentina, Italy, Japan, Germany, and Spain were young and had developed no long-term trust among the populations in general. Fascism often rose as a result of a large number of working poor in industrialized cities that seemed on the verge of open rebellion. The middle class and wealthy industrialists feared communism more than dictatorship; the saying that came out of Italy under Mussolini was, "At least the trains are on time," reflecting the desire for order and stability over individual freedoms (although the claim is false).

7. **C.** The presence of East and West Germany (a divided Germany) indicates this is Europe during the Cold War period, 1945–1991.

8. **C.** The Chinese declared a truce among themselves in order to fight the Japanese after they had already taken Manchuria in 1931. They could do little to defeat the Japanese, but the sheer size of China tied down many Japanese ground troops and aircraft. Beginning in 1941, the United States supplied materials to the KMT and trained several Chinese units fighting in Burma to keep the supply lines open to China.

9. **A.** Only the ability of women to provide for themselves has equalized gender roles in some societies, although not all. In addition, laws and medical technology (contraceptives like the birth control pill) supported women's rights, although not every society accepted these changes.

10. **A.** Other than the ousting of a government backed by the American government, although Baptiste had even lost U.S. support, little is shared in common. The Iranian Revolution worried the Soviet Union, rural populations played an important role as neither society was industrialized, and the Catholic Church, while supporting the poor, does not support communism. As a final point, they were both driven by internal forces, although Castro had Che Guevara (an Argentinean) as part of his inner group of advisors.

Free-Response Examples
Continuity and Change Over Time

Directions: You are to answer the following question. You should spend 5 minutes organizing or outlining your essay. Write an essay that:

- Has a relevant thesis and supports that thesis with appropriate historical evidence.
- Addresses all parts of the question.
- Uses world historical context to show continuities and changes over time.
- Analyzes the process of continuity and change over time.

Analyze the changes in Western economic and cultural influence in ONE of the following regions between 1914 and the present.

- China
- Latin America
- Sub-Saharan Africa

Comparative Essay

Directions: You are to answer the following question. You should spend 5 minutes organizing or outlining your essay. Write an essay that:

- Has a relevant thesis and supports that thesis with appropriate historical evidence.
- Addresses all parts of the question.
- Makes direct, relevant comparisons.
- Analyzes relevant reasons for similarities and differences.

Compare the role of the United State in global trade in the twentieth century to that of China in the sixteenth and seventeenth centuries.

THE BIG PICTURE: HOW TO PREPARE YEAR-ROUND

Even if the AP World History Exam is months away, the time to start preparing is now. This section will help you register for the test, prepare for the test in class and out, and manage the stress than an AP test brings. As the test gets closer, you can use the materials throughout this book to help review what you've already learned.

The **Strategies for Long-Term Preparation** are based on how much time you have to prepare. They're followed by a full-length **practice exam**, including in-depth answer explanations for the multiple-choice questions and sample responses to the free-fresponse questions. Make the most of your time before the exam, and when test day arrives, you'll be ready to earn a top score.

Strategies for Long-Term Preparation

Deciding to Take an AP Exam

When deciding to register for any AP Exam, you need to consider the following:

- Potential Credit
- Time
- Your Résumé
- Cost

First, if you have narrowed your choices for college, you need to check with them about what exams they accept and what scores will receive credit. Most universities will offer credit for students who receive a 4 or 5 on the exam. While the College Board considers a 3 passing as well, fewer universities will award credit for a 3. A score of a 4 or 5 requires commitment on your part. Look over your schedule. Do you have time beyond your normal schoolwork to use this book and other resources to prepare for the AP World History Exam—especially if you are also contemplating other exams? If you are considering taking several AP exams, schedule your time in advance to review for each. Not devoting enough time to preparing for each test could result in lower scores on each and subsequently no college credit.

Another factor you need to consider is, What does your college application look like? Colleges demand that students take a rigorous course load, meaning at least one or two AP classes on your transcript each year. With the courses on your transcript, you need to demonstrate your efforts with some solid scores on the AP exams; that is, you need to take the exams. If your transcript lacks AP courses, you need to demonstrate an ability to master college-level material; that is, you need to take some exams and score well.

One last factor involves cost. You must register and pay for each exam you take. The cost in the United States is $87 per exam (the cost is higher for students taking the exam outside of the United States). Some states and/or school districts will subsidize the cost of exams, so check with your school counselor or the AP coordinator for your school or district on the actual cost of each exam you plan to take. But remember, the possible earned college credit far exceeds the cost of an individual exam.

So now that you have decided to take the AP World History Exam, you need to set up a plan of action.

With a Few Months to Go

Start by reading the content sections of your *My Max Score* review guide. Use this to generate some questions in class (if you are taking an AP world history, pre-AP, honors, or regular course). Review your class notes and previous tests as well. Then, use the practice exams as a diagnostic to see what periods of history still give you the most difficulty. Go through the sections on answering the multiple-choice questions and the free-response essays. How might this advice have improved your score?

Now, make use of some online resources. Your textbook probably has an online resource site that includes practice exam questions. Go through the chapters that give you the most difficulties.

SOME ONLINE RESOURCES

Traditions and Encounters, Jerry Bentley	glencoe.mcgraw-hill.com/sites/2222555555/ student_view0/
World Civilizations: Global Experience, Peter Sterns	wps.ablongman.com/long_stearns_wcap_4/
The World's History, Howard Spodek	wps.prenhall.com/hss_spodek_worldhist_3/
The Earth and Its People: A Global History, Richard Bulliet	college.cengage.com/history/world/bulliet/ earth_peoples/3e/students/index.html

Each of these titles has practice questions to sharpen your skills. Also, check with your school librarian and local public library. Ask if they have any online databases such as ABC-CLIO. If they do, use them to supplement the content section of *My Max Score World History*. They contain too much information to just randomly read through, but vocabulary from the *My Max Score* book can help target specific bits of knowledge helpful in your preparation for the exam.

As the test date gets closer, sometime in early April, go through the "20 Things to Know" section. If specific information unfamiliar to you comes up on these pages, go back into the content sections to review the facts. Go online to the College Board's world history site (collegeboard .com/student/testing/ap/sub_worldhist.html?worldhist) and review more possible essay topics by downloading the course outline. Use the Free-Response Question suggestions in this book to draft some essay answers to these additional questions. Don't just think through the essay. Complete the brainstorming, and write a possible thesis. If other students are taking the exam, put together a study group. Go through the questions in the second practice exam together and discuss the different choices. Brainstorm the essay answers together and see who can write the best thesis. If you are on your own, see if you can get a teacher to review your essay answers and offer a critique.

With Only a Week or So to Go

If the test is only a few days away, go through the first practice exam then read the advice sections on answering the multiple-choice and free-response questions. Spend time on the "20 Things to Know" as they connect various time periods in history. If some of the information seems especially foreign, go to those content sections and review the material. Put together a study group if possible, and use the second practice exam (available for free download at mymaxscore.com) to lead the study session. Discuss each of the choices and arrive at a group consensus. For the essays, brainstorm the questions together and see who can come up with an agreed-upon best thesis. If a study group is not possible, take your time to go through the multiple-choice questions and try to remember your reasoning when you check your answers. For the essays, try to brainstorm and outline the essays all at once. Be sure to keep careful time of yourself, because many students find themselves running out of time before they even begin the final essay.

The Day before the Exam

No matter how early you started, eventually, it will be the day before the test. Run back through the sections on answering the free-response and multiple-choice questions. Do the review questions at the end of the content sections. You might even go back through some of the "20 Things to Know" pages. But early in the evening before the exam, put away your study materials and prepare what you need for the next day.

For the exam have

- Two #2 pencils
- Two black or blue pens
- A photo ID (if you are testing at your school, the school ID should do. If you are testing at another location, call a few days before to establish what you will need as proof of ID). Also, know your Social Security number.

- Bring a watch. The free-response section is not broken down into specific sections for each of the three essays. The suggested times are on the test, but the essays are not timed separately. There may not be a clock in the testing room, so you will want a watch to make sure you do not spend too much time on a single essay. You *may not* use a cell phone as a clock.

Go to bed early the night before the exam and set your alarm so that you wake up with enough time to eat a healthy breakfast.

On the Day of the Exam

Show up early to the testing site with the materials listed above. Make sure you have eaten a good meal. Once in the testing room, lay out your materials and have fun with the test. I know it sounds odd to say have fun, but at this point, only positives can occur; even a low score will not negatively affect your path toward college.

After the Exam

Wait. The scores will arrive sometime in mid-July. You will receive only a composite score, a number between 1 and 5. Review the information the College Board sends with your score to make sure you've listed the colleges to which you intend to apply, so that they will receive a record of your scores. They might earn you credit hours or enhance your application.

Also, unless you have graduated, use the scores to evaluate your preparation process if you will be taking more AP exams next year. What did you do correctly? What do you need to improve? How many exams can you realistically take? What *My Max Score* books do you need for the upcoming year?

This book contains one practice test. Visit mymaxscore.com to download your free second practice test with answers and explanations.

AP World History Practice Exam

Section I: Multiple-Choice Questions

Instructions (Based on those given on the actual AP World History Exam):

Section I of this exam contains 70 multiple-choice questions.

Mark all of your answers on the answer sheet included in the booklet. It is important to note that while you may write on the test itself, answers must be transferred to the answer document in the time allowed. Nothing written in the test booklet will be graded.

After you have decided which of the suggested answers is best, completely fill in the corresponding oval on the answer sheet. Give only one answer to each question. If you change an answer, be sure that the previous mark is erased completely. Here is a sample question and answer.

SAMPLE QUESTION	**SAMPLE ANSWER**
Japan is a	

A. state.
B. city.
C. country.
D. continent.

Use your time effectively, working as quickly as you can without losing accuracy. Do not spend too much time on any one question. Go on to the other questions and, if you have time, come back to the ones you have not answered. It is not expected that everyone will know the answers to all of the multiple-choice questions.

About Guessing

Each correct answer earns a point. There is no penalty for guessing; this is a change from previous years. You should mark the best answer you have for each question.

WORLD HISTORY
SECTION I
Time—55 minutes

70 Questions

Directions: Each of the questions or incomplete statements below is followed by five suggested answers or completions. Select the one that is best in each case and then fill in the corresponding oval on the answer sheet.

Note: This exam uses the chronological designations BCE (before the common era) and CE (common era). These labels correspond to BC (before Christ) and AD (anno Domini), which are used in some world history textbooks.

1. Which of the following best explains the changes during the Neolithic Revolution?

   A. New, metal tools increased the ability of hunting-gathering societies to kill large game.

   B. New building techniques allowed for the establishment of long-term settlements.

   C. Population increases forced hunting-gathering societies to expand into new areas.

   D. Agriculture allowed for permanent settlements and an increase in population.

2. A society is almost certainly a civilization if

   A. it has developed agriculture.

   B. it has developed a complex government.

   C. it has built a city.

   D. it has domesticated animals.

3. Which of the following statements is an accurate comparison of the Sumerian and Egyptian River Valley Civilizations?

    A. Both civilizations created a number of city-states but failed to establish a larger political union.

    B. Both Egypt and Sumer suffered from repeated invasions by nomadic groups, resulting in a series of short-lived empires.

    C. Egyptian civilization unified into a centralized empire while the Sumerian city-states were unable to form a larger political unit.

    D. The Sumerians developed an economic system based on long-distance trade while the Egyptians remained an agrarian society.

4. Which of the following was NOT a characteristic of a classical civilization?

    A. Complex political system
    B. Trade and cultural diffusion
    C. Complex philosophical tradition
    D. Movement from agrarian to urban society

5. Like the Qing, the Han dynasty gave the emperor absolute power over China, but in practice, who actually exercised political power?

    A. Military commanders
    B. Large landowning families
    C. Confucian bureaucrats
    D. The emperor and his immediate family

6. Which of the following best describes the status of women in the
    Han dynasty?

    A. Women enjoyed some economic rights but could not partici-
        pate in government.
    B. According to Confucian beliefs, women were only allowed
        the role of wife and mother and answerable to their father and
        husband.
    C. According to Confucian beliefs stressing a harmonious and
        egalitarian society, women were granted more economic and
        political rights than in other classical societies.
    D. As in most urban societies, women lacked status in the family
        and were not allowed any form of economic independence.

7. As a Chinese dynasty faced internal revolts, corruption in the
    bureaucracy, and external invasion, it was said to have

    A. lost the Mandate of Heaven.
    B. completed the cycle.
    C. lost its way (according to Taoist tradition).
    D. abandoned the emperor.

8. Which of the following political systems was practiced by many
    Greek city-states during the classical period?

    A. Feudalism
    B. Direct democracy
    C. Republicanism
    D. Absolutism (monarchy)

9. The columns shown above, located in modern Iran, but originally built in the fourth century BCE, are a result of the spread of what cultural influence?

    A. Hellenic
    B. Islamic
    C. Persian
    D. Mongolian

10. Which of the following civilizations most influenced the development of Roman culture?

    A. Persian
    B. Greek
    C. Phoenician
    D. Egyptian

11. In order to remain in control of the Roman people after overthrowing the republic, the Roman emperors

    A.   resorted to maintaining a large standing army in the city of Rome itself.

    B.   provided numerous public games for entertainment and provided handouts of free food to the poor.

    C.   continued to allow the Senate to make the laws and administer the empire while they only acted as a figurehead.

    D.   created a feudal system, granting lands and villages to noble families in return for their loyalty and promise of military aid.

12. As the Roman Empire began to decline, which of the following religious traditions converted many, including both slaves and emperors?

    A.   Islam

    B.   Greek mythology

    C.   Christianity

    D.   Eastern Orthodox

13. Which of the following statements accurately compares both the collapse of the Han dynasty and the Gupta Empire?

    A.   The Han were overwhelmed by external invaders while the Gupta broke up into regional kingdoms.

    B.   Internal corruption led to the overthrow of each dynastic family.

    C.   The Han dynasty broke into regional states due to bureaucratic corruption while the Gupta were overwhelmed by the Huns.

    D.   The Han dynasty faced a series of internal revolts that broke the power of the central government while the militarily weak Gupta failed to repel an external invasion by the Huns.

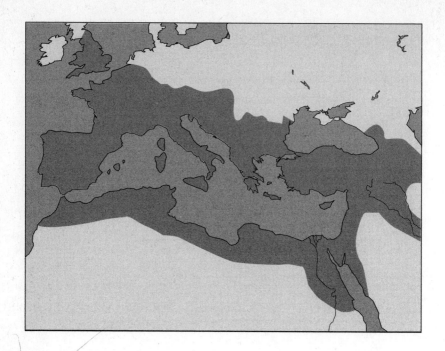

14. The shaded region on the map above shows

    A.   the spread of Christianity by 500 CE.

    B.   the conquests of Alexander the Great.

    C.   the Roman Empire at its greatest extent.

    D.   the extent of the conquest of the Germanic tribes.

15. All of the following were influences on Islam EXCEPT

    A.   Arab culture.

    B.   Persian culture.

    C.   Judaism.

    D.   Hinduism.

16. Which of the following explains a key factor in the early success of Islam?

   A. Islam supported a hierarchy, attracting local leaders to adopt the new faith.

   B. Islam was an egalitarian religion, attracting followers from the masses.

   C. Islam promised conquered peoples that they could continue their own systems of worship.

   D. Both Persian and Byzantine nobles were early converts to Islam.

17. Which of the following was the political successor to the Roman Empire in the East?

   A. The Safavid Empire

   B. The Byzantine Empire

   C. The kingdom of Rome

   D. The Russian Empire

18. Which statement is NOT correct about the spread of Islam between 700 and 1000 CE?

   A. Initial Arab conquests occupied much of the Middle East and then extended across North Africa.

   B. Islam benefited from the weakness of the Byzantine and Persian Empires as it moved to conquer their territories in the Middle East.

   C. Islam failed to expand into regions of Europe as it encountered resistance from Christian populations.

   D. The egalitarian beliefs of Islam made it popular with the lower classes, winning it many converts in the areas it conquered.

19. Which of the following statements accurately traces the movement of Buddhism into East Asia?

   A. The Mongol conquest introduced Buddhism into China, Korea, and Vietnam.

   B. Buddhist missionaries, traveling on the Silk Road, spread Buddhism into China; from there, it moved into Korea and Japan.

   C. Buddhist missionaries traveled along the coastal routes to Southeast Asia, then China, and finally Japan.

   D. Nomadic groups moving into northern China brought Buddhism with them; from there it spread to the rest of China and then moved to Korea and Japan.

20. Which of the following is an accurate comparison of the influence of Buddhism and Islam in India during the Delhi Sultanate?

   A. Islam was the dominant religion of the ruling dynasty while Buddhist influence was attacked by both Muslim and Hindu leaders.

   B. Islam established the sultanate, but resistance to foreign rule was led by Buddhist monks.

   C. Both Muslims and Buddhist were part of the ruling class during the sultanate.

   D. Islam came under attack by Buddhist and Hindu followers, losing all influence in the sultanate.

21. During the Mongol rule over most of Asia

   A. trade increased substantially because of the Mongol-enforced peace along the silk road.

   B. Buddhism, the religion of the Mongols, spread to China, Vietnam, and the Middle East.

   C. overland trade moved to safer sea routes.

   D. Europe, China, and India lost contact with each other, and the last of the classical civilizations vanished.

22. Which of the following African states, partially converted to Islam by caravan merchants, profited from trading gold and salt?

  A. Kongo, Zanzibar, and Zimbabwe
  B. Kongo, Mali, and Zimbabwe
  C. Mali, Ghana, and Songhai
  D. Ghana, Songhai, and Zimbabwe

23. Which of the following statements accurately describes the feudal political system dominant in western Europe by the year 1000 CE?

  A. Kings ruled as absolute monarchs with the backing of church authority.
  B. No central authority existed; individual nobles ruled small estates or manors.
  C. Kings distributed land to the nobles in return for loyalty and military service.
  D. Kings ruled a complex bureaucracy dominated by merchant and banking families.

24. A lasting result of the Crusades was

  A. Christian political and economic dominance in the Middle East.
  B. European control over the Mediterranean.
  C. reestablishment of trade contacts between Europe and Asia.
  D. the collapse of the last Islamic caliphate.

25. The Mongol conquest of China produced all of the following changes EXCEPT

   A. the decline of Confucianism as the dominant philosophy of Chinese civilization.

   B. Mongols were placed above Chinese officials throughout the official bureaucracy.

   C. China actively engaged in long-distance trade along the Silk Road and into Southeast Asia.

   D. the expansion of Chinese rule over Korea and an attempted invasion of Japan.

26. Which of the following describes the Japanese political system under the first shoguns?

   A. The shogun established a feudal system similar to that in Europe.

   B. The Shogun ruled as an absolute monarch, replacing the emperor.

   C. The emperor retained political power but relied upon the military power of the shogun to enforce his rule.

   D. The emperor ruled over a Confucian bureaucracy modeled on that in China, but real power rested with the shogun who commanded the military.

27. The Mongol invasion of the Middle East collapsed the Abbasid caliphate but was eventually stopped by

   A. the Seljuk Turks.

   B. the Persian Safavids.

   C. the Mamluks.

   D. the Bedouin.

28. After Arab dominance along the Indian Ocean trade routes faded, what civilization was the first to move into the region with advanced ships and navigational equipment?

    A. Portugal
    B. Ming China
    C. The Mongols
    D. The Spanish

29. After the Columbian Exchange introduced many new crops into the global economy, what impact did the potato have in Europe and the Far East?

    A. The potato opened up many new areas for cultivation, creating a population explosion in these regions.
    B. The potato required fewer agricultural workers, freeing up labor for industrialization.
    C. The potato was rejected by these areas because it was seen as peasant food that grew in low-quality soils.
    D. The potato became a luxury food because its nutritional value exceeded that of typical grains.

30. All of the following encouraged Medieval Europe to establish greater economic ties to other civilizations EXCEPT

    A. the Crusades.
    B. greater trade in northern Europe between cities of the Hanseatic League.
    C. the demand for luxury items from China.
    D. the collapse of the Eastern Orthodox Byzantine Empire.

31. Which of the following activities created the greatest demand for slaves from Africa?

    A. Tobacco production
    B. Sugar production
    C. Textile manufacturing
    D. Cotton production

32. Which of the following identifies a weakness of both the Aztec and the Incan Empires when faced by Spanish conquistadors?

    A. A civil war between branches of the royal family
    B. Uprisings by conquered tribes who allied with the Europeans
    C. Numerical superiority of the Spanish armies
    D. Spanish possession of advanced military technologies

33. Buddhism's increasing popularity in China resulted in

    A. the decline of the Confucian bureaucracy.
    B. the development of Neo-Confucian philosophy to incorporate Buddhist and Taoist ideas into Confucianism.
    C. greater contacts between China, Southeast Asia, and Japan.
    D. a rearrangement of the social order, giving more opportunities to women and the "mean" people described in Confucianism.

34. In order to secure their independence from the European powers in the seventeenth century, the Tokugawa shoguns

    A. adopted modern European weapons: firearms and cannons.
    B. allied with the Dutch, an enemy of Spain, in case Spain sought to establish control over Japan.
    C. expelled foreigners and limited trade to only Dutch and Chinese ships.
    D. encouraged greater trade with all European powers to avoid becoming dependent on any single one.

35. In the early eighteenth century, what nation used military force against the Ottoman Empire and the eastern European states to gain greater access to international trade?

    A. The Holy Roman Empire

    B. Prussia

    C. Russia

    D. The Safavid dynasty (Persia)

36. All of the following contributed to European absolutism EXCEPT

    A. the chaos and disorder of the fourteenth century.

    B. the ideas of Enlightenment philosophers.

    C. Humanist political philosophy.

    D. the Protestant Reformation and the subsequent weakening of papal authority.

37. Which of the following identifies a key component of Western European empires during the eighteenth century?

    A. Dependence on overseas holdings for both resources and markets for manufactured goods

    B. Economies supported by government policies that promoted free trade between nations

    C. Large land-based empires that were almost in continuous warfare with each other as they fought for a greater share of the European landmass

    D. An absolute emperor who controlled the empire through a large bureaucratic system

38. The Scientific Revolution developed as European thinkers focused on debate over

   A. evolution.
   B. the earth or the sun as the center of the universe.
   C. the power of the papacy over religion.
   D. creationism.

39. The ceramic vase shown above (with a blue design on a white vase) is an example of the high level of artistry and technical achievement reached by which of the following cultures?

   A. Tokugawa Japan
   B. Ming China
   C. The Ottoman Empire
   D. Mughal India

40. Which of the following statements best describes the Aztec social order at the time of the arrival of the Spanish conquistadors?

   A. Aztec society was basically egalitarian as conquest allowed the emperor to grant lands to warriors and farmers.
   B. A small Aztec nobility received the benefits of conquest while the lower classes had few opportunities to advance.

C. Aztec priests presided over a complex social hierarchy based on a family's military service and agricultural lands.

D. The Aztec social order rewarded military service, granting warriors lands and tribute taken from conquered areas.

41. Early in the nineteenth century, Mughal India, already suffering from internal fragmentation, came under the control of

A. France.

B. the Netherlands.

C. Spain.

D. Great Britain.

42. Which of the following statements is a correct analysis of the demographic changes in West Africa due to the Atlantic slave trade?

A. Populations in West Africa did not grow as much as in other regions of Africa, even as European technology and medicine came into the region.

B. West African villages suffered from a lack of working-age individuals, especially young men, since slavers favored this group over the very young or the elderly.

C. Populations in West Africa did not show a significant change because most slaves in the colonies were born there after the initial wave of slave shipments from Africa.

D. West African states saw significant population declines as people fled to the south to avoid the slave raiding parties operating along the Atlantic coast.

43. Which of the following statements is accurate concerning agricultural production and the Industrial Revolution?

    A. The Industrial Revolution failed to increase agricultural production, forcing many European nations to use their colonies for food production.

    B. Improvements in agricultural technology allowed excess labor to move to the cities to work in factories, reducing labor cost and increasing the rate of industrialization.

    C. Agricultural production decreased in industrialized nations because government policies drove many small farmers off of their land.

    D. Improvements in industry required fewer workers in the cities, allowing for an increase in agricultural production due to decreased labor cost.

44. Inspired by events in both the United States and France,

    A. Haitian slaves revolted against their owners and the French, winning freedom and independence in 1804.

    B. nineteenth-century Russian serfs revolted against the czar, demanding emancipation and land.

    C. twentieth-century Cuban revolutionaries overthrew the island's dictator in favor of a military-dominated republic.

    D. liberal revolutions spread to central and eastern Europe, forcing governmental change in Germany and Russia.

45. Which of the following statements is accurate about both the American and French Revolutions?

    A. Enlightenment ideas inspired members of the middle class to seek greater governmental representation.

    B. Enlightenment ideas inspired the poorest classes—peasants and the working class in the cities—to seek greater governmental protections of their rights.

C. The typical low wages and poor working conditions of the Industrial Revolution pushed the lower classes to revolution to better protect their rights.

D. Enlightenment ideas encouraged the initial revolutionaries but did not significantly influence the revolutionary governments established in each nation.

46. Which of the following statements best explains the Ottoman response to European industrialization and imperialism?

A. The Ottomans used their wealth to hire European specialists to modernize their military and industry.

B. The Ottomans failed to follow events in Europe, because they were more interested in extending their empire into the Middle East and North Africa.

C. The Ottomans failed to industrialize, becoming dependent on European manufacturing and finding themselves unable to defend their empire.

D. A wave of social and political reforms allowed for the small middle class to industrialize the empire during the latter part of the nineteenth century.

47. What factor restricted the growth of the middle class in many non-European areas during the nineteenth century?

A. Nations outside of Europe did not encourage education.

B. European nations restricted attempts at industrialization in their colonies.

C. Women outside of Europe were not allowed to actively participate in the economy.

D. Areas outside of Europe lacked coal and iron, the basic resources of industrialization.

48. In the nineteenth century, all of the following advantages allowed smaller European states to control large global empires EXCEPT

   A. Europe enjoyed an advantage in military technology over other civilizations.
   B. Europe's democratic political systems were able to mobilize greater manpower strength than the autocratic governments found in Africa and Asia.
   C. In many colonies, Europeans allied themselves with local elites to maintain control over the large populations.
   D. Innovations in communication and transportation allowed Europe to manage far-flung empires with great efficiency and to quickly put down local disruptions.

49. Which of the following civilizations maintained an independent government through the nineteenth century but were unable to limit foreign intervention in their territory?

   A. India
   B. China
   C. The Kongo
   D. South Africa

The nobles, while retaining their property rights on all the lands belonging to them, grant the peasants perpetual use of their domicile in return for a specified obligation; and, to assure their livelihood as well as to guarantee fulfillment of their obligations toward the government, grant them a portion of arable land fixed by the said arrangements, as well as other property.

While enjoying these land allotments, the peasants are obliged, in return, to fulfill obligations to the noblemen fixed by the same arrangements. In this condition, which is temporary, the peasants are temporarily obligated.

At the same time, they are granted the right to purchase their domicile, and, with the consent of the nobles, they may acquire in full ownership the arable lands and other properties which are allotted them for permanent use. Following such acquisition of full ownership of land, the peasants will be freed from their obligations to the nobles for the land thus purchased and will become free peasant landowners.

50. The above decree was issued by the czar of Russia in 1861. Who directly benefited from this new law?

A. The aristocracy
B. The urban middle class
C. The czar and his immediate family
D. The serfs

51. Latin American revolutions in the early nineteenth century

    A. rejected the ideas of the American Revolution in favor of the socialist movements of Europe.
    B. depended on populist leaders who created their own dictatorships once the Spanish were ousted.
    C. claimed inspiration from the American Revolution and the Enlightenment, but most failed to produce lasting republics or social change.
    D. depended on foreign help, either from the United States or Great Britain, to defeat the Spanish Empire.

52. Which of the following statements accurately describes changes in gender relations due to the Industrial Revolution in Europe?

    A. Women in the middle class had the opportunity to become more involved in social issues and become an important influence in the new consumer economy.
    B. Women in the lower classes were able to use factory jobs to establish independent lives, allowing them to live outside of their parents' home and choose when to marry.
    C. Women in the middle class were even more restricted in their social roles because society put greater social pressures on their husbands to meet certain standards in their public and personal lives.
    D. Women in the lower classes experienced fewer social restrictions because the attention of society focused on the urban middle class.

53. Which of the following occurred in China as a result of greater European contact with East Asia in the nineteenth century?

    A. China came under indirect foreign rule after losing a series of wars against the European powers and Japan.

B. China's Confucian bureaucracy was forced to adopt Western-style political reforms in order to maintain their control over the country.

C. China's Qing dynasty fell to European and Japanese conquerors.

D. China industrialized to avoid coming under the control of European powers.

54. The Opium War resulted from

A. Chinese attempts to stop the importation of opium to their country by British and other merchants.

B. efforts by the British to halt the production and sale of opium in the nineteenth century.

C. efforts by the Qing dynasty to reestablish their authority over southern China.

D. Chinese attempts to control the exports from their country into international markets.

55. How did the Japanese response to Western imperialism in the nineteenth century differ from that of Qing China?

A. Japan attempted to restrict foreign access to their nation until it suffered a series of military defeats.

B. Faced with superior military technology, Japan opened itself to foreign trade in an effort to rapidly industrialize.

C. Japan allowed only Dutch and Chinese merchants access to their trade while the Qing dynasty opened many ports to all of the Western powers.

D. Lacking sufficient resources, Japan opened itself to international markets as part of an attempt to industrialize.

"To liberate thought from the shackles of imitation and understand religion as it was understood by the community before dissension appeared; to return, in the acquisition of religious knowledge, to its first sources, and to weigh them in the scale of human reason, which God has created in order to prevent excess or adulteration in religion, so that God's wisdom may be fulfilled and the order of the human world preserved; and to prove that, seen in this light, religion must be accounted a friend to science, pushing man to investigate the secrets of existence, summoning him to respect established truths and to depend on them in his moral life and conduct."

—Muhammad Abduh, Islamic scholar (1849–1905)

56. The quote encourages Muslims to

   A. return to the traditional *umma*, or community of all Muslims, by restoring traditional values.
   B. respect reason and science as part of a religious life.
   C. free themselves of religious prejudices.
   D. focus on worldly matters by applying science to religion.

57. Which of the following statements best explains the changes in the Indian economic system during the nineteenth century?

   A. The British required greater industrialization of the textile industry in India to keep up with demand in Great Britain.
   B. The British encouraged Indian industrialization to make the colony more self-sufficient.
   C. The British required greater agricultural production, especially cash crops, including tea, opium, and cotton.
   D. The British forced the traditional industrial economy to return to an agrarian base in order to provide grain for many other areas of the British Empire.

58. During the late nineteenth century, nationalism created political
    instability in which of the following regions?

    A.   The Austrian-Hungarian and Ottoman Empires
    B.   Germany and France
    C.   Germany and Russia
    D.   Britain and the Ottoman Empire

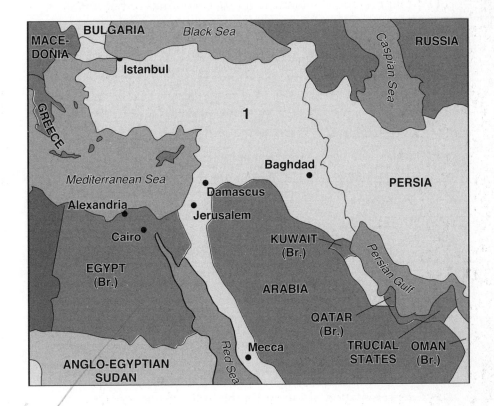

59. The area labeled #1 on the map above was controlled by what
    empire just prior to the outbreak of World War I?

    A.   The British Empire
    B.   The Ottoman Empire
    C.   The Russian Empire
    D.   The Persian Empire

60. All of the following were causes of World War I EXCEPT

   A. a complex series of alliances that rapidly drew the powers of Europe into conflict.
   B. an arms buildup that included naval units and overall troop strengths.
   C. increasing nationalism among ethnic groups in the Balkans.
   D. political and economic ideological conflicts in Europe.

61. Which of the following best describes the impact of World War I on many colonial areas?

   A. Colonial regions suffered official neglect because resources were concentrated in Europe to fight the war.
   B. Many thousands of colonial subjects died in Europe, Africa, and the Middle East, fighting for the European powers.
   C. Numerous colonial independent movements won freedom through the Treaty of Versailles.
   D. Colonial governments gained greater autonomy because the European governments granted freedoms for natural resources and manpower.

62. The initial goals of the Indian National Congress included all of the following EXCEPT

   A. representation of Indians in the Indian Civil Service.
   B. expanded representative government.
   C. a gradual end of British rule.
   D. industrial development.

	1965–80 (%)	1981–90 (%)
Low-income countries	7.3	8.2
China and India	7.0	10.3
Other	8.0	3.7
Middle-income countries	6.7	2.3
High-income countries	2.7	
OECD countries[a]	3.1	3.3

Note:

[a] Average annual growth rate for manufacturing in the OECD countries

Source: Adapted from the World Bank's World Development Report 1992 (given in Poulson, 1994, p. 378)

(OECD: the Organization for Economic Cooperation and Development; a group of 33 developed nations)

63. Which of the following conclusions is supported by the information on the table?

A. Middle-income countries were poised to become part of the high-income bracket in 1980 but fell behind during the next decade.

B. Middle-income economies did not focus on development of the manufacturing segments of their economies during the 1980s.

C. OECD countries failed to make significant investments in their manufacturing sectors between 1965 and 1990.

D. The manufacturing segments of the Chinese and Indian economies grew faster than any other nations between 1981 and 1990.

64. How did American and European responses to the Great Depression affect Latin America?

    A.   Latin America benefited from the industrialized powers' attempts to stimulate greater trade.

    B.   Protectionist policies greatly reduced the demand for Latin American exports, causing economic and political disruption.

    C.   Positivism had created economically independent, industrialized nations in Latin America that were able to isolate themselves from the worst effects of the Depression.

    D.   The failure of both American and European governments to take action to resolve key issues of the Great Depression created an opportunity for Latin American businessmen to capture new foreign markets.

65. Created at the end of World War II, which of the following missions was the United Nations best able to accomplish by the end of the twentieth century?

    A.   The eradication of nuclear weapons

    B.   The independence of former European colonies

    C.   The implementation of democratic reforms in each member state

    D.   The establishment of an internationally accepted standard of human rights

66. The creation of the State of Israel in 1948 resulted in

    A.   a long-term conflict between Israel and the Arab states of the Middle East.

    B.   the deportation of thousands of Jews from Europe to Palestine (Israel).

    C.   demands by other colonial territories for complete independence from Britain.

    D.   the inclusion of the Middle East into Cold War tensions between the United States and the Soviet Union.

67. Cold War tensions between the United States and the Soviet Union included all of the following issues EXCEPT

   A.   rising numbers of nuclear weapons.
   B.   military aid used to maintain nondemocratic governments.
   C.   access to dwindling global oil supplies.
   D.   a policy of containment directed at communist governments.

68. The Iranian Revolution overthrew a dictator

   A.   supported by the Soviet Union.
   B.   supported by the United States.
   C.   to establish a democratic republic.
   D.   who ruled over a fundamentalist Islamic state.

69. The nonaligned movement is best described as

   A.   a group of nations during the Cold War that sought to avoid being politically tied to the United States or the Soviet Union.
   B.   the neutral nations of Europe after World War I that sought to remove the restrictions of the Treaty of Versailles placed on Germany.
   C.   a group of newly independent nations that sought greater global contributions to international aid.
   D.   a group of nations at the end of the twentieth century wishing to avoid the effects of rapid international economic integration.

70. Which of the following terms describes the increased economic and social integration of societies at the end of the twentieth century?

   A.   Socialism
   B.   Imperialism
   C.   Globalization
   D.   Consumerism

END OF SECTION I

WORLD HISTORY
SECTION II

Note: This exam uses the chronological designations BCE (before the common era) and CE (common era). These labels correspond to BC (before Christ) and AD (anno Domini), which are used in some world history textbooks.

Part A
(Suggested writing time—40 minutes)
Percent of Section II score—33 1/3

Directions: The following question is based on the accompanying Documents 1–6. (The documents have been edited for the purposes of this exercise.)

This question is designed to test your ability to work with and understand historical documents.

Write an essay that:

- Has a relevant thesis and supports that thesis with evidence from the documents.
- Uses all or all but one of the documents.
- Analyzes the documents by grouping them in as many appropriate ways as possible.
- Does not simply summarize the documents individually.
- Takes into account both the sources of the documents and the authors' points of view.

You may refer to relevant historical information not mentioned in the documents.

1. Using the documents, analyze the actions and intent of Europeans as they colonized the New World. Explain what other documents would be necessary to complete the discussion of European intentions.

Historical Background: In 1492, Spanish explorers discovered the New World while attempting to establish a new trade route to China. They would soon realize that this New World offered even more opportunities. However, the exploitation of the continents accompanied the destruction of most of the Native American societies.

Document 1

Source: Simón Bolívar, Latin American revolutionary: "Letter from Jamaica" (1815)

"Three centuries ago," you say, "began the atrocities committed by the Spaniards on this great hemisphere of Columbus." Our age has rejected these atrocities as mythical, because they appear to be beyond the human capacity for evil. Modern critics would never credit them were it not for the many and frequent documents testifying to these horrible truths. The humane Bishop of Chiapas, that apostle of America, Las Casas, has left to posterity a brief description of these horrors, extracted from the trial records in Sevilla relating to the cases brought against the conquistadores, and containing the testimony of every respectable person then in the New World, together with the charges, which the tyrants made against each other. All this is attested by the foremost historians of that time. Every impartial person has admitted the zeal, sincerity, and high character of that friend of humanity, who so fervently and steadfastly denounced to his government and to his contemporaries the most horrible acts of sanguinary [bloodthirsty] frenzy.

Document 2

Source: Spanish missionary Cristoval de Acuña: New Discovery of the Amazons (1641)

If the Amazons then is the chief street,—the principal road by which to ascend to the greater riches of Peru, well may I affirm that she is the chief master of all those riches. If the lake of Dorado contains the gold which common opinion attributes to it; if, as many affirm, the Amazons inhabit the richest country in the world; if the Tocantins are so famous for their gold and precious stones; if the Omaguas were so famous for riches that a Viceroy of Peru dispatched a force under Pedro de Ursua in search of them; then all this wealth is now shut up in the great river of the Amazons. Here is the lake of Dorado, here the nation of Amazons, here the Tocantins, here the Omaguas, and here finally is deposited the immense treasure which the Majesty of God keeps to enrich our great King and Lord, Philip IV.

I gathered this from what happened with one of these Indians, who having heard something of the power of our God, and seen with his own eyes that our expedition went up the river, and, passing through the midst of so many warlike nations, returned without receiving any damage; judged that it was through the force and power of the God who guided us.

Document 3

Source: Spanish conquistador Francisco Vásquez de Coronado: Report on the northern expedition (1540)

Three days after I captured this city, some of the Indians who lived here came to offer to make peace. They brought me some turquoises and poor mantles, and I received them in His Majesty's name with as good a speech as I could, making them understand the purpose of my coming to this country, which is, in the name of His Majesty and by the commands of Your Lordship, that they and all others in this province should become Christians and should know the true God for their Lord, and His Majesty for their king and earthly lord. After this they returned to their houses and suddenly, the next day, they packed up their goods and property, their women and children, & fled to the hills, leaving their towns deserted, with only some few remaining in them.

Document 4

Source: Italian explorer Amerigo Vespucci: Account of his first voyage to the Americas (1497)

At this beginning, we saw nothing in the land of much profit, except some show of gold.... We landed in a harbour, where we found a village built like Venice upon the water: there were about 44 large dwellings in the form of huts erected upon very thick piles, and they had their doors or entrances in the style of drawbridges:

...and it was resolved that since this people desired hostility with us, we should proceed to encounter them and try by every means to make them friends: in case they would not have our friendship, that we should treat them as foes, and so many of them as we might be able to capture should all be our slaves: and having armed ourselves as best we could, we advanced towards the shore, and they sought not to hinder us from landing, I believe from fear of the cannons: and we jumped on land, 57 men in four squadrons, each one [consisting of] a captain and his company: and we came to blows with them: and after a long battle [in which] many of them [were] slain, we put them to flight, and pursued them to a village, having made about 250 of them captives, and we burnt the village, and returned to our ships with victory and 250 prisoners, leaving many of them dead and wounded, and of ours there were no more than one killed and 22 wounded.

Document 5

Sources: Spanish conquistador Hernando Cortés: Letter recounting greeting by Montezuma II, the Aztec emperor (1520)

Montezuma came down the middle of this street with two chiefs, one on his right hand and the other on his left. When we met I dismounted and stepped forward to embrace him, but the two lords who were with him stopped me with their hands so that I should not touch him; and they likewise all performed the ceremony of kissing the earth. When at last I came to speak to Montezuma himself I took off a necklace of pearls and cut glass that I was wearing and placed it round his neck; after we had walked a little way up the street a servant of his came with two necklaces, wrapped in a cloth, made from red snails' shells, which they hold in great esteem; and from each necklace hung eight shrimps of refined gold almost a span in length.

Document 6

Source: Queen Isabella I and King Ferdinand V of Spain: Privileges and prerogatives granted to Christopher Columbus (1492)

For as much of you, Christopher Columbus, are going by our command, with some of our vessels and men, to discover and subdue some Islands and Continent in the ocean, and it is hoped that by God's assistance, some of the said Islands and Continent in the ocean will be discovered and conquered by your means and conduct, therefore it is but just and reasonable, that since you expose yourself to such danger to serve us, you should be rewarded for it. And we being willing to honour and favour you for the reasons aforesaid; Our will is, That you, Christopher Columbus, after discovering and conquering the said Islands and Continent in the said ocean, or any of them, shall be our Admiral of the said Islands and Continent you shall discover and conquer; and that you be our Admiral, Vice-Roy, and Governour in them and that for the future, you may call and stile yourself, D. Christopher Columbus, and that your sons and successors in the said employment, may call themselves Dons, Admirals, Vice-Roys, and Governours of them…

END OF PART A

WORLD HISTORY
SECTION II
Part B
(Suggested planning and writing time—40 minutes)
Percent of Section II score—33 1/3

Directions: You are to answer the following question. You should spend 5 minutes organizing or outlining your essay.

Write an essay that:

- Has a relevant thesis and supports that thesis with appropriate historical evidence.
- Addresses all parts of the question.
- Uses world historical context to show continuities and changes over time.
- Analyzes the process of continuity and change over time.

2. Describe the continuities and changes in the pattern of European exploration and colonization between 1450 and 1914.

END OF PART B

SECTION II
Part C
(Suggested planning and writing time—40 minutes)
Percent of Section II score—33 1/3

Directions: You are to answer the following question. You should spend 5 minutes organizing or outlining your essay.

Write an essay that:

- Has a relevant thesis and supports this thesis with appropriate historical evidence.
- Addresses all parts of the question.
- Makes direct, relevant comparisons.
- Analyzes relevant reasons for similarities and differences.

3. Compare the internal and external forces that led to the fall of the Han dynasty and the Roman Empire.

END OF EXAM

Practice Exam Answers and Explanations
Section I, Multiple Choice
ANSWER KEY

1.	D	24.	C
2.	C	25.	A
3.	C	26.	A
4.	D	27.	C
5.	C	28.	B
6.	B	29.	A
7.	A	30.	D
8.	B	31.	B
9.	A	32.	D
10.	B	33.	B
11.	B	34.	C
12.	C	35.	C
13.	D	36.	B
14.	C	37.	A
15.	D	38.	B
16.	B	39.	B
17.	B	40.	B
18.	C	41.	D
19.	B	42.	B
20.	A	43.	B
21.	A	44.	A
22.	C	45.	A
23.	D	46.	C

47. B	59. B
48. B	60. D
49. B	61. B
50. D	62. C
51. C	63. D
52. A	64. B
53. A	65. B
54. A	66. A
55. B	67. C
56. B	68. B
57. C	69. A
58. A	70. C

ANSWER EXPLANATIONS

1. **D.** The introduction of agriculture during this time allowed for the first settled societies, opening up possibilities for permanent settlements and increased specialization that led to advances in tools and the use of new materials like metals.

2. **C.** The development of a city requires a great deal of sophistication: a surplus of food, job specialization, complex government, and written records. See the "Levels of Society" chart on page 13.

3. **C.** The Sumerians never developed a unified empire, but instead their many city-states fought each other for dominance, although no single one ever won. They were then incorporated into various empires when the region was conquered and reconquered.

4. **D.** While the classical civilizations did develop larger urban centers than before, the bulk of the population remained rural and agricultural. Political systems and trade both became far more complex and expansive during this period.

5. **C.** The Han instituted the first official adoption of Confucian philosophy into the national government. This system rested on the creation of a professional bureaucracy trained in the philosophy of Confucius.

6. **B.** Women were expected to marry and produce children, especially a male heir. They were not given a larger role in the family or society according to Confucian philosophy. Confucius sought to establish the family as the stable basis of a successful and peaceful society. Women were to provide that stability in the home, not concentrate on matters outside of the family.

7. **A.** The dynastic cycle came to a close as natural disasters and/or foreign invaders and revolutionaries exhausted the ability of the central government (the emperor and the bureaucracy) to address China's problems.

8. **B.** After about 500 BCE, many Greek city-states allowed adult, male citizens to debate and pass the laws of their city. This did not include a majority of the people, as women, foreigners (those who were not citizens; citizenship was also closed to most who were not born to citizens in many of the city-states), and slaves (a substantial portion of the population of city-states). Also, some of the city-states limited the authority of the assemblies of citizens.

9. **A.** Built by Alexander the Great, they are an example of the architectural influence of the Greeks that spread well into Asia.

10. **B.** Greek politics, religion, innovations, and arts all became the dominant influences in the Roman Republic and Roman Empire. The reputation of Greek learning and the Roman conquest of southern Italy's Greek colonies and Greece itself all contributed to this influence.

11. **B.** Many of the institutions of the republic, like the senate, continued, but real power belonged to the emperor, who enforced stability by providing the basic needs of the poor: food, and pubic distractions such as gladiatorial games. Together, these policies are referred to as "bread and circuses." Military forces around Rome only contributed to destabilizing the empire as they often involved themselves in politics, overthrowing an emperor for their commander, or even selling the office.

12. **C.** The egalitarian tradition of Christianity converted many in the lower classes as well as slaves. It also appealed to some at the top who rejected the religious ceremonies that went along with the crowning of an emperor and the rejection of the old republic.

13. **D.** This is the best answer, although C is similar. The bureaucratic corruption weakened the central government, but it was the revolts that eventually brought it down. Also, the reference to regional states implies something that the Chinese generally sought to avoid.

14. **C.** The key is to know that Rome dominated the areas around the entire Mediterranean, the Middle East, and the British Isles. Christianity covers many of these locations as well, but not the Persian Gulf. Also, Christianity does not dominate all of Europe until almost the year 1000 (and even then, Spain was under Islamic control).

15. **D.** The Arabs who were the initial society to practice Islam did not have direct contact with India. Muhammad was influenced by the monotheistic beliefs of Christianity and Judaism while Persian culture contributed a great deal to early Islam because it was the first area outside of the Arabian Peninsula to convert to Islam after being conquered by the Arabs.

16. **B.** Like Christianity and Buddhism, Islam offered salvation to all classes and attracted many of the poor to its ranks. While Islam did respect, in general, the rights of the "people of the Book," meaning Christians and Jews, it did not offer acceptance of any belief system among those who were conquered by the caliphate, and even some communities of Christians and Jews faced persecution during the caliphate.

17. **B.** The Byzantines were the eastern portion of the Roman Empire. They adopted a more Greek-centered culture but were founded on Roman political and cultural traditions.

18. **C.** While Christian populations did resist Islamic incursion (most famously in the eighth century in France), Spain fell to Islamic conquest.

19. **B.** Buddhism used missionaries to spread the word, similar to

missionary movements in early Christianity. The path of Buddhism into East Asia is through China, where it takes on the "Big Raft," or Mahayana, form of the religion to Korea and Japan.

20. **A.** The sultanate was an Islamic state while Buddhism was already a minority religion in India, having faced centuries of opposition from the Hindus.

21. **A.** The Mongols established a Pax Mongolia over Asia just as the Romans had done during their early empire. Stability and the active policing of trade routes by the Mongols caused a growth in trade inside the vast empire they built.

22. **C.** The West African states of Mali, Ghana, and Songhai were the origins of very valuable trading routes across the Sahara. This is basically a "know your economics and geography" question. Zanzibar is a trade island in the Indian Ocean. Kongo is a state in central Africa. Zimbabwe is a city-state in southern Africa. Of the three, only Zanzibar had a large Islamic population, and geographically, the three are not near each other to be part of the same trade caravan system.

23. **D.** This is the best answer, because C is more descriptive of the manor system and ignores the idea of a king with power over his country, although, in fact, they did not have great authority. For A, kings did rule with church backing, but they could not establish authority over their lands with any lasting success.

24. **C.** The exposure of Europe's aristocracy to the many luxuries available in the Middle East that originated in India, China, and Southeast Asia created a permanent demand in Europe that encouraged the growth of trade contacts and long-term changes to the economic system in Europe formerly dominated by feudalism.

25. **A.** While the Mongols did not adopt Confucianism as their philosophy, they did continue to use the Confucian bureaucratic system to run the vast Chinese empire.

26. **A.** The shogunate depended upon the great military lords, called

daimyo, to provide military support for the shogun's government. Like Europe, this system failed to provide for a stable central government, and by the third shogun, the system erupted into civil war.

27. **C.** The slave soldiers of Egypt, originally from the steppes, were able to halt the Mongol advance. Through revolt, the Mamluks created an independent Egypt that they would rule for many years.

28. **B.** Ming Chinese fleets under the eunuch admiral Zheng He traveled across the Indian Ocean and established communications between China and many small states in East Africa, Southeast Asia, and the ports of India. However, the Chinese withdrew from these ties by the mid-fifteenth century because their mission did not conform to the basic Confucian attitudes toward trade and the world outside of China.

29. **A.** The potato's ability to grow in formerly uncultivated lands and its high calorie-per-acre yield created a population boom because people enjoyed better health. This allowed women to have children over a longer period of their lives and to survive childbirth better. It also meant that people would live longer.

30. **D.** The collapse of the Byzantine Empire resulted from the expansion of the Islamic Ottoman Empire. The Western Europeans saw the Ottoman Turks as an enemy of Christianity, and while they did trade with them, periodic wars and general mistrust limited the amount of trade activity between the two regions.

31. **B.** Sugar production drove the economy of the New World colonies until the eighteenth century. It required a substantial amount of manual labor for harvesting and refining, creating the demand for slaves. The Industrial Revolution and the Enlightenment policies of Europe and independent colonies eventually resulted in the abolition of slavery.

32. **D.** The Incans were recovering from civil war and the Aztec faced rebellions, but both were completely unprepared for the military weapons and strategies used by the Spanish conquistadores.

33. **B.** Buddhism challenged the established bureaucracy, based on

Confucian philosophy. When the Empress Wu used Buddhist monasteries as a base of support for her rule, which violated traditional Confucian ethics, Confucian scholars in the bureaucracy sought a number of ways to address this treaty. Eventually, they taxed the monasteries and introduced certain aspects of Buddhist and Taoist teachings. Although many Confucians still firmly rejected both religions, Neo-Confucianism became the basis of the Song dynastic government.

34. **C**. The Tokugawa sought to remove all foreign interests in their country, going so far as to execute Christians and to tightly control the production of new firearms (reduced to just a small number of hunting weapons a year). Because of the distance from European centers of power and the greater interest in China, Japan's isolation was able to last until the mid-nineteenth century, when the Americans forced open the island.

35. **C**. After Peter the Great's rule, Russia continually sought a warm-water port for greater access to international trade. This brought it into conflict with the Ottoman Empire, Britain, France, and Japan.

36. **B**. The fourteenth century saw a weakening of the church and a new model for the centralized nation-state: France. Centralized government and the Reformation also strengthened the power of the king. Humanist philosophers like Niccolò Machiavelli and Thomas Hobbes also believed a strong king would benefit the European states. The Enlightenment argued for greater political rights for more individuals, not for concentration of power in the hands of a single ruler.

37. **A**. The Industrial Revolution encouraged Western nations to establish exclusive markets for their goods and to control the resources they needed to supply their manufacturing base. They had their own cheap labor and saw the development of manufacturing in the colonies as a threat to their economic base. Also, mercantilist policies dominated Western economics during the eighteenth and nineteenth centuries, restricting the free trade of goods.

38. **B.** Nicholas Copernicus published his heliocentric theory and touched off the Scientific Revolution.

39. **B.** China was famous for its porcelain, especially the blue-on-white designs made famous during the Ming dynasty.

40. **B.** The kings rewarded a small elite of nobles with the spoils of war while maintaining a strong hold over the peasants.

41. **D.** The British won the Seven Years' War and gained dominance over the Indian subcontinent. France lost its colonial areas in India due to this war.

42. **B.** The demographic changes were a result of the demand for young, strong individuals who could immediately go to work on the sugar and other agricultural plantations of Brazil, the Caribbean, and the American South.

43. **B.** Improvement in farming techniques that included some new machines, but not just this, allowed for fewer workers to produce more food. Improvements included the concentration of lands into larger farms, crop rotation that allowed the planting of all lands each year, and a reliance on some new crops.

44. **A.** The Haitian Revolution was inspired by changes in the United States and France. Russian serfs arose against a crushing economic situation and were not particularly inspired by Enlightenment ideas, nor were the Cuban revolutionaries of the twentieth century who ultimately followed a socialist-communist ideology. The Latin American revolutions were carried out by local elites in response to the fall of the Spanish king to Napoleon, not an Enlightenment-inspired cadre of revolutionaries. The 1830 and 1848 revolutions in Europe were met with a conservative backlash against some institutions of the Enlightenment and did not affect Russia.

45. **A.** This is true in both cases, although the French Revolution quickly involved the masses of Paris and the peasants who were motivated by severe economic hardships more than any philosophy about individual civil and political rights.

46. **C.** The Ottoman system did not allow for an industrial class to form, so the empire became dependent on purchasing manufactured goods from Europe and rapidly found itself unable to defend its interests without European assistance. Austria-Hungary, Britain, France, and Russia all focused on the Ottomans as part of their foreign-policy objectives. Austria-Hungary and Russia looked at quick opportunities for expansion while Britain and France both feared Russia's expansion into the Mediterranean and greater involvement in international trade. So during the nineteenth century, while the Ottomans did lose substantial lands in Europe, these generally did not become the territory of one of the great powers but instead became independent states, such as Greece and Bulgaria. The sultan shut down attempts at reform until just prior to World War I.

47. **B.** European governments depended on manufacturing economies for employment and income. They needed colonial markets for the goods they were manufacturing and therefore did not generally allow for development to occur in these regions.

48. **B.** Not all of the European powers adopted a democratic form of government, and those that did (like Great Britain) could not mobilize massive numbers of men for war anyplace around the globe. They depended on colonial troops, advanced technology, and manufactured armaments to control their empires.

49. **B.** China's Qing dynasty lost two wars over the opium trade, almost fell to the Taiping rebellion (but was aided by Europeans and local landowners), lost the Sino-Japanese War, and was humiliated by its participation in the Boxer Rebellion, yet managed to remain in power because the Europeans did not wish to face a new and potentially more resistant Chinese regime.

50. **D.** The decree by Czar Alexander II freed the serfs of Russia, although it did not lift them out of poverty, because they were still required to give restitution to the landowners. Many became indebted to their former masters or were pushed into the cities, which did not have the industrial jobs of the West to absorb the influx of new labor.

51. **C.** While some of the revolutionaries sought to establish the institutions of an enlightened (Enlightenment) republic, the ultimate result in Latin America were governments controlled by a Creole elite with few actual democratic institutions.

52. **A.** Women in the middle class found time to engage in a number of social reform efforts, including public health, prison reform, and public education. They also became a major economic force within middle-class families because they found themselves with more disposable income, which women used to fuel a consumer economy.

53. **A.** The opium wars and the Boxer Rebellion left China divided into European and Japanese spheres of influence. Treaties stripped the Qing dynasty of the ability to manage even the behavior of foreigners in China, who were granted extraterritoriality privileges.

54. **A.** The opium trade, fueled especially by production in British India, generated a positive trade balance for Britain and others in Chinese markets, and when the Chinese attempted to stop the trade, the British went to war to protect the property of their citizens.

55. **B.** Japan took the "if you can't beat them, join them approach," adopting a program of rapid modernization of their industry and military in an effort to regain independence from foreign influence and unequal treaty obligations like those imposed on China. By the 1890s, this was beginning to happen as Britain abolished its unequal treaties and supported Japan's demands that others do so as well.

56. **B.** Islam included intellectual currents that combined ideas about reason based on Aristotle and other Greek philosophers. Muhammad Abduh sought to coax Islamic societies into modernizing along Western lines in order to build greater economic and political independence.

57. **C.** The British pushed for greater commercial agricultural production and dismantled many preindustrial centers that manufactured textiles and other products, not wanting to have British-manufactured goods compete with similar goods from India.

58. **A.** While nationalism swept through most areas of Europe, the multiethnic empires of Austria-Hungary and the Ottoman Empire faced political upheaval as various ethnic groups sought greater autonomy or full independence.

59. **B.** The Ottomans controlled most of the Middle East until the end of the First World War.

60. **D.** The nations of Europe fought the war to build empires, not in the interest of democracy or to fight some political-social movement like communism or fascism.

61. **B.** The colonies provided manpower for the European nations, which were growing more and more desperate for troops while casualties mounted along the western front. Also, there were areas of conflict, especially in Africa, where colonial empires bordered each other.

62. **C.** The first resolutions of the congress did not call for independence due to a mix of issues. First, such a call would have caused a crackdown on the congress by British authorities. Second, the congress appreciated many of the influences of the British in India, including forced unity and access to higher education.

63. **D.** All of the other conclusions require information not available on the graph.

64. **B.** Protectionism devastated the manufacturing segments of the American and European economies. Without manufacturing, the demand for the raw materials supplied by many Latin American states plummeted.

65. **B.** This is the best answer because almost all regions capable of establishing an independent existence now have political freedom from Europe. While many nations have also instituted democratic reforms, not all have done so.

66. **A.** The Palestinian Arabs became a rallying point for Pan-Arab movements and for popular Arab opinion against Israel and its allies in the West, but it never unified the Arabs behind the Soviet Union during the Cold War.

67. **C.** The Soviets produced a large surplus of oil, and for most of the Cold War, oil supplies were not seen as a serious economic threat.

68. **B.** The Shah maintained a pro-American presence in the Middle East and near the Soviets in central Asia.

69. **A.** This movement sought to achieve a voice for its members—including states like India, Indonesia, and sometimes the People's Republic of China—outside of the politics of the Cold War. Generally, the members failed to achieve a unified political-economic agenda, and the end of the Cold War made the group basically obsolete.

70. **C.** Globalization, beginning at least as early as the eighteenth century, describes the increased economic integration of world markets.

Section II, Part A: The Document-Based Question

BRAINSTORMING-GROUPING

Document 1	By revolutionary
	Well after the period in question
	Cites evidence as credible proof of atrocities by Europeans against the Indians
	Could be using the atrocities to hurt the reputation of the Spanish government that he is against (revolutionary)
Document 2	Focus is on the "greater riches of Peru"
	Talks of the Amazon as the treasure chest of the king of Spain
	Emphasis on the natives accepting the power of "our" God (Christianity)
Document 3	Conquistador—out for gold and glory
	Conquered city; military conquest
	Says purpose is to make all Christians
	Also, all are to become subjects of the king

Document 4	Source is an explorer, but sounds like a conquistador
	Looking for profits, but seems disappointed at first
	Some gold
	Make locals friends, even though they are hostile
	Destroyed village (conquest) and returned with 250 prisoners (possible slaves, forced laborers)
Document 5	Conquistador playing the diplomat, but very interested in the gold shown
	Not clear on his talk with Montezuma as to the subject
	Real focus on gold
Document 6	Key sources: king and queen of Spain—they send out the people to the New World
	"Discover and conquer"
	Awards of titles (glory) for conquest

GROUPINGS

- Group 1: God
  - Many Europeans were motivated by the desire to extend Christianity into the New World.
  - Documents 1, 2, and 3
  - Key point is the idea of bringing in Christianity as a civilizing and controlling force

- Group 2: Glory
  - The conquistadors and others sought rewards for their efforts, not just financial, but long-term positions for their families: titles of nobility and government offices
  - Documents 3, 5, and 6
  - Key is the use of document 6 as it specifically addresses titles to be awarded to Columbus and his heirs for the discovery and conquest of islands and continents

- Group 3: Gold
  - The overriding intent of the European explorations was the gaining of material wealth, especially gold.
  - Documents 2, 3, 4, and 5 all reinforce this
  - Key point is the continued reference in the documents to gold; each is interested in treasure and the ease of taking it from the natives

THESIS

While the spread of Christianity and the desire for glory or fame inspired many Europeans who came to the New World, the quest for treasure drove most. The introduction of Christianity was seen as a way of bringing in a civilizing force to the native populations of the Americas. The Spanish saw themselves acting for God, and some truly worked in the interest of the natives. Other explorers saw the New World as a means of gaining titles and positions not available to them in Europe. But, above all, it appears from the evidence that the quest for gold or treasure dominated the thinking of many to cross the Atlantic.

BODY PARAGRAPHS

Spreading Christianity to the natives was clearly one of the goals of the Europeans in the Americas. Coronado, in document 3, makes a point to inform the natives that he intends to make them Christian. Cristoval de Acuña also seeks to awe the natives with the power of his God. As a missionary, he must be interested in ways of winning converts. The success of the voyage provides him with a way of swaying the natives by using the power of his God to protect him and the other Europeans. However, both Coronado and de Acuña also appear to have other motives as each talks about the lands coming under the control of their king. In document 1, Bolivar makes the best argument as to the sincerity of at least some of the Europeans at coming to the New World to minister to the natives. Bolivar gives an account credited to the bishop of Chiapas who is not afraid to criticize the Spanish for their treatment of the natives. As this would be a criticism of the government, the bishop could have faced some punishments for his account of the atrocities. The documents make it clear that while some came to minister to and convert the natives, this is not the primary intent of many.

Many came to the New World to win position back home. The conquistadors especially saw conquest as a way of achieving titles and other rewards from the king. In document 6, the king and queen of Spain establish this precedent with the very first voyage of discovery. Columbus is promised several titles—admiral, viceroy, and governor—if he conquers new territories for Spain. New lands allow the king and queen to reward their nobles and extend their power. Titles can establish a family's future beyond the current generation, as Columbus is allowed to pass on the titles of dons, admirals, viceroys, and governors to his successors. In document 3, Coronado is also quick to claim lands and subjects for his king. He may receive gifts of some value, but he clearly places greater importance on establishing his majesty's rule over the area. As this is a report to the government, his actions, as he recounts them, should demonstrate loyalty to the king, and he probably hopes they gain him rewards from the king more valuable than a little turquoise. Cortes, in document 5, acts the ambassador, greeting Montezuma and respecting the ceremony around addressing the Aztec emperor. Cortes, too, may be wishing to establish relations between his king and the Aztecs. This could win him rewards at home, although he is also clearly interested in the amount of gold the Aztecs may have, since he recounts the details about the necklaces he is shown.

The strongest theme in the documents as to the motivations of the Europeans is the quest for greater wealth. The conquistadors,

the missionary Acuña, and the explorer Amerigo Vespucci all refer to gold and other treasures available in the New World. It is
in their minds and must be one of the main motivations for the
European presences there. For the conquistadors, this is understandable, because part of conquering involves looting those you defeat.
But Acuña, even though he is a missionary, seems just as interested
in the wealth that the lands of the Amazon will provide for the
king. The explorer Vespucci also takes time from just mapping to
enriching his expedition with 250 prisoners to become their slaves.

WRAP-UP

The AP World History Exam essays do not require a conclusion, but
they do still have at least one component that may not have been part of
one of your body paragraphs: another document. There are several ways
to do this.

At the end of the first body paragraph, the following statement would
work:

A document by a native of the Americas giving a firsthand description of missionaries working in the New World might support the
statement conveyed by Bolivar in document 1. This could support the claims that the Europeans are only there to oppress and
use the natives or that there were also men there to bring them
Christianity and a better civilization.

As a conclusion, you could include the following:

To really evaluate the intentions of the Europeans, a document by
a contemporary native would provide a completely different viewpoint. This account could offer a better evaluation of the actual
actions of the Europeans and their impact on the natives, instead
of relying on just Europeans to explain their intent.

Section II, Part B: Change-Over-Time Essay

BRAINSTORMING

Motives	At first…
	Discovery of new routes to China and India
	Bypass Italian monopoly on trade
	Avoid areas where Muslims control trade (Ottoman Empire)
	Strong economy = strong nation
	Industrial Revolution
	Control raw materials for manufacturing
	Control of markets for the sale of manufactured goods
	Mercantilism: capitalist economic policy demanding the collection of hard currency into one's economy
	Technological changes increased the pace of European dominance
	Changes in transportation made overseas empires far easier to control
	Second Industrial Revolution and a crowded world
	By late nineteenth century world is full
	Scramble for Africa
	Opium wars, treaty ports, spheres of influence in China
	New imperialist powers: Germany, Italy, Japan, the United States
	Growing conflicts between the imperialist powers
Patterns	Exploration
	Isolated stations
	Agrarian colonies
	Colonists
	Company holdings
	Might of empires (colonies = power)
Continuities	Strong economy means a strong state; an empire strengthens the state

Changes	Exploration to permanent settlements
	Trade routes to destinations
	Demand for raw materials
	Demand for markets
	A crowded world

THESIS

Between 1450 and 1914, the European powers went from spon-soring exploration of the world to almost complete political and economic dominance of the globe. The initial drive for new routes to China and India was joined by European efforts to colonize the New World. Also, as European governments adopted mer-cantilism, colonization became an important part of each nation's survival. The Industrial Revolution further enforced the need to secure colonies for both raw materials and markets for manufac-tured goods. As the nineteenth century came to an end, the pow-ers in Europe found themselves more and more in conflict over colonies, pushing them toward a global conflict.

Note: The essay will focus on the continuity of seeking trade with China and India and add the influences of the Industrial Revolution and then imperial rivalry.

BODY PARAGRAPHS

Continuity: A good essay, to cover continuity, will discuss the demand in Europe for goods from China and India. Focus on silks and porcelains from China and textiles from India. Demand continues and expands to include tea from both areas and opium from India for the China trade.

Changes: A good essay will introduce at least two changes. First, the essay should introduce the change from exploration to colonization, especially in the New World. The New World offered many in Europe a chance for land that they could not get at home. The Spanish trans-planted nobles to Latin America while the British, Dutch, and French sent many settlers who found economic opportunities that were not available at home. Second, the essay should identify the changing role of colonization because of the Industrial Revolution. Industry created a greater demand for natural resources and cash crops in the manufacturing nations of Europe. Also, markets were needed for the output of the factories. Colonists and natives could be forced to be dependent on European manufactured goods. Mercantilist policies demanded this and enforced it with tariffs and other laws restricting trade between colonies and nations other than the home country. Finally, an essay could also include the buildup to the First World War as conflict over colonies and spheres of influence, especially initiated by newly industrialized countries like Germany and Japan, were a major cause of the war. A discussion of the "scramble for Africa," the growing conflict between Russia and Austria-Hungary over the territory of the declining Ottoman Empire, and the Russo-Japanese War would make a good close for the essay.

Analysis: The essay must explain the cause for each continuity or change.

- Desire for direct trade routes with India and China
- Continued demand for goods from both locations (as well as the large markets after the Industrial Revolution)
- Movement of Europeans to the New World and southern Africa in search of economic opportunities (and in some cases religious freedom) not available to them in Europe
- Insatiable demand for raw materials (like cotton for textile factories) created by the Industrial Revolution
- Need for markets for manufactured goods; colonial governments could even prevent the creation of industry to guarantee markets for the products of the home country, as was done in India
- Imperialism demanded that a nation build an empire in the late nineteenth century, but the world was mostly full and the European powers found themselves coming into greater conflicts over expansion

Section II, Part C: Compare-Contrast Essay

BRAINSTORMING T CHART

ROME	HAN
Internal	Internal
Lack of civic responsibility	Hardships for the peasant class
Weakening of the legions	Military cuts
Poor leadership	Corrupt officials
Overexpansion	Breakdown of central authority
Declining economics	
External	External
Invasion by steppe nomads (Huns)	Invasion by steppe nomads
Migrations of the German people into Roman territory	

THESIS

Toward the end of the classical period, both the Han dynasty of China and the Roman Empire fell due to internal political, economic, and social decline. Added to the internal difficulties, each also faced external attacks. In Rome and China, the quality of leadership declined drastically. Overexpansion in Rome and corruption of the bureaucracy in China both helped bring down the central governments. Economically, the failure of Rome to continue to conquer more lands led to an economic decline, while in China high taxes because of corruption devastated the peasant class, thus hurting agricultural production. Socially, the Romans found themselves unable to count on the sense of civic responsibility to get people to join the legions and work for the state. In China, the failure of the Confucian government caused a move away from Confucian social order and a rise in alternative Taoist sects, which led to revolts. These internal problems left the Romans open to attack by the Huns and Germans, who would eventually conquer the western portion of the empire. The Chinese also lost territory to steppe tribesmen: the Xiongnu.

BODY

Both Rome and China suffered from poor leadership before each empire eventually fell. In Rome, the emperors ruled based on the allegiance of military units and their ability to pacify the citizenship. As the empire stopped expanding, it became harder to reward the legions, and commanders turned against the emperors to increase their power and reward their troops. These internal fights became more frequent and severely hurt the ability of the empire to defend itself. Over time, the empire actually retreated from territories because it found them too hard to defend. In China, the emperors became absorbed in the politics of the palace, influenced more by their wives, concubines, and eunuch slaves. Confucian bureaucrats effectively ran the government of the Han while the emperors became more and more insulated in the palace. However, as bureaucrats began to focus on maintaining their positions and passing them on to their sons, corruption became an issue. With no effective central leadership, corruption drew off more and more tax revenue. Increases in taxes forced the poorest peasants to sell their lands to wealthier landowners. Since many wealthy landowners were exempt from taxes, this only increased the government's income problem.

In Rome, citizens were pacified with food handouts and public games. This kept the masses from rebellion, but it did nothing to increase the power of the state since people stopped joining the legions. To fill the legions, the Romans offered citizenship to the Germans who were migrating into Roman territory. This weakened the overall power of the legions and encouraged more migrations of Germans into Roman territory. In China, the peasants who lost their lands could not find work and many turned to banditry. Trying to control bandits, the government increased the size of the military and moved units from the frontier defenses. This increased the government's expenses and forced taxes up, which then drove more peasants off their lands. The Han were following what in Chinese history is called the "dynastic cycle." As the corruption problems grow and the central government loses the ability to manage the country, people begin to doubt the emperor's authority to rule.

These internal issues left both empires open to attack. In Rome, the Huns under the leadership of Attila attacked both the eastern and western portions of the empire. They were eventually defeated, but the Romans were forced to ally with the Germans to do so, and the reputation of the legions was severely damaged. Later, the Germans would force their way into the empire, and the legions proved unable to defend the frontier. By the fifth century, Germans were able to take the city of Rome itself and eventually the entire western portion of the empire fell. In China, the withdrawal of the military from the frontiers allowed Xiongnu tribesmen from the steppe to raid the borders. Internally, the failures of Confucianism led to Taoist sects (such as the Yellow Turbans) who led internal rebellions. Mixed with natural disasters, the people turned against the Han emperor who had lost the "Mandate of Heaven," the authority granted by the heavens to rule over China.

CONCLUSIONS

Both the Roman Empire and the Han fell due to internal difficulties. The Romans found themselves unable to maintain growth by conquest that was so important in the early centuries of the empire. Without new wealth and the promise of a better life offered by the legions, the system collapsed. Even some good emperors, such as Constantine, could not overcome the internal decline. In

China, the dynastic cycle predicted bad leadership, corruption in the bureaucracy, overtaxation, failure of the military, and natural disasters beyond the capability of the central government to deal with. In the end, the dynasty loses the Mandate of Heaven, and internal rebellions break up the state.

Remember that although conclusions are not required, they are helpful in your free-response essays.

About the Author

Kirby Whitehead teaches AP World History, AP European History, Model United Nations, and Modern East Asian Studies at Ronald Reagan High School in San Antonio, Texas. He has worked as a reader for the AP World History Exam and also writes questions for standardized state testing in the social studies area.

Also Available

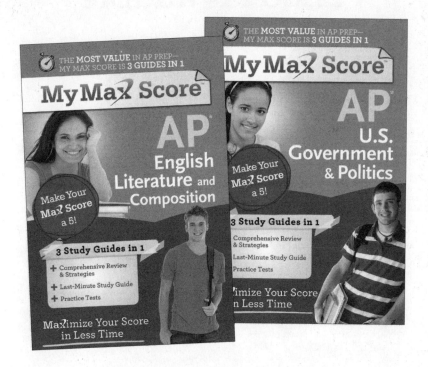

Also Available

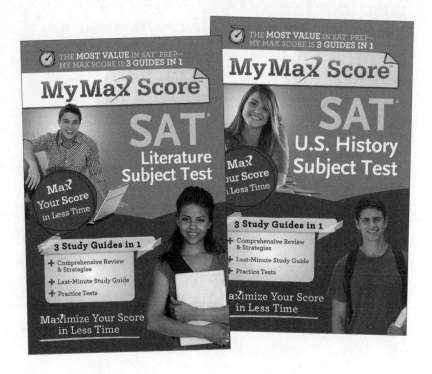

My Max Score SAT Literature Subject Test
by Steven Fox • 978-1-4022-5613-4

My Max Score SAT Math 1 & 2 Subject Test
by Chris Monahan • 978-1-4022-5601-1

My Max Score SAT U.S. History Subject Test
by Cara Cantarella • 978-1-4022-5604-2

• • •

My Max Score ASVAB:
Armed Services Vocational Aptitude Battery
by Angie Johnston and Amanda Ross, PhD • 978-1-4022-4492-6

$14.99 U.S./£9.99 UK

Essentials from
Dr. Gary Gruber
and the creators of My Max Score

"Gruber can ring the bell on any number
of standardized exams."
—*Chicago Tribune*

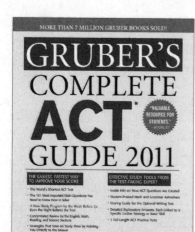

$19.99 U.S./£14.99 UK
978-1-4022-4307-3

$19.99 U.S./£14.99 UK
978-1-4022-5331-7

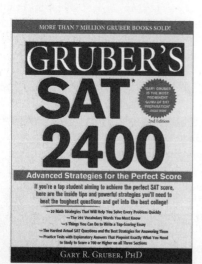

$16.99 U.S./£11.99 UK
978-1-4022-4308-0

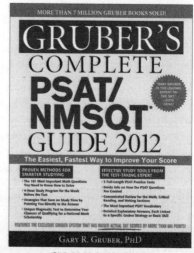

$13.99 U.S./£9.99 UK
978-1-4022-5334-8

"Gruber's methods make the questions seem amazingly simple to solve."
—*Library Journal*

"Gary Gruber is the leading expert on the SAT."
—*Houston Chronicle*

$14.99 U.S./£9.99 UK
978-1-4022-5337-9

$14.99 U.S./£9.99 UK
978-1-4022-5340-9

$14.99 U.S./£9.99 UK
978-1-4022-5343-0

$12.99 U.S./£8.99 UK
978-1-4022-6072-8

Notes